Groupthink
Versus
High-Quality
Decision Making
in International
Relations

Groupthink Versus High-Quality Decision Making in International Relations

Mark Schafer and
Scott Crichlow

Columbia University Press   New York

Columbia University Press
Publishers Since 1893
New York   Chichester, West Sussex
Copyright © 2010 Columbia University Press
All rights reserved

Library of Congress Cataloging-in-Publication Data

Schafer, Mark, 1962–
   Groupthink versus high-quality decision making in international
relations / Mark Schafer and Scott Crichlow.
      p. cm.
   Includes bibliographical references and index.
   ISBN 978-0-231-14888-7 (cloth : alk. paper) — ISBN 978-0-231-
14889-4 (pbk. : alk. paper) — ISBN 978-0-231-52018-8 (e-book)
   1. United States—Foreign relations—1945–1989—Decision making.
2. United States—Foreign relations 1989—Decision making. 3. United
States—Foreign relations—1945–1989—Decision making—Case
studies. 4. United States—Foreign relations—1989—Decision making—Case studies. 5. Group problem solving—United States—Case
studies. I. Crichlow, Scott, 1971– II. Title.
JZ1480.S32 2010
353.1'32330973—dc22   2009034847

∞

Columbia University Press books are printed on permanent and durable
acid-free paper.

This book is printed on paper with recycled content.

Printed in the United States of America

c 10 9 8 7 6 5 4 3 2 1

p 10 9 8 7 6 5 4 3 2 1

References to Internet Web sites (URLs) were accurate at the time of writing. Neither the author nor Columbia University Press is responsible for
URLs that may have expired or changed since the manuscript was prepared.

We dedicate this book to Cecil Eubanks and Stephen G. Walker. Great intellectuals, outstanding role models, and wonderful friends, they have taught us much about life in the academy, and otherwise.

Contents

Tables and Figures

Acknowledgments

This area of research began for us a long time ago, when Mark Schafer had just arrived at LSU as a new Ph.D. and assistant professor and Scott Crichlow had arrived there as a first-year graduate student. We published our first work in this area shortly thereafter. And while each of us continues to work separately in other areas of political psychology and international relations, our interest and work together in group decision making has continued since that time and is a major focus of our careers. This work has always been special to us because it combines the careful analysis of cases—which keeps us anchored in real-world phenomena—with social-scientific methods and generalizable findings.

Of course, since those early years many colleagues and students have provided insights, assistance, and support, and it would be impossible to acknowledge all of them. But there are some to whom we offer particular thanks. Over the last two years, four student workers at LSU have provided excellent assistance with various parts of the project: Cassie Black, Jessi deGruy, Christopher Nunez, Jonathon Nunley, Nicholas Smith, and John Turner.

We also thank our editor at Columbia University Press, Anne Routon. She was enthusiastic about the project from the start and did wonders to facilitate the process and the completion of the book. We thank her for her support and insights and for helping with a large number of tedious e-mail questions! She has been a joy to work with.

Rob Fellman, our copy editor at Columbia University Press, did a great job and was very helpful, responsive, and friendly along the way.

Joey Zimmerman was there at the very start and provided much support and encouragement along the way. He also helped specifically with some computer and IT components of the project, and we thank him very much.

We also wish to acknowledge and thank two individuals to whom we dedicate this book. Two of the finest and wisest individuals we have ever had the privilege of knowing, Cecil Eubanks and Stephen G. Walker, have provided much support, guidance, and encouragement, and they have inspired us in many ways. We strive to live up to their example, and we thank them for all that they have done.

Groupthink
Versus
High-Quality
Decision Making
in International
Relations

PART I

Groupthink and the Quality of the Foreign-Policy Decision-Making Process

One

INTRODUCTION

More than thirty-five years ago, Irving Janis published his now well-known book *Victims of Groupthink: A Psychological Study of Foreign-Policy Decisions and Fiascoes*. Janis's basic argument was that the quality of the process of foreign-policy making is likely to have an effect on the quality of outcomes that stem from the decision. Sometimes decision makers engage in a careful, deliberative process that seeks deep and varied information, specifies objectives, considers alternatives, asks hard questions, checks against biases in the process, questions assumptions, and reevaluates information and choices when needed. Citizens might generally assume that those in the upper echelons of government always conduct such careful, rational decision processes, especially when making major foreign-policy decisions that affect the blood and treasure of the country. Yet Janis's important work demonstrated that sometimes the process of foreign-policy making can be deeply flawed—and in such cases the probability of having a poor outcome goes up significantly.

His most famous case, the Bay of Pigs "fiasco," documents how an administration consisting of exceptionally bright individuals failed to conduct anything remotely close to a careful decision-making process. The Kennedy administration failed to question deeply flawed basic assumptions, kept important information out of the process when it challenged the direction the group was heading, and quickly quieted one individual who dared to try to disagree with the president and others in the administration. The result was one of the most embarrassing foreign-policy setbacks in the history of the modern presidency.

Janis referred to the broad pattern of decision-making problems in this case and others as "groupthink." Although he offers different definitions of the term throughout his work, he is referring generally to a process where group norms and patterns essentially take over and result in deeply flawed decision making. The "group" takes on a life of its own, one that is bigger than the sum of the individuals in the group. Group cohesion is valued above the quality of information processing; dissent is discouraged, suppressed, or eliminated; shortcuts are taken in the process; assumptions by the leader or key advisors go unquestioned; and biases lead to policy. The result of these flaws in the process is that the group reaches "premature consensus" (Janis 1972). The group feels good about its decision, and group cohesion has been maintained, because, after all, dissent was minimal.

Janis supported his argument with a series of case studies (1972, 1982). Some, such as the Bay of Pigs, demonstrate that when groupthink occurred, the outcome was very poor. Others, such as the Cuban Missile Crisis, demonstrate that high-quality decision making—which avoids groupthink—resulted in a very good outcome. There is great intuitive appeal to Janis's argument. We hope leaders at the top of governments conduct careful decision-making procedures, and when they do not, it makes sense that the outcomes should be less than optimal. Yet, while Janis's work remains the locus classicus in this area, it also raises many questions. How often does groupthink occur? Is groupthink an either-or condition, either there or not? Or, on the other hand, is the quality of decision making more variable than that? Might some cases display decision making of very poor quality, some display very good decision making, and some in between? How often does poor decision making result in poor outcomes? What conditions give rise to poor decision making? Are there different stages, components, or factors in decision making that affect quality? What can be done by policymakers to improve the quality of decision making?

Despite its intuitive appeal and its popularity, Janis's original work has some important limitations that simply cannot address these questions and others. Janis's work was strong on providing qualitative narratives of cases but weak on modern social-science methods. He selected a small number of cases that—one could argue—merely exemplified his working thesis. Related to this concern is that Janis himself chose cases that he judged either as successes or failures, and then he subsequently made judgments about the quality of the processes that went into those cases, a method that runs the risk of researcher bias (or at least opens the door to such criticisms). Janis's qualitative case studies also do not lend themselves to any type of meaningful comparison. We do not know if there is "more" groupthink in one case compared to another, or how much better the quality of decision making is in some cases, or if there is a systematic correlation between qualitative levels of decision-making processes and the quality of outcomes that stem from those processes. Finally, there is the issue of the timeliness of Janis's work. Since he published this seminal book on groupthink (1972), there have been six different U.S. presidents (Ford, Carter, Reagan, G. H. W. Bush, Clinton, and G. W. Bush), numerous new foreign-policy events and issues, the end of the cold war, the nonstate-actor challenges of the twenty-first century, and a host of other changes in international politics. In addition, there have been many contributions to the foreign-policy decision-making literature and much advancement in social-science research methods. Our broad objectives in this book are to revisit Janis's hypothesis, report new case studies, apply new social-science methods that let us investigate his hypothesis more broadly and rigorously, and generally expand the scope of the questions he posited so long ago.

Groupthink is now a famous term in many different disciplines, including political science, international studies, psychology, sociology, and business management and administration. It is a term we will use frequently in this book. However, the term is limiting. Janis himself offered several different definitions of groupthink throughout his career. In addition, since Janis's book was first published, there have been many different studies that looked not only at the phenomenon of groupthink but also at other components related to the quality of decision making. Thus our work looks more broadly at the *quality of the decision-making process*, of which groupthink is only one part. In some circles, the term groupthink is synonymous with poor-quality decision making—and indeed, when groupthink is present, it is an indicator of poor-quality decision making. However, a case may have poor-quality decision making and not be emblematic of groupthink. All squares are rectangles, but not all rectangles are squares. Therefore, while we clearly place our work in association with the groupthink research program, we think of our analytical frame as being broader than that. We look at the quality of group decision making in its broadest possible terms, one part of which is groupthink.

Groupthink as Part of a Larger Research Program

It is important to place our work and the groupthink research program into the broader context of research in the field of international relations. In short, this study is one component of the broader research area called foreign-policy decision making (FPDM). More than fifty years ago, Snyder, Bruck, and Sapin (1954) revolutionized foreign-policy analysis by imploring that we get inside the "black box" of the decision-making process to better understand and explain the factors affecting policy. By arguing that "the state is its decision makers" (Snyder, Bruck, and Sapin 1962, 65), these scholars realized the importance of the human element in decision making. Foreign-policy making is not simply a matter of a rationalist calculus, which merely requires realist inputs about power and interests to determine choices and outcomes. Instead, we must think of the decision process as a fundamentally human one that includes diverse personalities, competing—and sometimes unclear—role assignments, misperceptions, biased processing, wishful thinking, problematic group dynamics, ineffective lines of authority and communication, and other common human elements. To understand how a state arrives at a decision, we must carefully examine the human processes behind that decision. Without this, we have an incomplete understanding of the case. Every single decision a state makes must flow through humans and human interactions in one form or another.

Essentially, the FPDM research program takes us inside the state. This is different from other schools of thought in international relations exemplified by the "billiard-ball" metaphor. This metaphor suggests that state interaction in international politics is similar to balls interacting on a billiard-ball table: the solid balls periodically come into external contact with one another, causing collisions and caroms. The part of this metaphor most relevant to our discussion here is the idea that states are solid entities and that whatever exists inside the state is irrelevant. One school of thought related to this notion is the rational-actor school. It assumes that states are rational calculators trying to achieve their interests. In this conception, think of a state as a computer program: it takes the inputs from the system and simply calculates the output, with the decision rule specified as maximizing state interests. It weights the same factors the same way every time; it does so without error, biases, or emotions; and it does not allow for variance in interaction patterns because, conceptually speaking, there are none. In short, there is no *human* element in the billiard-ball model.

The FPDM school strongly diverges from this conception, and indeed, Snyder, Bruck, and Sapin so long ago wrote quite the opposite—that the decision process within a state is quintessentially a human process, fraught with those things that are human: biases, errors, emotions, interpretations, projections, personalities, and many others. This does not mean that actors within states are irrational. Nor does it mean that actors are not trying to maximize interests. Of course they are. But they are human beings, and they have human limitations. In fact, human beings are involved every step of the way in decision making—from trying to discern what "interests" are, to interpreting ambiguous information, to weighing possible alternatives designed to accomplish those "interests," to conducting the implementation of the policy. And since each human being is unique, who the individuals are inside the apparatus of the state matters. If someone else had been president at the time, would the United States have employed a blockade in the Cuban Missile Crisis? Invaded Iraq in 2003? Opened relations with China? Who governs can matter, and states are not solid entities.

Once we grasp this, then many avenues of research are opened to us. Research coming out of the FPDM school includes such areas as the psychological study of leaders; analysis of public opinion; consideration of bureaucracies and their role in the process; and the analysis of the media, special-interest groups, particular governmental structures, the political culture and norms, and many other areas. The groupthink research program is one of the most well-known programs to emerge out of FPDM. It fits well with the notion that decision making is a human process and that in order to understand what a state does and how it arrived at that decision, we must get inside the state and look at the processes within.

The particular contribution of the groupthink research program is its thesis that the quality of the process in decision making is likely to be connected to the quality of the outcome associated with the decision; poor process is likely to increase the probability of a poor outcome, and vice versa. Sometimes human beings interact more effectively than other times; sometimes group norms overwhelm group members who might otherwise oppose a policy; sometimes power plays in a group can override good analytical processes. When decision making breaks down at the top of the state apparatus, problems such as poor information search and biased information processing are much more likely to emerge. Under such circumstances, human-interaction patterns result in something that does not look like the precise functioning of a software program.

The quality of the decision-making process certainly is not the only explanation for poor outcomes. They may come about because of a variety of factors associated with the case: the other side may take a totally unexpected action, public opinion may decline quickly, or the international community may react very negatively. Janis's thesis suggests that the quality of the decision-making process is one key variable—though not the only one—affecting the quality of the outcome. Importantly, the quality of the process is something over which decision makers can have great influence. While it is not always possible to influence the other side's action, public opinion, or the international community, it is possible to set up better structures and procedures for decision processing within the administration. For that reason, a better understanding of these matters can have powerful prescriptive benefits. By altering the way a government is designed and decision making is carried out, political leaders have the ability to affect the likelihood that their endeavors will be successful, and the countries they lead may see major benefits as a result.

Going back to two of Janis's cases, the Bay of Pigs and the Cuban Missile Crisis, we have an example of a decision-making process he describes as terribly problematic and one he describes as excellent *within the same administration*. In our research, this kind of major transformation is rare, but it exemplifies the possibility that an administration can implement better structures and procedures. And implementing such structures and procedures can have a tangible, positive effect on policymaking. Kennedy quickly and publicly took personal blame for the Bay of Pigs disaster and then went to his administration and told them that new and better decision-making procedures were needed. He introduced a system where some advisors were assigned the role of challenging assumptions and asking hard questions. He included a larger number of advisors in the process and brought in outsiders who had different kinds of expertise and could challenge intra-administration perspectives. Concerned that his own presence might hinder free discussion at meetings, he pointedly stepped out of some meetings, allowing his advisors to speak their minds more freely and reducing the potential appearance of leader bias (Janis 1982). Each of these acts created structures and processes that allowed for more critical thinking and better information processing.

Advancing the Groupthink Research Program

While Janis's work was groundbreaking and important, it also has some limitations and leads to many new questions. We do not approach this project as doubters of Janis's basic thesis or as critics of his findings—indeed, quite the opposite. Janis's cases provide intriguing evidence, and reading histories of foreign-policy cases over the years shows abundant anecdotal support for the hypothesis that there is an important connection between the quality of the decision-making process and the quality of the outcomes associated with that process. Nonetheless, the limitations in Janis's research and the new questions that emerge out of it must be addressed. Janis's cases included not only the two from the Kennedy administration but such others as the level of naval preparedness before Pearl Harbor, U.S. escalation in Vietnam, and the development of the Marshall Plan. These are major matters that affected life and death, and they fundamentally altered international politics. If the quality of the process mattered in them—and many other cases since—then indeed the stakes are very high in this research, and it is incumbent upon us to be as rigorous as possible.

There are several important methodological innovations and advancements in the research presented in this book. While Janis himself judged both the outcome and the quality of the case, we separate the evaluation of these two parts of the puzzle. The dependent variable—the outcome of the case—is judged by a survey of foreign-policy experts from around the country (who were kept blind to the research hypotheses). The quality of decision making—our primary independent variable—was separately assessed by us, using case-study techniques. With these case studies our work looks similar to Janis's. We gather high-quality materials for each case. We include such things as memoirs, autobiographies, accounts by journalists and historians, and other works that, as much as possible, let us get inside the decision-making process. We read these materials, identify key actors, cross-check the facts, develop timelines, and generally come to know what went on inside each decision process as much as possible.

However, our methods also make improvements over Janis's approach. Before beginning the research, we specified a set of operationalized variables pertaining to the situational conditions and variables relating to the quality of decision making. These allow us to consistently and systematically evaluate these factors across the set of cases in our research. These operationalizations are derived from earlier research on the quality of group decision making. For example, Janis argues that one symptom of groupthink is poor information search in the case. Based upon other existing research, we specified a definition of this concept that could be applied the same way across every case in our study:

> *Poor Information Search*: The group fails to pursue information that may be available and necessary for critically evaluating policy options. This can be the result of a variety of problems, including arrogance, ignorance, misguided deference, or even a conscious decision to not contact someone who has relevant information and is available to talk.[1]

These operationalizations add a higher level of objectivity, consistency, and structure to our reading and evaluation of the case studies. In addition, these operationalized variables lend themselves to quantification of the underlying concepts. For example, based on the above definition, we are able to code every case for the presence or absence of poor information search. When we combine this variable with others (such as stereotyping, biased processing, and suppressing dissent) in the decision-processing stage of a case, we end up with a numerical value—essentially a measurement—for the number of decision-processing faults in that case. Though Janis never took his research to this level, from his overview of the cases we can be certain that in the Bay of Pigs case there were more decision-processing faults than there were in the Cuban Missile Crisis. Janis never precisely measured that difference. Our approach allows for more precise measurements and the ability to more accurately compare cases. This is essential if we hope to find generalizable patterns in our analysis that can both help us better understand the dynamics of decision making in the past and point us in directions by which we may be able to improve decision making in the future.

Our analysis also differs from Janis's work in that we selected our cases so that we would be studying a wide variety of decision-making events. We wanted to understand decision making across policy domains and decision making that resulted in a wide variety of outcomes. Janis, on the other hand, focused on events that were deemed to be either clear successes or clear failures. But not every foreign-policy case is so clearly cut, and by systematically choosing cases that had either bad decision-making quality or good decision-making quality and the corresponding, expected outcomes, Janis limited his work. What about those cases that are not as straightforward? In our research we chose major foreign-policy decisions (because those are the ones that are most clearly made at the top of governments) without any predisposition to the quality of the decision making or the quality of the outcome. We let the foreign-policy experts judge the quality of the outcome, while our reading of the cases, with our operationalized variables, produced evaluations of the quality of the process. And, indeed, we did *not* end up with two polar-opposite types of cases, good and bad. Instead, there are some cases where the quality of the process was good, some where it was bad, and many in between. Our quantified measurements of the quality of the process let us make systematic and meaningful comparisons of cases.

Thus in our research we end up with measurements, separately derived, on both the quality of decision making and the outcomes of the cases. When combined with a larger number and more diverse set of cases than Janis investigated, we are able to conduct rigorous statistical analyses of our substantive questions and produce generalizable findings. Statistics reveal patterns in the underlying research materials. They tell us the probabilities of different factors affecting the process. They let us test hypotheses and draw both broad and specific conclusions regarding the phenomena under investigation. The best statistical analysis shows us things that we could not otherwise have seen. But it is important to remember that our research methods are grounded in case studies. Sometimes, statistical research feels like it has been removed from reality and that the data are a collection of numbers sterilized from the underlying meaning. Nothing could be further from the truth in our research. As with Janis's research, our research entails deep and careful investigation of each case. Each one is a story, a piece of history, a real-world event driven by real human beings. Our research centers on getting inside those events. Where we differ from Janis is in the number and type of cases we investigate, the systematic and consistent way we investigate the cases across the whole set using the operationalized factors, and the fact that after investigating the cases we are able to translate the results into measurements that let us make meaningful comparisons and conduct statistical investigations.

Another important innovation in our research is our analysis of psychological traits of leaders and their effects on the quality of decision making. While many, including Janis, talked about the possibility that the leader's psychology would have an effect on the quality of decision making, there have been very few investigations of this puzzle. This research takes us further back in the causal chain and asks the following question: do individual-level psychological characteristics of the leader have an effect on the quality of decision-making structures and processes in the administration? The dependent variables are primarily the variables on the quality of decision making discussed as independent variables above. In other words, given that there are differences in the quality of decision processing across cases, here we examine whether those differences might be influenced by the psychology of the leader. For instance, a leader who has a high control orientation might be less open to contradictory comments made by an advisor during a decision episode. A leader who is low on conceptual complexity might set up decision structures that limit the amount of information coming into the process. Measurements on the independent variables here (psychological characteristics) are derived using "at-a-distance" methods developed by Margaret Hermann and her colleagues, called leadership-trait analysis (Hermann 1980, 1984; Hermann and Preston 1994; Kaarbo and Hermann 1998; Preston 2001).

To summarize, as with Janis, our research is grounded in case studies of actual foreign-policy decisions over the last thirty-five years. We add innovations that at once increase the rigor and reliability of the research and allow for conclusions that are more generalizable. We separate out the analysis of the quality of the outcome of the case, which is done by our panel of foreign-policy experts, and the quality of the decision-making process, which is done by ourselves, using extensive case-study procedures. We specify in advance what variables we consider and how they are measured, based upon existing literature. This allows us to develop quantitative indicators across the set of variables, which means that we can make comparisons across cases and conduct statistical analyses. Finally, we focus specifically on the psychology of individual leaders and ask if their psychological traits had an effect on the process.

The Plan of the Book

Since Janis first published his work on groupthink, there has been extensive research done on both group and individual components of the decision-making process. This has resulted in a large literature on the two main areas of focus in the book: group decision making and individual-level psychology. The literature provides key theoretical contributions and empirical findings that are appropriate for review, which we undertake in chapter 2.

We discuss Janis's classic conception of groupthink and review the revisions to that work and how it has been expanded over the last thirty-five years. We examine whether or not such a thing as "bad group processes" really exist, what facilitates their construction, and specifically what it is about them that has detrimental effects on the quality of decision making. We also look at some of the seminal works on individual-level psychology, and we introduce readers to modern psychological-analysis methods known as "at-a-distance" assessments. In addition, we tie individual-level psychology to groupthink by hypothesizing about what kind of psychological characteristics are likely to matter in foreign-policy decision making.

These literatures form the basis for the development of our own model of the decision-making process, which we specify and discuss in chapter 3. Our model includes four broad categories of influences—psychological, structural, process, and situational—that interact to shape the course of a country's foreign policy. We discuss how the individual-level characteristics of decision makers affect group membership, structure, and processes; how group structures affect group behavior; how the processes that groups employ during specific decision-making events affect their policy choices; and how all these matters are shaped by the situational environment in which decision-making exists. There are two primary causal components of our model: (1) the effect of psychological traits of leaders on the quality of group structures and processes in decision making, and (2) the effect of group structures and processes on the quality of decision outcomes.

Since case studies are the starting point of our methods, in the next two chapters (4 and 5), we present a series of case studies that take the reader inside the decision-making process of some well-known U.S. foreign-policy cases. Modeled somewhat after Janis's approach, we have selected cases that exemplify poor decision-making quality and resulted in negative outcomes (chapter 4) and cases representing much better decision processes, which resulted in beneficial outcomes (chapter 5). This is overly generalized, but these chapters provide in-depth narrative case studies that investigate the connection between processes and outcomes. The case studies also give the reader a chance to see our operationalized variables at work and how we apply them to individual decision events. Chapter 4 includes the following cases: the Carter administration supporting the Shah of Iran in 1978, the Reagan administration funding the Contras in 1981, the proposal for the Strategic Defense Initiative by Reagan in 1983, and the decision to impose stiff tariffs on steel by the G. W. Bush administration in 2002. Chapter 5 includes the restrained actions by the Carter administration in the Ogaden War in 1978, the decision by the Reagan administration in 1986 to ease Ferdinand Marcos out of power in the Philippines, and the decisions and actions by the Clinton administration during the 1998 Pakistan-India nuclear crisis.

Chapter 6 is the first of our two chapters presenting statistical tests of our model. This chapter represents the heart of our research—analyses of the effect of the quality of the decision-making process on the quality of the outcome of the case. The analyses include two different sets of process variables: (1) the structure of the decision-making process by the administration and (2) the decision processing done during the case. Each of these two sets includes many variables that cover a broad range of factors in decision making (all of which are covered in chapter 3). The dependent variables here are the scores from our panel of foreign-policy experts, who rated the outcome of each case in terms of national interests and the level of international conflict. Chapter 7 continues our statistical analysis, here by looking at the effect of the leader's psychological characteristics on the quality of decision making. Whereas in chapter 6 the variables regarding the quality of the process were the independent variables, here they are the dependent variables. The basic question is: does it matter what type of psychological traits the leader has in terms of how effective his or her decision-making process is?

In chapter 8, we present a more extensive signature case study, this one pertaining to perhaps the most significant post–cold war foreign-policy decision to date: the decision by the G. W. Bush administration to invade Iraq in 2003. Using our framework, we show how flawed decision making at both the individual and group levels contributed to poor analysis of available information, disregard for input from area experts, virtually no consideration of the potential costs of the initiative, a general lack of postwar planning, and other major faults and errors that imperiled U.S. interests at home and in the region. While low-quality decision making was not the only factor limiting U.S. success in the conflict, our account will illustrate for readers how the matters at the heart of this book played a central role in affecting the outcome of a top-level foreign-policy decision.

The decision-making process variables in our study are not always determinative—certainly other factors matter. Sometimes, even with good processes outcomes can be poor, and sometimes certain factors allow for good outcomes even when there are poor decision-making processes. In our concluding chapter (chapter 9) we discuss some of these contrarian cases in our research, which helps place the study in the broader context of other international-relations literatures. But, as we note in that chapter, despite the contrarian cases, our research demonstrates that there is a probabilistic relationship between the quality of decision making and the outcome of a case. In this concluding chapter we summarize the research in the book, both from the data and from the case studies, and talk about specific structures and practices that will contribute to better decision-making processes.

Two

THE GROUP AND THE INDIVIDUAL IN FOREIGN-POLICY DECISION MAKING

Our primary focus in this book is what happens inside the "black box" of foreign-policy decision making at the very highest levels of government. Factors at other levels certainly matter as well, such as the role of bureaucracies, the power of the military, and the influence of public opinion, and these have been studied extensively in other places. But in many cases, even these other factors matter only if decision makers at the top care to take them into account. For example, as our case study of the decision leading to the 2003 war in Iraq shows, parts of the bureaucracy did a good job of analyzing Iraq's potential for weapons of mass destruction, ties to al Qaeda, and potential complications in a postwar Iraq. But decision makers at the top put that information aside and moved forward with the decision to go to war regardless.

This does not mean that there are no constraints on decision makers coming from other forces in the process or that decision makers get to do whatever they want. Sometimes factors beyond the decision-making group, such as overwhelming public opinion or the level of military power, are so important that they by themselves constrain a decision. But it does mean that what goes on inside the black box—who is in the decision-making group and how the group operates—matters tremendously when decisions reach that level: hence our focus on the final decision unit, the group at the very top.

There are two principal areas of research that focus on these top decision units. The first area deals with the group itself, including such things as norms and standard procedures, channels of communication, psychological patterns in the group, and levels of expertise and teamwork. Sometimes the way the group is organized and functions has a major effect on how well the group does. The second area of research regarding top decision makers focuses on individuals and individual-level psychology. Sometimes what matters most are particular psychological characteristics of the leader or a prominent advisor in the process. Of course, these two areas are not separate and distinct. Certainly the psychological characteristics of a strong leader would likely influence the organization and functioning of the decision-making group, something we return to later in the book. Over the years, extensive literatures have developed in each of these two areas and they offer us much. In this chapter, we review these existing literatures.

Group Phenomena That Can Impair Decision Making

Decision-making groups are social entities. They are composed of multiple individuals. They have different types of leaders, with varying degrees of power, who seek to use the groups in a variety of ways. The groups develop their own norms and rules. Other norms and rules may be imposed upon them. They expand and contract. They may alter their behavior in the face of new information. Then again, they might not. Their workings depend upon whom they are composed of, who leads them, the structures and circumstances in which they exist, their norms of behavior, and, of course, on the goals and purposes they are created to address.

There is a large literature across a number of academic and professional fields that has studied whether specific behaviors or characteristics—be they small-group phenomena or associated with individual group members—enhance or inhibit a group's performance. But surprisingly little rigorous, systematic work has addressed exactly what constitutes "high-quality" group decision making and what group characteristics further or block groups from performing at that level. This is somewhat understandable, as different groups exist to fulfill many different types of needs. But if we truly hope to understand the way groups work and to facilitate their functioning, these topics need to be directly addressed.[1] Our research does this, and it has a particular type of group in mind—the small decision units that are the last venue for the consideration of major foreign-policy decisions.

Are There "Bad" Processes; or, Is That Contingent?

In bridging the work that focuses on both individual decision makers and the small groups that are often charged with thrashing out policy disputes on major international issues, it is important to note something that is sometimes overlooked in this literature. While there may indeed be certain behaviors that a group should generally seek to foster or suppress if its goal is to efficiently achieve specific ends in an optimal or near-optimal manner, which procedures and rules will work best for any specific group may depend on that group's leadership, membership, and aims. While we will see evidence that there are indeed certain phenomena that the average group should seek to avoid, we must keep in mind that groups are not led by or composed of average individuals. People who compose groups have different thinking and working styles, and the success of a particular group may depend on achieving the right fit between the needs and traits of a group's membership and its behaviors and norms. In specific instances, particular group phenomena may be especially helpful—or especially problematic— depending upon the characteristics of the individuals involved in the group and the particular strengths and weakness of its leader.

One of the most thorough studies to make this point is Paul Kowert's (2002) *Groupthink or Deadlock?* That work features a set of comparisons of President Eisenhower and President Reagan. The two thrived in very different working environments and learned in different ways. Eisenhower's decision making was more likely to suffer when he lacked advice or allowed his decision-making group to become closed off from outside views. Reagan suffered from a similar problem in that for him "consensus was closely tied to validity" (93). But Reagan's learning style and personality also meant that his decision making often suffered when he faced many choices and open debate. It "paralyzed" (148) him, and receiving conflicting advice made Reagan "angry and depressed" (149).

Of course, it is not simply the characteristics of the leader of the group that make it difficult to say that there are inherently good or bad group processes. What is good or bad might also depend on the level of hierarchy in the group, the size of the group, and the speed required for making a decision, among other matters. It is important to keep this point in mind as we proceed.

All that said, there is a preexisting literature that has examined the likely effects of a number of group behaviors on the policy outcomes produced by different types of decision-making groups, and there appear to be several characteristics and behaviors that, in general, can either assist or harm groups as they seek to achieve their ends. Even Kowert notes that some group processes seem on balance to be good (learning and collecting information) regardless of the leaders involved, while other phenomena and characteristics seem on balance to generally be harmful. He notes that "the most closed modern presidents . . . all suffered a great deal politically from pursuing policies endorsed by ideologically unified top advisors but not subjected to wider scrutiny" (164). This literature, which has tried to establish prescriptive rules for how groups can better pursue their aims (and avoid fiascoes), informs our hypotheses.

The Groups We Will Examine

Since we are primarily interested in group phenomena that are likely to be associated with the workings of decision-making bodies at the pinnacle of foreign-policy decision making, certain parts of this literature may be more relevant than others. These groups differ from many other bodies that affect policymaking in key ways. For example, the groups under study in this research may have a great deal more latitude and access concerning their ability to collect information from a variety of sources than a group that exists inside a specific governmental bureaucracy. In addition, the decision makers who are part of these bodies may have considerably more leeway to propose a variety of actions or speak on a variety of matters than would a member of a lower-level decision-making group. This could make their beliefs, personal preferences, perceptions, and expertise all the more important.

The design and function of a group like the National Security Council means that it engages in considerably different interactions than the deliberations and analysis that occur in groups located within a more specialized branch of the government. In groups like this, the number of roles that group members have to fill is likely to be unusually high, and group members may be "subject to and exposed to the pull of contradicting social interaction influences because they are simultaneously members of more than one peer group and are often attuned to persuasion by different reference groups" (Vertzberger 1997, 276). The fact that these decision makers have an unusually high number of interests and affiliations (they are supposedly on the president or prime minister's team, they are also often the voice of one or more organizational interests, and, presumably, they hold their own personal beliefs and preferences) may mean, for example, that at this level there may be many more opportunities to overcome otherwise insurmountable bureaucratic conflicts or the inertialike power of entrenched routines.

These groups may also have to perform an unusually large number of tasks over an unusually high number of issue domains, and the consequences of their actions are doubtless of a higher magnitude than the enterprises undertaken by most groups in government or business. Group members will often be aware of the scope of these consequences when choosing to work with one another (or not), and because of this groups facing choices of this magnitude may operate under unusually high levels of stress. This can be exacerbated by higher levels of uncertainty than are usual, given the scope of the matters affecting and affected by the issues at hand. The peculiar composition of these groups, as well as the gravity of the issues they deal with, mean that they may work in ways that differ from the behaviors of an average small group, and thus the ideal processes at this level of decision making might be different from those of a group that is operating on low-level or mid-level topics deep in the heart of a specific bureaucracy.

It will also be obvious as we proceed through this text that the groups we focus on are different from many policymaking groups in another important way. Their limited lifespan (they change in fundamental ways with every change in administration, and their format, design, and practices may be greatly altered during any particular government) means that they will often be in flux. They are less likely to be bound by enduring norms of procedure than many other groups (Stern 1997). Their standard operating procedures may change with greater frequency, and even when set, they may entail considerably more flexibility in their operations than groups that function at lower levels of government and are embedded in more lasting, set bureaucracies. Indeed, we will see as the text progresses that the nature of the rules and operating procedures that are utilized at different times by these groups often change. And that is a matter of no small consequence given that there is a good deal of evidence in this work and other texts that point to variation in these structures, and this plays an important role in determining whether or not a decision-making team will successfully achieve its desired ends.

Groupthink

Keeping in mind these points concerning whether or not there are processes that are always beneficial or harmful to a group's performance and
the unusual nature of the groups under study (including the elasticity one
may find in their structures and processes over time), let us address the
preexisting literature examining the effects of particular group behaviors
and attributes on the quality of the deliberation and the decisions that these
groups produce. It could be fairly asserted that the groupthink phenomenon
lies near the heart of this research project. Groupthink is possibly the best-
known group-level phenomenon affecting foreign-policy decision making
(and of course policymaking groups more generally). And it encompasses
several separate phenomena that a variety of literatures have held are harmful to the decision-making process and inhibit the ability of decision-making
groups to achieve successful outcomes.

Formally, the model is clear and direct. "Groupthink (Janis 1982) is a
linear model of how seven antecedents increase the likelihood of premature concurrence seeking (groupthink), which leads to eight psychological symptoms of groupthink, which lead to symptoms of defective decision
making, which lead to poor decision outcomes" (McCauley 1998, 143).
Janis saw a cohesive group of individuals seeking consensus as the center-
piece of this phenomenon. According to Janis, "high cohesion is necessary
but not sufficient to produce groupthink" (McCauley 1989, 252). The other
six antecedent conditions include four structural faults (insulation, a lack
of a tradition of impartial leadership, a lack of norms requiring methodical
procedures, and a homogeneity of members' background and ideology) and
two elements associated with a provocative situation context (high stress
stemming from a threatening situation in which there is limited hope and
low self-esteem induced by recent failures, a lower sense of self-efficacy, or
moral dilemmas that violate ones ethical standards).

Moving on in Janis's causal chain, the symptoms of groupthink include
possessing an illusion of invulnerability, a belief in the group's inherent
morality, the use of collective rationalizations, stereotyping the out-group,
self-censorship, illusions of unanimity, directly pressuring dissenters, and
the presence of self-appointed mind-guards. The symptoms of defective decision making include gross omissions in surveying objectives; gross omissions in the survey of alternatives; conducting a poor information search;

processing information in a biased manner; failing to reconsider rejected alternatives; failing to examine the costs and risks of the preferred choice; and failing to work out detailed implementation, monitoring, and contingency plans (Janis 1982). These behaviors increase the probability of low-quality decisions and outcomes.

This work has been critiqued on many occasions, and its tenets have been tested using a wide variety of methodologies. These critiques have varied from investigations into the particular emphasis that should be placed on various parts of the theory to fundamental discussions on whether or not Janis's emphasis on procedural phenomena is misplaced. Some simply doubt the scope of the effects of procedural behaviors on policy choices and outcomes; others think the prioritization of the procedural over the political is misplaced, given the explicitly political nature of the events that Janis studies (Kramer 1998). Adherents to the latter school of thought believe Janis is improperly focused on process and politics-free evaluations of "quality," whereas politicians often rate those outcomes that are political wins as those that are the "best" (Peterson et al. 1998). And, of course, since parts of Janis's theory are connected in various ways with specific factors that have been said to affect the nature of human decision making, parts of it have been examined outside of studies specifically examining groupthink. After all, the components of Janis's model were not newly discovered influences on decision making: "Janis simply selected a subset (of influences) and wrapped them in a metaphor" (Fuller and Aldag 1998, 172). Patterns can be seen in these studies and critiques written over the last two decades that raise serious questions about Janis's conception of groupthink. However, even if there seem to be flaws in Janis's originally proposed outline of the causes and effects of groupthink, after undergoing numerous examinations, parts of his theory still appear to be useful concepts for understanding the quality of group decision making (notably his focus on the importance of how decision-making groups are structured), and Janis's thoughts have served as a valuable jumping-off point for other scholars to further consider the value or harm that particular group processes can have on the quality of group decision making. But considering the work of those who have critiqued Janis is important. It shows how this research has moved forward over time and points to how it may be further refined in the future. With that in mind, consider some of the contributions of the following four scholars who have worked to improve our understanding of groupthink.

Critics of Janis's Groupthink

Clark McCauley

Clark McCauley has written thoughtful studies of groupthink, including an article in the February/March 1998 issue of *Organizational Behavior and Human Decision Processes*, which was devoted to reviewing the groupthink literature twenty-five years after Janis's *Victims of Groupthink* (1972) was first published. In an earlier work, he dealt with the issue of whether or not group cohesion was really at the root of groupthink. McCauley's 1989 study saw groupthink's true roots in structural and procedural faults like promotional leadership and group insulation, not in the presence (or lack) of cohesive groups. Other studies of groupthink that have reached similar conclusions include Flowers (1977), Tetlock et al. (1992), and Peterson et al. (1998). Furthermore, in the same study McCauley held that Janis improperly combined a number of disparate behaviors under the "groupthink" rubric. Importantly, McCauley stressed that some of what Janis saw as groupthink was truly only compliance, a point also stressed in Paul 't Hart's (1991) review of the groupthink literature in *Political Psychology*. This has a number of important implications, muddling both our understanding of the exact nature of groupthink and our understanding of the exact nature of its causes and symptoms. If, for example, the same situational stimuli can lead to both groupthink and compliance, as McCauley states, can they be usefully included in models examining one, the other, or both?

McCauley (1998) went even deeper in reconceptualizing groupthink. Whereas Janis had put a heavy emphasis on the importance of self-esteem, discussing its key role in maintaining an amiable, functioning group and how the threat of failure could undermine self-esteem, McCauley reverses that emphasis. He sees uncertainty as being the underlying threat in this causal chain. It is uncertainty from which a threat of failure emerges and from which a lowered sense of efficacy, damaging compliance and excessive concurrence seeking can emerge.

Glen Whyte

Like McCauley, Whyte (1998) sees many of the behaviors associated with groupthink occur in decision making and believes that they can have negative consequences. However, also like McCauley, Whyte does not believe that these are brought on by the specific influences that Janis stresses. In particular, Whyte believes that Janis's prioritization of group cohesiveness is misplaced. Instead, Whyte believes that the focus should be on the sense of collective efficacy that groups develop. The basic problem is that groups often believe they can do more than they can. And this inflated belief in their own efficacy can lead to the structural and procedural faults in decision making that Janis attributes to group cohesion. It can also lead to excessive risk taking and at least partially account for the group polarization phenomenon that holds that a "group will be inclined to be more risky than its average individual member was prior to participation in group discussion" (Whyte 1998, 195).

A heightened sense of collective efficacy (or perhaps merely a desire to believe in the group on that matter) maybe be tied to a number of other factors often associated with groupthink. For example, overoptimism has been linked to groupthink in several studies ('t Hart 1991), and this may also be linked to the so-called runaway norm. The latter stems from the political pressures that exist within groups and the fact that "it is sometimes highly desirable to be a *bit more* risky than other group members" (Raven 1998, 357). This tendency can lead groups to be more risky than individuals, as the various group members try to out-risk-take each other. Developing an inflated sense of the group's capabilities may spur this behavior. Other scholars have also highlighted how groupthink can make groups more willing to take risks. As 't Hart writes, "the characteristics and consequences of de-individuation contain forces which provoke a negligence of risks" (1991, 266). Not surprisingly, 't Hart (1998) thinks that one of the most important things groups can do to ensure that they do not behave in excessively risky ways is to ensure that individuals remain responsible for their contributions to group decision making and to ensure that small, isolated groups are not allowed to control policymaking.

Whyte's analysis is not wholly dissimilar from that of Janis. He sees collective efficacy as a necessary but not sufficient cause of groupthink. Whyte believes that Janis's structural faults remain as "enabling conditions of groupthink" (1998, 191). The conditions that give rise to collective efficacy likely also lead to directive leadership and insulation and a lack of methodical procedures. And he sees social-identity theory connecting his interest in collective efficacy with Janis's focus on cohesiveness, for "if identification with the group increases commitment to group values and norms, then collective efficacy will increase as identification increases" (Whyte 1998, 203). But the centrality of collective efficacy in Whyte's analysis of groupthink does change our understanding of the phenomenon in key ways and reduces the importance of some of the variables Janis prioritized. Another example of this is that Whyte believes stress should not be highlighted in our understanding of groupthink, because "people's beliefs in their capabilities determine not only their level of motivation, but also how much stress they experience in threatening situations" (1998, 191). Once again, for Whyte, collective efficacy appears to be the central variable influences other behaviors and dynamics.

Paul 't Hart

Paul 't Hart has written frequently on groupthink and associated phenomena, as he has spent much of his career studying how small groups function in the political arena. He has made many notable findings, and he has pushed along our understanding of groupthink a great deal, for example, by pointing out that Janis too often blurred the line between two distinct types of groupthink: collective avoidance and collective overoptimism ('t Hart 1990). But here we want to highlight his work on how we can evaluate group performance. This is a central issue to this project and to the work on groupthink. Janis believed that groups should be judged on the basis of the outcomes that stem from the concrete actions and orders a particular group produces. However, as 't Hart, Stern, and Sundelius (1997) have pointed out, groups exist to fulfill many functions, so evaluating the quality of a group's performance may be a much more complex matter. How can we "cope with the multiple functions that groups in government fulfill, and the conflicting evaluation criteria that are associated with these functions" ('t Hart 1998, 307)?

Policymaking groups exist to perform multiple functions, according to 't Hart (1998). In his first model, groups exist to solve problems. They function as think tanks. In this model, it is perfectly appropriate to judge a group according to its ability to collect information, the manner in which it processes information, and the quality of its deliberations—all matters that interested Janis. But groups function as more than just problem solvers, and 't Hart's second model of policymaking groups focuses on their role in articulating and adjudicating value disputes. In this model, groupthink can be a hindrance, but it can also help groups operate effectively. In order to manage competing values effectively, many voices must be heard, and a group's decisions should reflect "the plurality of views and stakeholders" ('t Hart 1998, 312). Groupthink can block that from happening. But it can also create the type of congenial atmosphere that assists with managing these types of matters, and that is of central importance in this model of policymaking. "Whereas from a model 1 perspective, government failure is the product of bad decision making, the ultimate threat to good government in the model 2 world is not bad policy but political paralysis, that is, the inability to resolve conflict and to reach any collective decision at all. Groupthink is an effective antidote to indecisiveness and political impasse" ('t Hart 1998, 312).

The third model of policymaking proposed by 't Hart views group behavior as aimed at fostering institutionalized action. This can be accomplished through substantive actions, but much of this work, both inside the group and outside of it, is symbolic and expressive ('t Hart, Stern, and Sundelius 1997). Creating and maintaining support for a decision can be a key purpose behind a group's existence (Fuller and Aldag 1997). But Janis does not leave much room for this group purpose, and it is hard to square it with his notion of what groups should do. This model of policymaking lacks a precise description of "good" decision making that fits with Janis's ideas. To the extent there is such a thing, the existence of groupthink can often actually be said to promote it. After all, groupthink can raise morale and resolve, matters of considerable consequence if a key purpose for a group's existence is to legitimate its existence and actions.

Randall Peterson et al.

While much of 't Hart's work has pushed forward new theoretical frames for looking at these issues, there are many scholars who have engaged in empirical and experimental studies of groupthink and the techniques Janis said should be utilized to avoid it. They have investigated a number of parts of the groupthink phenomena and their results have not always fit with Janis's expectations. For example, Callaway et al. (1985) found that whether or not groups contained high-dominance members did matter, as Janis expected. But it mattered in a way that Janis did not predict. Groups with such individuals made better decisions and in less time than other groups. Most of the empirical investigations into groupthink are discussed in 't Hart's (1991) review article in *Political Psychology* and James Esser's

(1998) review in *Organizational Behavior and Human Decision Processes*, and further empirical work in this area has continued since those articles were written. But while groupthink and associated phenomena have been a popular subject of research, many of these studies have raised as many questions as they have answered and left our understanding of certain key points muddled by contradictory findings.

One of the articles of this sort that is indicative of a number of others in this research program is Peterson et al. (1998). This research is quite interesting, both in the ways it supports Janis and in the findings that challenge his views of groupthink and the processes leading to high-quality decision making. Randall Peterson and his colleagues examined the behavior of seven top management teams using a Q-sort technique (GDQ), to see what types of groups produce the best outcomes (Peterson et al. judged outcomes on the basis of whether or not they "satisfy strategic constituencies"). While finding support for some of Janis's ideas, they also produced findings that clashed with the vigilant decision-making processes favored by Janis. Their findings suggest that the most productive groups (measured in terms of satisfying "strategic constituencies") will feature "greater leader strength, more centralization of authority, greater rigidity, more willingness to take risks, less legalism, and more optimism than the ideal type for vigilant decision making" (Peterson et al. 1998, 291). While Janis and several experimental studies have called for highly impartial leadership that does not stifle debate, the most successful groups they observed featured biased leaders who were trying to persuade their colleagues. Another key finding, one that fits with Tetlock et al. (1992) and other critiques of Janis, is that the influence of strong group cohesion has been overstated as a determiner of poor group performance.

The Costs of Janis's Solution

Finally, Peterson et al. (1998) are among a number of scholars who have pointed out that even if Janis's understandings of the basic phenomena he is considering are accurate, the potential solutions he proposes to "fix" the problem raise another set of concerns. After all, if policymakers are to practice the "vigilant" decision making Janis favors, they will be placing heavy demands on themselves and their organizations, which will make it more difficult to make a decision and may break down collegiality in government. After all, to "be 'vigilant' in decision making, groups are required to carefully survey their objectives, conduct an extensive and dispassionate search for relevant information, and make contingency plans once an option has been selected" (Peterson 1998, 274). Strategic management "critics have argued that advocates of vigilant decision making underemphasize the advantages of simple decision rules" (Peterson 1998, 275), and "in many contexts, decision makers quickly reach the point of diminishing marginal returns for further information search and analysis" (Peterson et al. 1998, 275). In light of this concern, it is apparent that almost every part of Janis's theory has (and in many cases continues to) come under close scrutiny.

Other Group Dynamics–Related Research Programs

Our research falls in the vein of work that follows and builds upon the work of Janis and other scholars who are interested in how group processes affect foreign-policy choices. Much of this research is directly tied to studies that focus on groupthink, but there are other lines of research in this area that we should briefly discuss, as they feature similar dynamics.

While these dynamics are certainly touched on in the groupthink literature, there is a vibrant literature outside of the particularly focused work on what is sometimes termed group-attribution bias or out-group-homogeneity bias. Basically, this deals with the fact that when people are working in group settings they are even more likely than usual to attribute the behavior of others to the personal dispositions those others are presumed to possess and to see others as more united and conniving than they actually are (McDermott 2004).

Another reason for why groups may behave in less than "vigilant" ways is that they are simply engaging in the routines and shortcuts called for according to the preexisting standard operating procedures they are supposed to follow. There is a considerable literature, most of which is associated with work on governmental or bureaucratic politics, that details institutional reasons for why groups act as they do. The pressures on groups from the organizations in which they are a part and the institutional structures in which they exist may block the sort of deeper, broader examination of the facts surrounding a decision-making event that Janis's work would seem to call for. Groups do not tackle problems in a vacuum. They collect information and deliberate in ways that are in accordance with norms, rules, and procedures set down prior to any one particular decision-making event (Allison 1971; Halperin 1974; Welch 1992).

And the circumstances when small, high-level decision-making groups are likely to wield the most influence over U.S. policymaking, according to the likes of Holsti (1972) and Hermann and Hermann (1989), are often crisis situations. These situations are often perceived to require quick action and sometimes grand high-profile responses. This suggests that it may be important to consider situation variables when trying to account for how prominent a role a decision-making group is likely to have in setting policy. And it also suggests that small groups operating in high-stress, surprising, crisis situations may be acting under enormous pressures that limit their ability to act in the "vigilant" ways prescribed by Janis (though it is also possible that the stakes involved and the short time frame of decision making may in fact move decisions closer to those ideals, as some of the "noise" and politics surrounding decision making in other situations is necessarily dispensed with in these types of situations).

Finally, the research on decision units and decision-making style includes a number of facets that would seem to fit with the groupthink literature. Of particular interest might be the conditions during which the process of decision making is most likely to have an effect on the policies that are decided upon, whose voices are likely to be the most influential, and how the characteristics of particular leaders are likely to lead them to be more or less likely to favor particular decision-making techniques and even specific policy proposals (Preston 2001; Hermann 2001; Hermann, Preston, Korany, and Shaw 2001; Kowert 2002). Among the variables that this literature focuses on are the experience of the lead decision maker and the relative experience and relationship that exists between the executive and his advisors. Other key variables would include whether the leader and the group value disagreement as part of "good" decision making and whether or not gatekeepers are employed to limit the spread of information and access within the group. Relatedly, just how well does the group function as a cohesive team, what types of norms does it adopt, and what behaviors does it engage in? This also touches on ideas from a number of other literatures, such as the work that has been done on the stages of group development (Tuckman 1965; Tuckman and Jensen 1977; Stern 1997; Stern and Sundelius 1997).

Group-Related Variables Requiring Examination

The research on groupthink, governmental politics, foreign-policy decision making, and related literatures clearly illustrates a host of ways that group-level behavior can affect foreign policy. But clearly there is much left to be firmly determined when it comes to the exact nature of these relationships. Throughout this review, many of these effects have seemed to be conditional, and there is obvious disagreement about which of them are strongest. This research is aimed at providing greater clarity on these matters, enabling us to better see the effects of a wide variety of group-level characteristics by studying them systematically across a wide variety of cases. In chapter 3, we will discuss the nature of the variables in our model in deeper detail, but this review of the relevant literature clearly points toward a number of matters that need to be investigated in our study, given previous research.

First, it appears clear that we will need to include a variety of variables that account for the nature of the context within which the groups we examine are performing. Both the groupthink literature and the larger foreign-policy decision-making literature suggest that decision-making groups may act differently given their situational environment. Is there a crisis at hand? What is the stress level? Is there a short time constraint? How do the decision makers perceive the nature and extent of the challenges or threats they face? Finally, given the arguments of groupthink critics like Kramer and the host of scholars who study the political roots of foreign-policy choices (Snyder 1991; Milner 1997), what is the political milieu in which the decision makers are operating? Do they have domestic opposition? Do they have support from foreign powers? What does the public think? While no single one of these contextual variables represents the basic nature, behavior, or characteristics of the group itself, there is a large body of literature suggesting that at least some of these variables will shape how the group functions, the choices it makes, and the policies it opts to pursue.

Second, it appears that there are several characteristics that groups possess that may affect how they act (or do not act) in specific situations and the quality of the outcomes that result from those choices. Here we mean somewhat longstanding structural attributes that decision-making groups will possess. There appear to be several ingrained characteristics of a group that the literature is largely united in labeling harmful—the lack of a tradition of methodical procedures, insulation, and overoptimism (an illusion of invulnerability), among others. From the debates in the groupthink literature, it appears that there are also other key characteristics that many scholars think are important determinants of a group's performance, but the exact nature of their effects is somewhat controversial. These include how cohesive a group is and whether or not the group leader engages in biased, promotional leadership. Among the other variables that group-oriented literatures discuss as affecting the quality of foreign-policy decision making are the level of interest a leader has in the topic, whether the group values or even allows disagreement among its members, and whether certain opinions are suppressed by gatekeepers.

Finally, there are the behaviors that a group performs when it is dealing with specific foreign-policy operations or decisions. These are not characteristics that the group necessarily has over time and across cases of decision. These are specific actions taken in particular circumstances and mostly encompass what Janis termed "information processing errors," matters like the quality of the information search, the reliance (or not) on stereotypes, and how deeply objectives and alternatives are considered. A number of studies have suggested that some of these variables are important determinants of how well a group functions and how likely it is that it will achieve "good" results.

In the coming chapters, we will investigate the impact of these variables. While many of these matters are central to the groupthink literature, our interest is wider. We are not testing the validity of Janis's causal chain or whether groupthink or compliance has more of a negative effect on political behavior. In terms of the literature on groups and foreign-policy decision making, our contribution is to systematically examine what are "good" and "bad" group traits and behaviors (and how does that vary depending on the situational context), given the variables that a variety of literatures (and critiques of those literatures) have presented as being particularly influential on the quality of political action. We are looking at how these relationships existed in a wide variety of key decision-making moments in international politics in order to present findings that are at once the most generalizable in the field (at least in terms of how these variables affect foreign relations), while also providing extensively detailed summaries of certain decision events to note how our basic findings can vary, depending on specific situations.

Individual-Level Psychology and the Foreign-Policy Process

It seems intuitive to many students of international politics that the psychology of individual actors makes a difference in the process of foreign-policy making. Nonetheless, many of the major schools of thought in the field have disregarded or ignored individual-level psychology in most of their research. These schools include realism and neorealism, rationalist approaches, and constructivism. In addition, many major empirical research programs fail to include any psychological variables. These include large-n research projects dealing with correlates of war, militarized interstate disputes, cycle theories of war, and research that focuses on operationalizing realist concepts such as power and interests. While each of these schools and programs have provided us with important insights, virtually none of them have looked at the role of individual actors and their psychological characteristics.

Meanwhile, the field of political psychology has grown and developed over time, resulting in important theoretical and empirical advances in how to study the psychology of individuals. The purpose of this section is to review that literature and tie it into the main focus of our work on better understanding foreign-policy decision-making processes. There is an abundance of literature on individual-level psychology, and while we cannot review all of it, we will provide some historical review on the evolution of the field and then spend some time on more recent developments that result in quantitative psychological variables.

Where do we think individual-level variables are likely to affect the foreign-policy decision-making process? One can imagine that we might see their effects in many different areas, but our present work focuses on two broad areas in particular: process and policy. We know from existing research that there is great variance in how administrations conduct their decision making. We see this variance in terms of such things as thoroughness of information search, tolerance of dissent, level of consideration of alternatives, and many other factors that we discuss elsewhere in this book. Given that there is such variance across administrations, we wonder if individual-level psychology plays a role. Perhaps a president with a high level of cognitive complexity is going to demand more and better information in the decision-making process, perhaps a more controlling president will have a lower level of tolerance for dissent, and perhaps a dogmatic president is more likely to have a process that limits consideration of alternatives. In all of these simple examples, we see the possible effects of psychological factors affecting the process of decision making.

It is even more intuitive to consider the possibility of psychology affecting the direction and content of policy. We think that something *within* leaders such as Hitler, Stalin, Patton, Churchill, Gandhi, Mao, and Truman had a causal impact on the kinds of policies they each pursued. If their individual-level differences did indeed matter, then we are inherently talking about their psychology. This may include such things as level of distrust, conflict orientation, images of others, need for power, dominance orientation, and many other possible constructs.

How do we begin to organize our conception of the content of policy? Rarely in the field of political psychology specifically or international relations more generally do we think we can accurately predict specific policy choices. But there is a general, broad organizing notion that underlies much work in this area, namely something like a cooperation-conflict continuum. Most policies of interest in the field of international relations move in one of these two directions. Indeed, many schools in the field—such as game theory, event data analysis, large-n conflict studies, and others—conceptualize their dependent variables in terms of some kind of a conflict scale. Of course, there are plenty of controversies (whether it is one continuum from conflict to cooperation or two separate ones; whether we can actually scale actions using something like an interval or ratio-level measurement or if they should be simply dichotomized; where certain kinds of policies, such as surrender or retreat, belong on a continuum), but many nonetheless recognize the general directionality of conflict and cooperation.

In a later section of this chapter, we will return to these two areas where we think individual-level psychology may make a difference in foreign-policy decision making. But first we turn to a general overview of the development of individual-level political psychology that includes broad methodological approaches. After that, we look at several specific constructs that researchers have used to organize psychological variables. We then discuss some ongoing controversies and issues in the assessment of psychological characteristics. We finish this chapter by returning to our dependent variables of interest: process and policy.

The Development of Political Psychology

The convergent study of politics and psychology is perhaps as old as the earliest political philosophers. Both Plato and Aristotle had something to say about psychological phenomena in the realm of politics. In more modern times, Bloom (1993) notes that perhaps the greatest minds in psychology, such as Freud, Erikson, and Mead, all focused some of their work on psychological phenomena affecting society and politics, namely in the area of identity politics. Lasswell's (1930) *Psychopathology and Politics* provided one of the earliest systematic treatments of political psychology and is frequently referred to as the origin of the new academic field (Deutsch and Kinvall 2002, 15). Though sometimes criticized for its focus on pathology (the criticism being that many, if not most, political actors do not have a mental disorder rising to the level of a pathology), Lasswell's work nonetheless made explicit connections to mental functioning and its effects in politics.

In the wake of Lasswell's work, scholars investigated specific political puzzles by looking at underlying psychological phenomena. Leites (1951, 1953) sought to explain why Soviet bargaining behavior after World War II did not fit Western expectations. He argued that there was a default social-psychological operating mechanism in the Soviet Politburo that was largely driven by the personalities of Lenin and Stalin. To understand Soviet behavior, one needed first to understand the "operational code" of the Politburo and, therefore, the psychology of Lenin and Stalin.

Several scholars took up another puzzle regarding the unusual political behavior of President Woodrow Wilson (see, for example, George and George 1956). Wilson displayed a pattern of frequently approaching success throughout his career only to seemingly engage in some form of self-defeatism, the most famous of these incidents being the failure of the United States to ratify the Treaty of Versailles, which, as one of its provisions, created the League of Nations. Explanations included such things as competition with his father, physiological causes, high control orientation, among other things, and while the collection of essays on the topic makes for fascinating reading, if they reach different conclusions, they generally agree on the underlying notion that Wilson's mental functioning played a causal role in his self-defeating political behavior.

As the foreign-policy decision-making school developed as a field in international relations, several scholars made contributions in the form of frameworks that explicitly included psychology in their causal chains. Snyder, Bruck, and Sapin (1954) made what many consider the seminal contribution to the field of foreign-policy decision making. While they include many different factors, both internal and external, which they suggest are likely to have an impact on the decision-making process, their thesis is quite clear: in the end, it is individuals who make decisions and, therefore, the "state is its decision makers" (Snyder, Bruck, and Sapin 1962, 65). Inherent in this, of course, is that individual psychological differences are critical factors in the process. They devote a major section of their book to discussing "motives" of decision makers as critical variables.

Similar frameworks were offered by Sprout and Sprout (1965), who talked about the role of "cognitive behaviorism"; Brecher, Steinberg, and Stein (1969), who focused on the "psychological environment" including attitudes and elite images held by decision makers; and M. Brewster Smith (1968), who was the most explicit in talking about psychology in process, including such things as object appraisal, ego defense, and engaged attitudes. In none of these frameworks do they focus on the psychology of individuals simply to better understand them. Rather, they focus on individuals as the central actors in a multifaceted process that results in state behavior. While factors external to the actor are clearly important in these frameworks and undeniable to many objective observers, their "reality" must always be interpreted, weighted, processed, and acted upon by one or more individuals in positions of power within the state. If a tree falls in the woods, and the decision maker does not hear it nor believe that it fell, then for all intents and purposes the state does not acknowledge the fallen tree.

A vivid historical example of this occurred during the Cuban Missile Crisis, when Kennedy received two relatively contradictory letters from Khrushchev, one more conciliatory and the other more hostile, without any intervening communication by Kennedy. Upon careful advice from key advisors, Kennedy chose simply to ignore the second, hostile letter and acted upon only the information in the first. There was a clear reality that the second letter had arrived, yet Kennedy acted upon an entirely different reality, the one he felt would be most helpful in resolving the crisis. In this case, Kennedy made a conscious choice in the matter. In many other cases, decision makers are not aware of the effect of their own heuristics, biases, or cognitive shortcuts. But the point remains the same: incoming information must be processed, consciously or unconsciously, well or poorly, through one or more individuals before action is taken; human agency is a central fact of state decision making.

This does not mean that factors external to the decision makers do not matter, nor does it mean that decision makers always misconstrue incoming information. It means simply that all incoming information, before being acted upon (or not) by the (reified) "state," must first go through some level of processing by human agents. And given that, it becomes essentially a truism that individual psychological differences are going to matter in the process—perhaps more or less so (which becomes an empirical question and subsequently perhaps a question of parsimony), but they will matter.

Walker and Schafer (2006a, 2006b) agree with this assessment that decision makers are essential components of the process, and they acknowledge that conceptually there may be variance in the extent to which an individual's psychology affects the process. They note that decision makers may accurately reflect stimuli and situational constraints, or they may bring their own psychological predispositions to the process. Walker and Schafer refer to the former phenomenon as "mirroring effects," where the actor simply reflects existing external realities, and the latter as "steering effects," where the actor's psychology becomes a crucial intervening variable. Of course, the extent to which a decision maker mirrors reality or steers the process is itself idiosyncratic and may therefore be a psychological variable.

Many other scholars have pointed out that situational and psychological constraints result in variance in the extent to which an individual's psychology makes a significant difference in the process. Greenstein (1969), Hermann (1976), Byman and Pollack (2001), and Winter (2003) offer somewhat different conceptions of when the psychology of an actor is more likely to matter, but they generally agree on certain factors, such as the role or power position of the actor, or if the situation is novel or changing, a crisis or institutional conflict, or symbolically significant. Having discussed some of the seminal works regarding the role of psychology in decision making and some of the important frameworks contributing to the topic, we now turn to a discussion of the approaches and constructs used for psychological assessment by scholars.

Approaches and Constructs

There are several ways to distinguish approaches that have been used to assess the psychology of individual actors. In this section, we focus on two such distinctions: (1) idiographic versus nomothetic approaches and (2) cognitive versus personality psychology. Another distinction, which we will reference throughout this section, is whether the methods involved are qualitative or quantitative.

Idiographic Versus Nomothetic Approaches

Must psychology be thought of as an idiosyncratic, one-individual-at-a-time endeavor (idiographic), or are there generalizable patterns or universal principles that can be applied across individuals or in large-*n* studies (nomothetic)? The question is more one of methodological and philosophical approach, as both approaches, whether explicitly so or not, are interested in contributing to generalizable knowledge; idiographic approaches just tend to do so one individual at a time. But the underlying philosophical differences are important.

Idiographic, or single-case, approaches are generally qualitative in nature, limited in their number of subjects, and provide holistic, often depth-psychology analysis of subjects. The product from such an analysis is often referred to as a psychobiography; it looks at the subject's whole life with the aim of explaining adult patterns of political behavior. The contributions on Woodrow Wilson noted earlier use such an approach. Greenstein (1969; see also Winter 2003) notes that there are often three interrelated parts of a psychobiography. The *phenomenology* is the puzzle the researchers are interested in trying to solve—the unusual adult political behavior that is difficult to explain given the immediate circumstances. The *dynamic* is the adult existential psychological characteristics in the individual that would seem to provide an explanation for the puzzle in the phenomenology. Finally, *genesis* is the explanation given for the onset of the dynamic: these are events, usually happening in childhood, that gave rise to the particular psychological makeup of the adult individual. In addition to some of those cited earlier, there are many excellent examples of idiographic research including Erikson's (1958) study on Luther, Post (1993) on Saddam Hussein, Glad (1980) on Jimmy Carter, and Renshon (1996) on Bill Clinton.

As noted above, while idiographic approaches tend to be in depth and provide "thick" analysis of the subject, they still nonetheless hope to contribute to generalizable knowledge. In that regard, the point is not to know more about Woodrow Wilson per se (though of course that is one of the important ends) but rather to know more about Wilson such that we know more about psychological functioning in humans in general. However, nomothetic approaches are much more explicit about looking for patterns across individuals, generally by looking at a small number of psychological characteristics across a larger number of subjects at any one time. They may be qualitative or quantitative with their methods. Nomothetic approaches include such things as developing typologies of leaders across a small number of characteristics; measuring characteristics of subjects using psychometric scales; and using survey research, content analysis and experimental methods to look for psychological patterns.

Some illustrative examples of nomothetic research include Barber (1968a, 1968b), who looked at U.S. presidents and built a four-category typology consisting of two different psychological characteristics; Hermann (1980), who correlated psychological traits of forty-five heads of state with several different state-behavior variables; Robison (2006), who, controlling for several other factors, demonstrated the effect of the operational codes of U.S. presidents on the state's cooperative and conflictual policies under their administration; Schafer (1999), who demonstrated the effect of certain psychological characteristics of U.S. presidents on the propensity for groupthink in their decision-making processes; Winter (1987), who looked at motive congruence between a U.S. president and society at the time and correlated those with the leader's appeal and the leader's performance; Crichlow (2002), who investigated the effect of the psychological characteristics of members of Congress on openness to international trade; and Tetlock (1981), who content analyzed U.S. senators' speeches and correlated those with isolationist tendencies.

Both approaches, of course, contribute to our understanding of psychology in the field of politics, but they provide very different kinds of information and answer very different kinds of questions. Because our own research tends to be nomothetic in nature, much of our attention in the sections that follow will focus on those kinds of approaches and constructs.

Cognitive Versus Personality

Greenstein (1969) pointed out that the term "personality" is the broadest, most inclusive term when referring to any type of mental or behavioral activity. As classically used by psychologists, personality includes such things as attitudes, cognitions, motivations, and other ego-defense mechanisms. However, we have found it helpful to use the distinction, made by many political scientists, that separates cognitions and attitudes from other components of personality such as motives and ego-defense mechanisms (Greenstein 1969;

Schafer 2000). Cognitions and attitudes are products of mental functioning that involve relatively *conscious* thinking about a subject or object; their manifestations are such things as beliefs, prejudices, images, schemata, and operational codes. On the other hand, motives, ego-defense mechanisms, personality traits, and other components of depth psychology are generally considered to be more *unconscious* responses and reactions.

The conscious/cognitive versus unconscious/personality distinction is certainly not perfect (and there are many other ways that researchers have divided up personality into categories). Indeed, though conscious thinking may form cognitions, they often function at a level below our conscious awareness. And, though motives or ego-defense mechanisms often come from sources outside of our conscious awareness, we sometimes become aware of some of their manifestations. Still, the distinction is helpful in organizing constructs in political psychology.[2] Across this divide there have been both qualitative and quantitative methods used by researchers. We turn now to a discussion of many of the different specific constructs that have been developed and used by researchers in political psychology. Again, our intention is not to be exhaustive in this review but rather to focus on some of the seminal contributions, some of the more recent advancements, and some that are part of our own empirical contribution later in the volume.

Constructs

James Barber's (1972) book *Presidential Character* is an often-cited seminal typological work in political psychology, and, as with many early efforts in any field, it has since been the target of some criticism. But it retains value as a pioneering work. Indeed, Greenstein (1969) offers critical praise of Barber's (1968a, 1968b) initial publications of his typology. Barber developed a scheme for classifying presidents based upon two variables, each having two values, activity level (high or low) and attitude or outlook (positive or negative), resulting in a 2x2 typology. While other research has developed more clearly operationalized and more theoretically developed variables, Barber's contribution continues to be cited today because of its initial effort at systematizing how personality shapes presidential leadership.

Lloyd Etheredge made two early and important contributions to trait analysis in political psychology. His first (Etheredge 1975) is one of the few empirical pieces that has used "real-world" subjects (foreign-policy specialists in the U.S. State Department) and correlated their psychological traits to their behavioral propensities using survey-research techniques. He found that three traits in particular correlated with higher conflict propensities: a high level of distrust, a desire for power, and a low level of self-esteem. In his second and more famous work, *A World of Men* (1978), he looks at two trait variables: extraversion and dominance. Using blind-coding methods, Etheredge ascertained scores for thirty-six U.S. presidents and key foreign-policy advisors on these two variables and found that those high on extraversion were more likely to favor inclusionary policies, while those who were higher on dominance were more likely to favor force.

One construct in political psychology has produced a large number of findings using only one variable, integrative complexity. Whereas other cognitive constructs that are discussed later focus on the content of cognitions, this variable, along with other versions of "complexity," focuses on cognitive style and the structure of cognitions, thus putting it more on the personality/unconscious side of our divide.[3] Peter Suedfeld and Philip Tetlock are the most well-known and prolific researchers in this area. Complexity research has demonstrated that lower complexity tends to correlate with high conflict propensities and that complexity tends to decline in the six-month period prior to the onset of a war (Driver 1977; Levi and Tetlock 1980; Suedfeld and Bluck 1988; Suedfeld and Tetlock 1977; Suedfeld, Tetlock, and Ramirez 1977).

One of the major research programs at the individual-level of analysis in political psychology focuses on motives, motive imagery, and needs analysis. David McClelland (1951, 1961) made some of the early and important theoretical and empirical contributions. In more recent times, David Winter (1993, 1987, 1980) has been the most prolific scholar using motive imagery as an analytical tool, particularly focusing on needs for power, affiliation, and achievement. Using content-analysis methods, Winter codes for motive imagery in verbal material of subjects, one example of "at-a-distance" assessment methods that will be discussed in greater detail later in this chapter. Among the findings from this research program are that those higher in need for power tend to be more aggressive and favor more hostile foreign policies (Winter 1987, 1993); those higher in need for affiliation tend to be more peaceful and cooperative, except under conditions of threat (Winter 1992, 1993); and those scoring high on need for achievement tend to be better entrepreneurs but not successful politicians (McClelland 1961; Winter 2002).

Another well-established research program using at-a-distance techniques is leadership-trait analysis (LTA), pioneered by Margaret Hermann
(1974, 1980, 1984, 1987). While there have been a few changes over the
years in Hermann's variables, the core have remained largely the same, and
today the research program looks at seven different psychological characteristics: need for power, distrust, conceptual complexity, self-confidence,
belief in ability to control events, task (versus relationship) orientation, and
in-group bias. From these seven characteristics, Hermann constructs three
derivative variables, each of which has two levels, which then result in an
eight-fold typology of leaders. The three derivative variables are: (1) whether
the leader respects or challenges constraints, (2) whether the leader is open
or closed to contextual information), and (3) whether the leader's focus is
more on problems and tasks or on relationships.

Here are some examples of the types in Hermann's eight-fold typology
of leaders. The *expansionist* is someone who challenges constraints, is generally closed to contextual information, and is more problem focused than
relationship focused. This type of leader is focused on expanding the power
of the leader and/or the state's influence and role. The *influential* is someone who respects constraints, is closed to information, and has a relationship focus. This leadership style is likely to result in building cooperative
relationships as a way to constructively advance one's own interests. The
opportunistic leader respects constraints, is open to information, and has a
problem focus. This type of leader tends to focus on what is possible in the
given situation with the given, realistic constraints.[4]

Hermann's 1980 article was groundbreaking in showing an important
connection between LTA variables and several different dependent variables
regarding state behavior. For instance, she found that distrust and need for
power correlated negatively with interdependence (versus independence)
of action, while need for affiliation and conceptual complexity correlated
positively with this variable. High distrust and control orientations correlated negatively with state commitment, while a participatory orientation (one
of her earlier derivative categories) correlated positively with commitment
(for additional findings, see Herman 1980).

Using our personality/unconscious versus cognitive/conscious divide, we
see that most of the variables discussed in the constructs thus far tend toward
the personality/unconscious side, though some of the variables in LTA seem
more cognitive in nature. Other research programs have been much more

explicit in their focus on cognition, and here we will spend a little time on three of them: image theory, cognitive mapping, and the operational code.

Kenneth Boulding provided a seminal contribution to the study of images fifty years ago with his well-known book *The Image* (1956). In it he argued that images of self and other mattered in foreign-policy decisions. Other classic contributions were offered by Holsti (1970) and Jervis (1976). The most cohesive and prolific research program dealing with images originated with Richard Cottam (1977) and has been expanded upon particularly by Richard Herrmann (1984, 1985; Herrmann, Voss, Schooler, and Ciarrochi 1997; Herrmann and Fischerkeller 1995) and Martha Cottam (1985, 1986, 1992, 1994). The idea is that individuals have inherent cognitive limitations, meaning that they must constantly filter, interpret, and limit the information they take in and process. Developing an image of an opposing country (or a friendly one) is therefore not only a common occurrence but also a necessary one. They argue that external images are likely to have three different components: (1) threat versus opportunity, (2) culturally similar versus culturally inferior, and (3) level of power. Various combinations of these three variables form ideal types of images, such as the "enemy image" (threat, culturally similar, similar level of power) and "dependent ally image" (opportunity, inferior culture, lower level of power).

Much of the research in this area has been qualitative and interpretative and has generally supported the argument that differences in images result in different foreign-policy preferences. (Cottam 1985, 1992, 1994; Herrmann 1984, 1985). Herrmann and Fischerkeller (1995) looked more systematically at the connection between images and behavior and found support for their hypotheses in two dyads: U.S.-Soviet Union during the cold war, when prevailing enemy images by each side resulted in containment and deterrence policies but no direct military engagement; and Iran-Iraq, where sometimes "mutual enemy images" (also marked by containment and deterrence policies) changed to "enemy-degenerate images," the latter being marked by threat, inferior culture, and similar level of power, and where conflict was much more likely to erupt.

The seminal work on cognitive maps was done by Axelrod (1972, 1976), though others made important early contributions that generally built on Axelrod's work (Bonham and Shapiro 1976; Roberts 1976; Hart 1976). The idea with cognitive mapping is that the analyst would make a visual "map" of the causal connections in the subject's cognitive content. The human mind makes many connections between objects as part of its standard operating procedures, and those connections tend to repeat and form patterns. Axelrod focused on causal connections between concepts because of the role of causal inference in problem solving and decision making in the human mind. If the analyst is effective at mapping the range of causal connections in the subject, then she or he presumably would be able to make better predictions about a subject's choice of behavior. The objective of prediction was explicit in the work of Bonham and Shapiro (1976), though Axelrod's (1976) objective was different. He thought that exposing a subject's cognitive map would enhance the quality of decision making by making explicit the cognitive shortcuts and assumptions that the subject was probably using implicitly, resulting in unnecessary oversimplification.

Content-analysis procedures have been the basis of cognitive mapping, with the analyst focusing on verbs (which mark the relationship between concepts) in the subject's spoken material. Once all causal connections are identified, they are aggregated and cross-referenced to produce the cognitive map. As with many of the psychological at-a-distance approaches, the early work in this area was done by hand, making the process quite labor intensive. Michael Young (1994) provided a crucial breakthrough by developing a computer-based system to conduct the aggregation and map-production part of the process. Some recent work on cognitive mapping moves the focus from the individual to the small decision-making group (Shapiro et al. 1988). Research on cognitive maps has provided insights on expert advice to policymakers (Bonham and Shapiro 1976), adjustments in cognitive content in response to a major event (Bonham et al. 1978), Jimmy Carter's response to the Soviet invasion of Afghanistan (Young 1994), and process versus causal reasoning in international negotiations (Bonham et al. 1997).

Operational code analysis (OCA) is one of the oldest and most-cited research programs in political psychology. In 1951, Nathaniel Leites published *The Operational Code of the Politburo*, in an effort to better understand unusual bargaining behavior by the Soviet Union. He concluded that members of the Politburo were essentially imprinted with the psychological traits of Lenin and Stalin. This explanation combined individual-level psychology—with a focus on depth psychology—with social-level psychology and group processes. Alexander George (1969, 1979) converted the operational-code construct to a primarily cognitive one, with a focus on the belief systems of individuals. Gesturing to the cognitive revolution in psychology in the 1960s, George believed it appropriate to focus primarily on the cognitive beliefs of subjects. In particular, he conceptualized the operational code as a belief system entailing a fairly small number of cohesive beliefs in the subject's cognitive makeup. George posited two broad categories of beliefs: philosophical beliefs, which summarized the way that the subject generally viewed international politics and other actors in the system, and instrumental beliefs, which summarized the views that the subject held about his or her own approach to political strategies and tactics.

After George's conceptual work, a number of operational-code studies were published (for example, Johnson 1977; McLellan 1971; Walker 1977; Stuart and Starr 1981; Walker and Falkowski 1984). Most of these followed a similar methodology involving qualitative content analysis and interpretation of the subject's words and deeds, either while in office or prior to taking office. The results of these studies were generally promising and demonstrated many times that a better understanding of a subject's cognitions helps provide insight into state behavior.

In the late 1990s, Stephen Walker began conceptualizing a quantitative content-analysis system for the operational code, which would be similar to other at-a-distance psychological assessment techniques such as LTA and motive analysis. This system would provide numerous advantages, including such things as reliability, replicability, direct comparisons, and statistical models (Walker, Schafer, and Young 1998; see also Schafer and Walker 2006b). While qualitative and interpretative operational codes no doubt provide valuable insights that cannot be captured by the quantitative operational code, the system of Walker et al. has led to a major expansion in this research program, with numerous studies and publications to date (see, for example, Walker et al. 2003, 1999, 1998; Walker and Schafer 2007, 2006, 2002, 2000; Schafer and Walker 2007, 2006a, 2001; Schafer and Crichlow 2002; Schafer et al. 2006; Marfleet 2000; Marfleet and Miller 2005; Malici 2005, 2006; Robison 2006; Thies 2006; Drury 2006; Stevenson 2006; Feng 2006, 2005; Crichlow 2006, 1998).

Walker and his colleagues called the content-analysis system for operational-code analysis the Verbs in Context System (VICS). It identifies each verb in the subject's verbal material—as verbs are key signifiers of power in relationships—and codes those verbs on a conflict-cooperation continuum. The results are used to construct indices that represent broad patterns in the subject's rhetoric and hence the manifestation of his or her belief system. Philosophical beliefs are indexed with the verbs used by the speaker when others are the grammatical subject of the clause, thus providing a representation of the way the speaker views others in the political system. Instrumental beliefs are indexed with verbs whose subject is the speaker or other key in-groups for the speaker, thus providing a representation of the patterns of strategies and tactics the speaker attributes to self (Walker, Schafer and Young 1998).[5]

Quantitative At-a-Distance Psychological Assessment

How does one get measurements of psychological characteristics for individuals who cannot be assessed directly in person, as obviously it is not practical nor generally possible to have direct access to many of the subjects we wish to study? Given this challenge, researchers have developed effective and efficient techniques for assessing many different psychological characteristics of individuals "at a distance," meaning they make assessments and derive measurements using available materials without direct access to the subjects. The central premise in the development of these research programs was the assumption that what people say and how they say things can tell us much about what they think and who they are. For instance, we all know the old adage that an optimist refers to the glass as half full, while a pessimist calls the same glass half empty. By specifying that specific traits or beliefs are associated with the usage of particular words, phrases, or speech patterns and then looking for these kinds of patterns in a subject's verbal material, we can assess many different psychological traits and characteristics. For instance, a person more inclined to engage in conflict is likely to use more conflict-oriented words in his or her rhetoric (operational code); someone who uses more black-and-white terms, such as *absolutely, definitely,* and *always,* as opposed to more gray terms, such as *possibly, maybe,* and *perhaps,* is presumed to be lower in conceptual complexity (LTA); and someone who has a high need for power is likely to use language with a higher number of references to asserting power and influence over other people (motive analysis).

Over the years, each of these research programs has refined the operationalizations of their constructs, assessed and measured the characteristics in more and more subjects, conducted different validity tests, and developed research tools such as norming samples that include averages and standard deviations for regional or world leaders. While virtually all of these research programs use verbal material to assess psychological characteristics, there are significant differences in the content-analysis methods employed by them. Two research programs, LTA and operational-code analysis, are based primarily upon dictionaries of words and phrases developed by the research-ers that are indicative of the characteristics under investigation. LTA, which as noted above includes seven different psychological characteristics, has fourteen different dictionaries, one for each characteristic showing posi-tive manifestations of the characteristic and one for each showing negative manifestations of the characteristic, the characteristics being trait variables such as distrust and in-group bias. The computation for each characteristic is then a ratio of the positive to negative manifestations.

The primary dictionary for the operational code consists of verbs and verb phrases that are categorized on a conflict-to-cooperation continuum. A secondary dictionary specifies whether the subject in each verb-based utter-ance is self or other. Taken together, these two dictionaries allow researchers to assess how conflict oriented the actor sees others in the political universe and how conflict oriented she or he sees herself or himself.

Because LTA and operational-code analysis are dictionary based, it has been possible in recent times to develop automated coding systems for each of these constructs. This means that personal computers can now do virtu-ally all of the content analysis for these two systems in a fraction of the time that hand coders would need—and with outstanding reliability: there is no coder fatigue, bias, or error. Both research programs use the same underly-ing software program, Profiler Plus, which is a full-language parser devel-oped by Social Science Automation. Once the verbal material of interest is parsed by Profiler Plus, the software then uses the specified dictionaries to conduct the content analysis.

Other research programs using at-a-distance techniques continue to be driven by hand coding, such as motive analysis and integrative complexity. In these programs, the broader content and context of the rhetoric play a larger role, and so dictionary development and automated processing have not yet been developed, though there may be some efforts to do so in the future.

Taken as a set, these quantitative programs have opened political-psy-chology research questions on many fronts. Measurements allow compari-sons of subjects, assessments of subjects over time, comparisons of groups of subjects, statistical modeling, and analysis of many other types of effects.

While these research programs have provided an important break-through in political psychology, they have their critics and limitations, though most of these are empirical questions that have simply not yet been fully investigated. Some concerns deal with the extent to which the subject actually authored the verbal material or perhaps was coached into using certain "sound bites" by his or her political handlers. The argument goes as follows: if the words are not the subject's own, then how can one use them to assess her or his psychological characteristics?[6]

Another set of concerns deal with trait stability—this is sometimes called the trait-state debate. The argument here is that perhaps certain situational constraints trigger different psychological characteristics in the subject, and thus psychology depends upon the "state" of the individual and is therefore not so predictable. Finally, one might wonder how far we have to cast our research nets to capture the relevant psychologies at work in a state's decision-making episode. The inclination, for obvious reasons, has been to focus on individual chiefs of state. But virtually no leader makes a decision in complete isolation, and in many instances, key advisors may be even more important than the chief of state (Crichlow 2005).

While these concerns point out that the state of the art today in political psychology may not be a panacea, we return to the general point that the concerns raised above are primarily empirical ones. We can test the extent to which leaders differ when speaking spontaneously or using prepared, written remarks authored by others (see, for example, Schafer and Crichlow 2000). We can also examine the extent to which psychological characteristics change over time and under different circumstances (for example, Schafer et al. 2006; Crichlow 1998; Robison 2006; Renshon 2008). Rates and ranges of change may well vary by individual, but at-a-distance methods will let us investigate those and account for them in our models. We can also run and compare models that include leaders only, key foreign-policy advisors with leaders, or even larger circles of advisors (Marfleet 2000; Robison 2006; Walker and Schafer 2000; Walker, Schafer, and Marfleet forthcoming). We certainly are not arguing that all these issues have been resolved; we note only that the state of the art today has made such important breakthroughs that many more kinds of questions can now be systematically investigated than was the case in the recent past.

Psychological Characteristics and State-Level Political Behavior

Earlier we noted that our interest in individual-level psychology centered around two broadly construed dependent variables at the state level of analysis: variables concerning the process of decision making and state-behavior variables focused primarily on directional (conflict versus cooperation) foreign-policy choices. While it makes intuitive sense that psychological characteristics are likely to affect these dependent variables, in this section we increase our specificity of this assumption by talking about some of the specific variables noted above and how they might affect state behaviors and processes.

Several individual-level psychological characteristics seem likely to correlate with behavioral propensities toward *conflict*. On the personality side of our divide, we have the need for power (which is included in the research programs on motive/need analysis or LTA), low self-esteem or self-confidence (from Etheredge's work or LTA), dominance orientation (from Etheredge), and low complexity (from integrative complexity or LTA). On the cognitive side, several more psychological characteristics seem likely to correlate with conflict propensities: distrust (from Etheredge or LTA; this may also be related to Barber's negative outlook), nationalism or the re-lated concept of in-group bias (from LTA), negative images of the opponent (from image theory), and negative worldviews or conflict propensities for self or other (from operational-code analysis).

Likewise, several characteristics seem likely to correlate with more *coop-erative* behavior. On the personality side we include the high need for affili-ation (motive/need analysis or LTA, where affiliation is conceptualized as the opposite end of the continuum for high task orientation, the idea being that individuals tend to be either task- or people-oriented or someplace in between on a continuum), optimism (or, perhaps relatedly, Barber's posi-tive outlook), and a high level of complexity (from integrative complexity or LTA). And, of course, since we are dealing with inverses on each side of the equation, we would expect that the opposite scores on the variables discussed under conflict in the previous paragraph would tend to correlate with cooperative behavior as well, such as low need for power. Likewise, on the cognitive side, we expect cooperative images of others and positive op-erational codes to correlate with more cooperative behavioral propensities.

Hypothesizing about where psychological traits might affect the pro-cess of decision making is a bit more complicated, because, as opposed to the single continuum of conflict-cooperation discussed under state policies, there are multiple areas where psychology might matter. Some of these are information processing, leader dominance, biases, organization, commu-nication, deliberative and analytical skills, and judgment. Though where psychology might matter is more complicated when analyzing the decision-making process, it nonetheless is still intuitive that it is likely to matter. For instance, it seems reasonable to think that those scoring low in complexity (from integrative complexity or LTA) are less likely to facilitate broad and far-reaching information searches, counterfactual explanations, or thorough lists of objectives and alternatives than are their high-complexity counter-parts. On the cognitive side, biased information processing may be predicted with information related to image theory, operational-code analysis, distrust, or in-group bias (the latter two from LTA).

Irving Janis's classic work on groupthink (1982) is clear that a biased or dominant leader is likely to stifle discussion, short-circuit information searches, and may create premature consensus. This tendency of some leaders to act that way is directly related to Etheredge's dominance orientation and may also show up in his or her need for power (motive/need analysis or LTA), high control orientation (LTA or OCA), or even Barber's active orientation.

Other psychological characteristics might have an effect on the decision-making process as well. High need for affiliation (from LTA, as the opposite of task orientation, or motive/need analysis) might correlate with better communication patterns in decision making or perhaps with more effective use of soft-power resources. Distrust, also from LTA, might result in a closed-off decision-making system or one that systematically biases information to fit preferred expectations. Individuals with a high need for achievement, who Winter identifies as having good organizational and entrepreneurial skills, may facilitate setting up effective organizational structures in decision-making processes. High task-oriented individuals might follow a similar pattern. Still other traits might matter, though their hypothesized effects remain unclear, such as Barber's positive orientation or Etheredge's extraversion.

Finally, we point out that the strengths of some characteristics might also produce countervailing negatives, and vice versa. For instance, high-complexity individuals might be much more thorough with their information search, but this might result in a much slower process or perhaps policy stagnation or indecision. On the other hand, individuals with a high need for power might dominate and intimidate other participants in the process but also may be more decisive and provide firmer leadership under stressful conditions.

Conclusion

Today, the field of political psychology is more advanced than ever. Not only are there well-developed, clearly operationalized, valid constructs that can be used to measure psychological traits of leaders, but there is also a large and growing number of studies that have demonstrated how these characteristics affect state behavior. While many questions remain (some of which we investigate later in this volume), for now we are encouraged by the "state of the field." Today we know much more about how individual-level psychology affects state behavior, and we have good tools, which are becoming better every day, to effectively investigate many more puzzles in the future.

Three

THE DECISION-MAKING MODEL

The Interplay of Group Processes and Psychological Characteristics

Having reviewed the existing literature on groups, individuals, and how the interplay between them shapes foreign-policy decision making, it is time to construct a model in which we can integrate this literature and move it forward. While our focus on groupthink remains central, given the preceding chapter it is clear that we should broaden our approach to include key variables that fit with Janis's hypotheses but not merely mimic his framing of the components of decision making. Here we take those ideas and synthesize them with the other literatures discussed in the preceding chapter. In doing so, we hope to show that the group phenomena that Janis warned about have a central role in policy making, but we broaden our investigation, aware that those pressures and behaviors exist in a wider decision-making context.

Foreign policy stems from an intertwined network of roots. National decision makers, the top-level governmental groups they work in, and the broader political and situational context that surrounds them come together and influence the process of decision making. Foreign-policy decisions are made in an environment where fundamental structural pressures and political tides that often spur or restrain a government's actions come into contact with the psychological characteristics of individuals and the dynamics of decision-making groups. It is the purpose of this book to elucidate these connections in a way that has explanatory and prescriptive benefits. By better understanding these relationships, we can both illustrate how patterns in them help explain the course of foreign affairs and provide knowledge that will leave readers better able to evaluate why specific foreign policies succeed or fail. By looking at decision making as a multistage process, whose component parts (group structures, group processes, and the decision makers themselves) vary and can be changed, we will aid readers' abilities to understand what factors are the most likely to produce better foreign policies and where breakdowns in decision making are most likely to occur. Later in this chapter, we discuss and demonstrate how each of these categories interact and affect the outcomes of a case.

We posit a model of decision making in which four broad categories of influences—situational, psychological, structural, and process—shape the course of a country's foreign policy. The first of these four, the situational context, includes matters related to time constraint, the level of threat at hand, the balance of power among the involved parties, and the positions of other potentially relevant political actors. These include, for example, the opinions of the national legislature and international organizations, both of which could make certain policy options more or less costly enterprises. Situational-context variables can affect both the processes a government engages in when trying to set government policy on a specific matter and the choices a state later makes regarding that policy.

The chain of decision making for an administration begins with individual-level factors—our second category—since humans are responsible for creating state action. Given this, we see foreign-policy choices stemming, at least in part, from the psychological characteristics of the decision makers themselves. The beliefs and personality traits of the country's chief executive affect, among other matters, who he or she will name to high office, the group decision-making processes the leader will prefer, the issues that will command attention, and basic predispositions relating to engaging in cooperation or conflict. For example, a leader high in conceptual complexity is more likely to be sensitive to information in the surrounding environment, while a distrusting leader may tend to escalate conflict. Understanding the key role that the personal attributes of individual decision makers have in setting the parameters of debate and the structure of top-level institutions is essential to understanding foreign-policy decision making.

While decision-making structures, our third category of influences, may, of course, depend on the personal attributes of the key leaders who design and inhabit them, these structures, once created, dramatically affect the course of decision making in small groups. They constrain the behaviors of individuals in the process, whose actions are conditioned by the rules and norms of the policymaking group, and they create process channels that often privilege or hinder the influence of certain actors. This is a matter of even greater importance in foreign-policy decisions, because those decisions are more likely to be the product of small groups than any one individual or large governing coalition (Hermann and Hermann 1989).

These structures include such things as how insulated the group is, how methodical the procedures are, whether the group has a general tolerance for disagreement, how experienced the team is, and how well they work together. They exist prior to the commencement of policymaking on particular instances of state action. The variation in the rules, norms, and staffing of these institutions affects the process of decision making that occurs during discrete decision events. These structural frameworks shape policymaking both directly and as a mediating mechanism between the traits and behaviors of individual decision makers and the processes and working practices of groups engaged in specific decision events.

The process of decision making during specific episodes is our final category of influences on a government's foreign-policy choices. These come after the personnel involved in a case of decision making and the institutional structure of the decision-making environment are set, and they include a wide variety of group-level dynamics that can affect a state's choices. For example, does the group collect and process information in a thorough and unbiased manner? Does it rely on stereotypes? What is the scope of the objectives that a group considers? How many and what kind of policy alternatives are placed before the group? These factors are affected by both the basic traits of the decision makers themselves and the fundamental structures of the decision-making environment. They may also, of course, vary depending upon the situational events at hand during a particular period of decision making. Therefore, unlike the other foci of our study, they are affected by all of the other broad sets of independent variables. It is this stage of decision making that attracted the most attention in Janis's work. For example, stereotyping the out-group and conducting a poor information search during a specific decision-making episode are classic "symptoms of groupthink" (Janis 1982).

The linkages between each of these sets of factors and foreign-policy behavior are well established in the international-relations and decision-making literatures. Our model is geared to provide a greater level of detail on the intra-administration matters that lie at the heart of decision-making models while also incorporating influences from the broader situational environment. Our research is firmly planted in the foreign-policy decision-making research program. But such studies should never be disconnected from the broader political, social, and power structures in which decision makers operate. As the research on systemism has shown (James 2002), international relations cannot be fully understood through designs built on individualism or holism. For a comprehensive understanding, one needs to model behavior in ways that incorporate both microlevel and macrolevel influences. We model our investigation with this in mind.

Dependent Variables

In seeking to better understand how key individuals, structures, processes, and the situational environment shape foreign policy, it is of course necessary to define what types of variation in the dependent variable we seek to explain. Foreign policy can, of course, be categorized and evaluated in a variety of ways. However, for those pursuing a research agenda aimed at creating prescriptive benefits that can improve the quality of foreign policy, and for most in the broader international-relations literature as well, two basic standards of evaluating foreign policy are prevalent: its effects on the national interest and the level of international conflict (Herek et al. 1987; Renshon and Larson 2002). The former is typically considered by realists and those who believe that domestic political forces drive foreign policy. Therefore it is an appropriate measure to use in considering whether or not a foreign policy is achieving its aims. As to the latter, explaining the sources of cooperation and conflict is one of the most vibrant ongoing research programs associated with international relations. That question is central to the discipline. Here we are interested in understanding how the process of decision making might ameliorate or heighten international conflict. Therefore, for our two dependent variables, we examine a nation's success in achieving its foreign-policy goals and how its decisions mold the basic contours of international interaction in terms of conflict and cooperation.

National Interest

Many would argue that the most appropriate way to evaluate foreign policy is on the basis of how that policy affects the national interest. Those who see foreign policy as essentially a fight to preserve or strengthen national resources and prerogatives will prioritize this measure. So will those who see decision makers as political actors who prioritize the accumulation of resources and prestige that they can use to maintain and further their political influence on both the national and international scenes.

We focus on "the national interest" given its longstanding, prominent role as a motivator of, or constraint on, action across a variety of international-relations theories and approaches to the study of foreign policy. As Morgenthau noted, "interest is the perennial standard by which political action must be judged" (1978, 10). It is necessarily a broad concept, as it is interpreted through the lenses of a variety of decision makers, and it entails both material and nonmaterial matters. It may work in tandem with variations in capabilities, the other primary concern of classical realists, but it may have other nonmaterial aspects that matter for both domestic and international politics. Fundamentally, an increase in one's interests adds to one's security and ability to influence others, which are central concerns of a government.

However, while this will be the concept that weighs most heavily on the minds of many decision makers as they conduct the nation's business, the "national interest" is a notoriously ambiguous concept. Quite apart from concerns about how individual leaders will define it differently and seek to shape evaluations of it in a personally beneficial manner (this can be overcome somewhat by having it rated by people other than those who are trying to claim a success or stump for a particular cause), as one gets further away from the moment of the decision, more and more events across an increasingly wide set of policy areas and regions may, arguably, have been affected by that initial decision, which greatly complicates an evaluation of the decision's impact. And as one gets further away from the initial decision, that plethora of action is ever more the product of other stimuli as well, and thus matters that might seem directly connected to the event being examined are also the product of an increasing number of other factors. Necessarily, then, it is considerably easier to evaluate the short-term implications of an action on the national interest than it is to examine one policy's long-term effects. Similarly, it is also the case that most politicians, especially in democracies, are interested in increasing their own power and influence in the near term. As a result, many politicians are more likely to be concerned with the short-term effects of their actions than with distant effects that will not occur until after the coming election cycle or beyond the immediate policy debate or crisis. For these methodological and theoretical reasons, we focus primarily on the short-term effects of a decision on national interest.

Level of International Conflict

For reasons akin to those stated above, our basic measure of the effects of a policy choice on the level of international conflict is focused on the short-term effects of that policy. As one moves further from the decision under examination there is an ever-increasing number of other stimuli that could actually be partially responsible for what appear to be long-term effects and an ever-increasing level of noise in the international system that makes it difficult to unpack exactly which previous moves were truly responsible for longer-term peace or conflict. And again, in terms of what is likely to be on the minds of the decision makers in the democracies we are examining, at the time they are acting, those leaders are likely to be more interested in the short-term implications of their choices than in the nature of the political world they will leave to their successors in office.

Independent Variables

We consider four broad sets of factors that affect the process and shape the choices made by a foreign-policy creating group. These are (1) the individual-level psychological characteristics of the leader that are relevant to foreign policy–making behavior, for example his or her control orientation and conceptual complexity; (2) the outside situational and political context, for example the level of stress involved, the power differential between actors, and the concerns of allies; (3) the structure of the decision-making group, for example the role of the leader and whether or not the group has a tradition of using methodical procedures; and (4) the methods a group engages in during the decision-making process under examination, for example the extent of the information search and whether or not information is processed in a biased manner. Research across the field of foreign-policy decision making argues that these influences shape leaders' choices. On the basis of that work, we have constructed operational definitions to consider the effects of a host of matters that fall under these categories.

Leader's Psychology

Many who study foreign policy, political psychology, and general international relations have made the point that states do not directly act in the international system; a state is a legal and social construct that can only behave to the extent that individuals inside it choose to operate it. Therefore, the human element should not be overlooked when evaluating how a state makes and implements foreign-policy decisions.

The individual decision makers who compose a state's brain trust bring to their job a set of psychological characteristics that affect the likelihood that their state will pursue one or another course of action. These also affect their preferred decision-making styles and will likely shape the design of the foreign-policy apparatus they inhabit. Each of the following psychological characteristics may have an effect on the quality of the decision-making process under the direction of the leader, and they may also affect the direction or intensity of policy, thus affecting the outcome of a case.

In our analysis of the cases, we consider the role of seven different psychological traits. As we discuss in a later chapter, modern psychological methods allow us to measure these traits in leaders, which means we can consider the effect of higher and lower scores of each trait on different aspects of the decision-making process. For example, is it the case that lower scores on conceptual complexity correlate with limited information processing? Another example: is a higher level of distrust associated with more conflictual outcomes? The methods for these measurements come from a research program developed by Margaret Hermann, which she calls leadership-trait analysis (LTA), and we cite her work extensively below.

Belief in ability to control events.
This is the extent to which the leader sees himself or herself in control of situations. Leaders who score high on this variable "will want to maintain control over decision making" and "are less likely to delegate" to others (Hermann 1999, 14). These are classic problems associated with groupthink (Janis 1972, 1982), because they indicate a leader who is likely to dominate the process, be inflexible, and not delegate to or rely upon others. We might expect such a leadership style to result in problematic group structures and poorly executed decision processes, which could in turn be harmful for the national interest.

Need for power.
This is about having an impact on others and enhancing one's power and influence. High scores on this trait indicate individuals who will challenge conventional constraints (Hermann 1999, 10) and "are good at sizing up situations and sensing what tactics will work to achieve goals" (Hermann 1999, 16). This suggests that such leaders may get the most out of subordinates, push them to perform at high levels, and make the most of situations, things that seem likely to reduce groupthink and improve the quality of decision making. That would seem likely to benefit an administration's ability to achieve results that are in the national interest (Callaway et al. 1985). But such a tendency could also result in a forceful foreign policy that would see high levels of conflict.

Self-confidence.
This is "an individual's image of his or her ability to cope adequately with objects and persons in the environment" (Hermann 1999, 20). This trait may affect decision making in two different ways. Self-confidence, perhaps manifested as self-righteousness or overconfidence, may make one "immune to incoming information from the environment" (Hermann 1999, 21), which would lead to poorer-quality decision making. However, high self-confidence may manifest as healthy self-esteem, "which is involved in regulating the extent to which the self system is maintained under conditions of strain" (Ziller et al. 1977, 177). An individual who reacts well to pressure because of self-confidence may be more comfortable hearing contrarian information, may maintain a better decision-making apparatus, and may elicit more efficient processes from advisors.

In-group bias.
This is described by Hermann as "a view of the world in which one's own group (social, political, ethnic, etc.) holds center stage. There are strong emotional attachments to this in-group" (Hermann 1999, 29). Hermann expects that in-group bias will result in biased information processing, particularly in terms of external actors. This would correlate with information-processing patterns associated with groupthink. However, Hermann's conception of the variable suggests components of positive in-group maintenance as well. Higher involvement with and reliance upon the advisory in-group may help to counter groupthink by enhancing teamwork and

empowering dissenters. This leaves us with rival possibilities regarding this trait's effect on the quality of decision making.

Task focus.

According to Hermann, this trait is a continuum with two poles: one end is a focus on the task while the other end is a focus on relationship building. Those scoring high on this trait indicate individuals who move "the group toward completion of a task (problem solving)" (Hermann 1999, 24). Hermann discusses these leaders as "always pushing a group to work on solving the particular problem of the moment . . . constantly asking for movement on a project . . . [and] for options to deal with a problem" (Hermann 1999, 26). These characteristics—problem solving, focusing on the task, and pushing for options—would seem effective at countering groupthink. On the other hand, low scores on this trait indicate leaders who focus on the "morale and spirit" of the group and "foster a sense of collegiality" (Hermann 1999, 26–27). These are things, according to Janis (1972, 1982), that may contribute to groupthink, particularly in the form of premature consensus, where maintaining the collegiality and morale of the group may take precedence over thorough analysis of information and options.

Conceptual complexity.

This is the propensity "to differentiate things and people in one's environment" (Hermann 1999, 10). People higher in complexity are thought of as information seekers and open to alternative explanations and possibilities. As groupthink includes components of shutting down, closing off, and ignoring alternatives and contradictory information, it may be that low levels of complexity will correlate with higher levels of groupthink, while those higher in complexity will be more likely to avoid groupthink. On the other hand, high complexity may lead to a leader who is inundated with information or feels overwhelmed with the intricacies of the environment. This could produce problems in decision making, such as undue equivocation, mixed signals to advisors and international actors, or putting off important matters.

Distrust.

This "involves a general feeling of doubt, uneasiness, misgiving and wariness about others—an inclination to suspect the motives and actions of others" (Hermann 1999, 31). We might expect high levels of distrust to contribute to groupthink in at least two ways. First, individuals who are distrusting may not adequately rely on others, delegate tasks to others, or trust the information provided by others within the advisory system. All of these strongly relate to Janis's conceptions about the onset of groupthink (Janis 1972, 1982). Second, an individual with a high level of distrust may be reticent to seek or believe information coming in from outside sources. In both cases, it seems likely that individuals who are distrusting will be more closed to information, particularly contradictory or disconfirming information, which is a classic problem associated with groupthink. Decision making flawed in this way may overlook a variety of possibilities and result in a lower quality of outcomes and a tendency toward preferring force to cooperation.

Situation and Context Variables

No model of decision making should look solely inside the minds and workings of those who fill the executive branch. Those individuals may have a major impact, but they do not exist in a vacuum. Every policy move affects other possible policy moves. Some policies must be set more quickly than others due to time constraints. Some situations may involve high stress levels that could lead to the decision makers seeing their options quite differently than they would in a different environment. Domestic or foreign political actors may constrain one's choices. And, of course, the overall balance of power and the nature of security concerns that may be present may also affect how a state behaves in the international system. It is with such concerns in mind that the following situational factors are added to the model. Variation in them may alter what is possible, what is likely to be done, and precisely when and how it is likely to be done. Therefore, here we consider the impact that things such as time, stress, threat level, military balance, and domestic and international political constraints have on decision makers — all matters contingent, at least in part, on circumstances and forces beyond the control of the decision makers we are examining.

Stress level.

A number of studies have found that a group's effectiveness, its ability to function in such a way as to attain its interests, and its tendency to engage in heightened levels of conflict are related to the level of anxiety that exists among the members of the group (Holsti 1972; Janis and Mann 1977).

Crisis.

Decision makers sometimes face an unexpected, highly threatening situation that must be dealt with in a short time period (Hermann 1969). Several works on decision making have asserted that groups function differently than normal when facing such a situation (Brecher 2008; 't Hart 1990; Krasner 1972; McCalla 1992).

Short time constraint.

The decision-making group believes it must act within a short time window. This may cause it to discard or favor certain policy options prematurely. Some otherwise promising policy options may not be considered at all, and the group may strikingly alter its usual routines (Janis 1982; Lebow 1981). In the years since Janis's work, the research associated with the International Crisis Behavior Project has shown that a finite time for decision making (similar to our *Short Time Constraint* variable) can have important effects (Brecher and Wilkenfeld 1997).

Threat level.

The options a government considers and the manner in which it works may vary depending upon the level of the stakes at risk. If vital interests are at stake, as compared to strategic or peripheral interests, the group may be more diligent with decision making, or there may be a greater willingness to use force. Such a threat may also cause the decision-making group to work in abnormal ways (McCalla 1992).

Recent failure.

If a recent political or military defeat is weighing on the minds of policymakers, their decision-making processes and the policy moves they consider and implement may be notably different from how the group would behave absent such concerns (Janis 1982; Khong 1992; Welch 2005).

Military capability differential.

Policy processes and choices may be affected by decision makers' perceptions of the military-power balance that exists in the situation at hand (Schafer and Crichlow 2001; Wittkopf et al. 2007).

Allies' views.

The stance taken by a country's allies may affect how a decision-making group sees a situation and the policy options the group considers (Wittkopf et al. 2007).

International organizations' views.

Similarly, the stance taken on the issue by leading international organizations may affect how a decision-making group frames a situation and the specific policy options it considers (Karns and Mingst 1987; Wittkopf et al. 2007).

Public opinion.

Foreign-policy decision makers are political beings. As such, their deliberations, preferences, and choices may be affected by public opinion. Whether or not the public is interested in a topic—and the direction of their interest, if it exists—may affect how policymakers behave (Holsti 2004; James and O'Neal 1991; James and Hristoulas 1994; Powlick 1995; Russett 1990; Wittkopf et al. 2007).

Legislative opinion.

Relatedly, the decision-making group may act differently depending on whether there is a great deal of interest in an issue from the national legislature, and if such interest exists, whether or not it is in line with the preferences of foreign-policy decision makers (Hagan 1993; Milner 1997; Schafer and Crichlow 2001; Wittkopf et al. 2007).

Situational distractions.

There may be other contextual factors that affect decision makers while they are weighing a particular issue. We have created this category to account for a variety of situational pressures that may distract decision makers' attention from the issue at hand. This could be anything from a sudden crisis across the globe to a precipitous decline in the group leader's health.

Group Structures

Formal structures through which a government is constituted and formal and informal structures that set the rules and norms of a government's behavior have been found to have a key influence on both the actions a government will pursue during a specific foreign-policy event and on the quality of the outcomes that stem from that behavior. In this study we consider the effects of the following group structures.

Group insulation.
A group is insulated if decision makers isolate themselves from others not in the central decision-making circle. They exclude a wide variety of voices that could bring valuable perspectives to decision making, including intelligence officials, midlevel bureaucrats, military specialists, and those on the scene of a crisis. A group is considered to be insulated if it relies primarily on its own members for counsel and information. Several researchers have found that this is a dangerous practice that can lead to decision makers lacking basic facts and accurate knowledge on which to base their actions (Hybel 1993; Janis 1982; Schafer and Crichlow 1996, 2001; Thomson 1968).

Biased leadership.
A group is said to have biased leadership if the leader has historically led the group in a manner that cuts off the consideration of a wide variety of alternatives, especially those that are at variance with his or her known preferences. Such a leader often makes known his or her preferred course of action before consulting with advisors. This has been found to have negative consequences in many instances, as the decision-making group engages more in supporting and approving what appears to be a fait accompli than in actually carefully considering the wisdom of that action or alternative courses of action (Ahlfinger and Esser 2001; Haney 1997; Schafer and Crichlow 1996, 2001).

Methodical procedures.
This variable accounts for whether or not the decision-making group has established a tradition of using methodical procedures. This can entail a variety of matters, including such things as systematized procedures for the sharing and dissemination of information, regularly scheduled and clearly organized meetings, and consistent approaches to the evaluation of policy alternatives. Such structures are often seen as conducive to efficiency and the careful consideration of information and options ('t Hart 1990; Janis 1982; Schafer and Crichlow 1996, 2001).

Group homogeneity.

This variable is included as it is assumed that processes such as groupthink may depend, at least to a degree, on how alike group members are to start with. It is presumed that a group whose members are more alike to begin with will be more likely to develop stronger in-group feelings and associated behaviors, potentially shutting out other voices and perspectives from being heard (George 1980; Janis 1982; Schafer and Crichlow 1996).

Illusion of invulnerability.

This variable is included to account for the group's general sense of its own collective efficacy. Strong arguments have been made for the proposition that groups that perceive themselves as having more control over events than they actually do are more likely to make mistakes, take excessively dangerous risks, and engage in sloppy analysis of the situations that they find themselves in. The negative behaviors associated with groupthink may stem from groups having unrealistic assumptions about their knowledge of and control over political events (Janis 1982; Schafer and Crichlow 2001; Whyte 1998).

Gatekeepers.

The group features one or more members who actively pressure those with whom they work in order to keep certain information and arguments from being presented to the group. This is often done to block a policy that the gatekeeper personally opposes from gaining support or to prevent a policy he or she favors from being undermined. However, gatekeepers need not necessarily be silencing information that they personally wish to see blocked. They may be operating in that fashion in order to keep a leader uninformed, to maintain comity within the group, or for other reasons. It is often asserted that the presence of gatekeepers harms decision making, as it keeps group members unaware of pertinent information and may signal that a group is more interested in following an ideological agenda than in pursuing information, carefully considering arguments, and thoroughly thinking through its actions (Hoyt 1997; Janis 1982; Schafer and Crichlow 2001).

Group values disagreement.

The group has a general atmosphere that values the presentation of a variety of opinions. Its members do not try to quash dissent. Rather, they believe that the presentation of alternative points of view and multiple policy options will strengthen the quality of decision making (George 1980; Haney 1997; Janis 1982; Schafer and Crichlow 2001).

Foreign-policy interest.

The group leader is interested in, and regularly engages in, the design of foreign policy, as opposed to merely approving decisions made by others or simply ignoring foreign-policy matters. A lack of leadership can be highly problematic, as it leaves room for both unending in-fighting between various factions in the group and for little oversight over the implementation of group orders. And, of course, leaders who are interested in foreign policy are more likely to invest their own time in it (thereby increasing their personal stake in getting it done "right") and to become better informed. The latter means they are likely to seek out more information and over time become better readers of that information. This should lead them to make more carefully and thoroughly considered decisions (Hermann 1980; Hermann and Preston 1994; Schafer and Crichlow 2001).

Knowledge and experience.

The group charged with directing foreign policy at the highest level is knowledgeable about and experienced with the matters that come under its domain. Expertise is presumed to help leaders work more efficiently, be grounded in a better knowledge base, and have better judgment about the choices that come before them (Haney 1997; Preston 2001; Schafer and Crichlow 2001; Thomson 1968).

Teamwork.

The group charged with making foreign policy has established itself as a unit that works well together, even if there are policy disagreements. Channels of communication function well. The group is not frequently impaired by divisive fights over its rules and procedures, nor does it feature incessant jockeying for position or members who spend much of their time trying to pull down one or more of their colleagues. Behavior of that nature can lead to actions being taken that are more about intragroup prestige than the national interest, and they can harm efficiency and the group's ability to function in a variety of ways ('t Hart 1990; George and Stern 1998; Schafer and Crichlow 2001).

Unusual structural factors.
This category is included to account for relevant structural factors, generally unique to the particular case, that do not precisely fit into the preceding categories.

Decision Processing

In Irving Janis's classic conception of groupthink, he saw the presence of certain lasting characteristics of a decision-making group, like some of those listed above, as shaping the group's tendency to demonstrate "symptoms of groupthink" (Janis 1982). Thus to Janis the central dynamics of group-think turned on how certain group structures resulted in decision-making groups adopting processes during specific decision episodes that impaired the group's ability to function effectively and responsibly. Whether or not these symptoms stem from the precise reasons posed in Janis's classic work, a large body of research has developed in foreign-policy decision making, presidency studies, and related literatures that has stressed the negative implications of these "symptoms" and the need for decision makers to engage in what Janis termed "vigilant" decision making during the process of decision making itself. The symptoms represent the failure to carry out certain basic decision-making tasks or carrying out these tasks in such a way that they will fail to meet their objective purposes. Again, the focus in this section is on actions that are carried out in each specific decision-making event rather than on relatively more stable structures and organization of the group that exist across longer periods of time.

Poor information search.
The group fails to pursue information that may be available and necessary for critically evaluating policy options. This can be the result of a variety of problems, including arrogance, ignorance, misguided deference, or even a conscious decision to not contact someone who has relevant information and is available to talk. Decision makers who make their choices off of unnecessarily incomplete information stand a greater risk of seeing their plans fail (George 1980; Haney 1997; Herek et al. 1987).

Biased information processing.
The group shows a tendency to accept new information only when it supports the preferred alternative and to ignore, refute, or rework other infor-

mation to which they are exposed. This tendency can go beyond simply how a particular decision maker responds to a piece of information. It is also possible that some involved in the decision-making process will actively pursue or block information from spreading among the members of the decision-making group, depending upon whether or not its content fits with preexisting biases. As is the case with our *Poor Information Search* variable, this type of behavior can lead to decision makers acting on poor, incomplete, or inaccurate information, and thus it can heighten the likelihood of policy failures and conflict (Haney 1997; 't Hart 1990; Herek et al. 1987; Janis 1982; Jervis 1976; Schafer and Crichlow 2001).

Survey of objectives.

The group reviews, discusses, and carefully considers its objectives and the nature of its goals in a situation before deciding on a course of action. Several works that address the variance in the quality of performance by decision-making groups stress the value in being clear about the goals one hopes to achieve. Carefully establishing objectives can make it easier to judge what tactics will best achieve those ends (George 1980; Haney 1997; Herek et al. 1987; Janis 1982; Schafer and Crichlow 2001).

Survey of alternatives.

Much of the same literature points out the value in systematically evaluating a variety of alternative paths of action. This includes considering the likely risks, costs, and prospects for success of these alternative options (Haney 1997; Herek et al. 1987; George 1980; Janis 1982; Schafer and Crichlow 2001).

Stereotype of out-group.

Does the group stereotype members of the out-group that it is focused on? Does it rely on cursory, often negative, judgments about that group instead of learning more about its true nature and intentions? A variety of literatures have found that relying upon stereotypes can have negative consequences for decision makers, as they lack data that is vital to effectively dealing with the out-group in a more efficient manner. Relying upon stereotypes has also been linked to the use of higher levels of conflict in the pursuit of one's ends (Boulding 1959; Herrmann 1986; Herrmann and Fischerkeller 1995; Hybel 1993; Jervis 1976; Khong 1992; Schafer and Crichlow 2001; Thomson 1968).

Stereotype of situation.
This variable is similar to the one preceding it, except that the target of the stereotyping is the situation that a decision-making group sees itself in, not the out-group. In both instances, the group is relying upon possibly problematic short cuts and is not gaining a rich understanding of the context. Here the concern is that the analogy, which never fits perfectly, will be misleading or will result in inaccurate conclusions. As with the other form of stereotyping, previous research has found it can have a negative effect on a state's ability to achieve its aims (Hybel 1993; Jervis 1976, 1985; Khong 1992; Schafer and Crichlow 2001; Thomson 1968).

Pressures toward uniformity.
Are there practices that exist in the decision-making group aimed at limiting the free exchange of perspectives on the issue at hand? These can include self-censorship, an illusion of unanimity, and direct pressure on would-be dissenters. These behaviors in the decision-making process itself, which can vary from self-imposed compliance to the exclusion of a variety of voices, have been found by a number of studies, particularly works stemming from the groupthink research agenda, to impair the ability of decision makers to plan and execute policy as effectively as possible ('t Hart 1990; Janis 1982; Schafer and Crichlow 1996).

Unusual process factors.
This category is included to account for relevant methods or processes, generally unique to the particular case, that do not precisely fit into the preceding categories.

A Model of Foreign-Policy Decision Making

Needless to say, there are many variables to take into account in the foreign-policy decision-making process. Figure 1 organizes and models the effects of these variables. We begin, actually, at the end point in the model: the outcome of the decision, our dependent variables. In foreign-policy analysis, this is what we are trying to explain. We wonder how a state ended up at this point and not some other one. We have two measures for this endpoint: *National Interest* and *Level of International Conflict*. In any given case, a state's decision may end up advancing or hindering national interests and raising or lowering the level of international conflict. Clearly, in international poli-

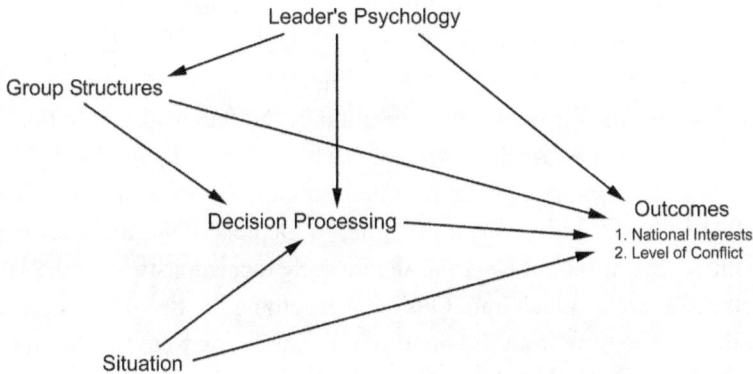

FIGURE 3.1   A model of foreign-policy decision making

tics there are many examples of each of these kinds of outcomes. It seems intuitive that things might have turned out differently than they did. This is particularly the case because, as we argued early on, the process of making a foreign-policy decision is essentially a human one: the actors involved could have processed information differently than they did, changed the weights they assigned to competing values while making their decision, or turned the ship of state in an entirely different direction. This means the outcome of a case is never predetermined or automatic; our puzzle is explaining how things turned out the way they did.

We then turn to the factors that might have affected the decision in the case. These are our explanatory, or independent, variables, and we group these in the four areas noted earlier in the chapter: *Situation* factors (for example, stress, power differential, and political pressures), the *Leader's Psychology* (including such traits as conceptual complexity and need for power), *Group Structures* (such as group homogeneity, traditional use of methodical procedures, and the expertise of advisors), and *Decision Processing* during the case (including, for example, poor information search, biased processing, and pressures for uniformity). These four categories serve as an analytical prism that helps organize relevant factors in the decision-making process. And, as seen in figure 3.1, we expect that each of these categories of variables may have effects on the decision process and on the outcomes of a case.

The unit of analysis in our research is the "case," defined as the occasion for a significant foreign-policy decision by the administration. In most instances, the beginning point of the case is the moment it first appears on the policy radar screen for the top decision makers in the administration. For example, the Entebbe case started when the Tel Aviv flight was first hijacked, provoking the occasion for decision by the Rabin administration. In some instances, the case deals with a preexisting situation, but the situation reaches a new turning point for the administration. For example, though the conflict was well under way at the time, in October 1990, the George H. W. Bush administration began to significantly escalate its forces to a level it felt necessary to attack Iraq. Our focus regarding the decision-processing variables is the time from the onset of the case to the time that the major decision is made by the administration in the case.

Each case we investigate in this research features a given set of constraints pertaining to the context of that case; we call these *Situation* or *Context* variables. They are things that are generally outside of the immediate control of the decision makers, such as the amount of power each side has, the international and domestic political climate, time limits, and the interests at stake in the situation. These factors may place limits on information processing during the decision episode and may shape the choices considered by the decision makers. In figure 3.1, we see these possibilities represented by two arrows. The first arrow goes from *Situation* to *Decision Processing*, meaning that context variables might have an effect on the internal decision making of the group. For instance, high levels of stress and short time constraints might significantly hinder the careful processing of information in the case. The second arrow goes from *Situation* to *Outcomes*, suggesting that these context factors might have a direct impact on how things turn out. For example, if one country is significantly stronger than the other in a conflict episode, this factor alone is likely to have an effect on the outcome.

Our next set of variables deals with the leader's psychology. In our research we include seven psychological traits, such as conceptual complexity and need for power, drawn from Margaret Hermann's research program (1980, 1999). As seen in figure 3.1, we anticipate that the leader's psychology may affect three different stages of decision making. First, as seen by the arrow going from *Leader's Psychology* to *Group Structures*, it is likely that the psychological characteristics of the leader will affect such things as organizational structures, precedents in decision making, and who the leader chooses for advisors. Psychology is also likely to affect what goes on during the actual decision making of an episode, which is marked by the arrow going from *Leader's Psychology* to *Decision Processes*. Here, we expect that the traits of the leader, such as his or her complexity or control orientation, will play a role in information processing, use of stereotypes, consideration of alternatives, and pressures for uniformity. Finally, it may be that the leader's psychology will affect how the case turns out. For example, a leader high in distrust may be more likely to escalate a conflict. This is represented by the arrow going from *Leader's Psychology* to *Outcomes* in figure 3.1.

Next we have a set of variables dealing with structural components of decision making. Before the case begins, many attributes of decision making are already in place. These are the organizational structures and previously established procedural norms that have been put in place by the leader and his or her advisors; we call these *Group Structures*. It is probably this area that decision makers have the most control over; the leader chooses his or her advisors, decides how to organize the process, establishes routines, sets up channels of communication, and creates precedents and traditions for the decision-making process—all in advance of actual decision making in any particular case. These structural factors may have an effect on outcomes, which is represented in figure 3.1 by the arrow going from *Group Structures* to *Outcomes*. But, perhaps more importantly, we expect these group-structural factors to have an effect on the quality of processes used during a decision-making episode, which is represented by the arrow in figure 3.1 going from *Group Structures* to *Decision Processing*. If effective structures are put in place, then good processing during any one case is much more likely to happen.

Finally, our fourth set of variables refers to the process that goes on during the decision episode itself. Most of these factors pertain to the processing of information in the case, such as thoroughly searching for information, carefully considering objectives and options, stereotyping the out-group or the situation, or creating pressures for uniformity. Here we are wondering what happens during the actual decision making in the case: does the group carefully consider information, objectives, and options, or do they take shortcuts, distort information, and arrive at premature conclusions? While components of groupthink exist in both group structures and decision processing, it is the latter that frequently receives more prominent attention when talking about groupthink: poor information processing seems to be at the heart of what Janis called "premature consensus" in decision making. This relationship is represented in figure 3.1 by the arrow going from *Decision Processing* to *Outcomes*. Poor information processing is likely to have a detrimental effect on outcomes in terms of both national interests and the level of international conflict.

While there are already plenty of arrows in figure 3.1, it would be possible to add more. Perhaps the most prominent of these would be a set of feedback arrows going from the outcome of a case back to each set of independent variables. For instance, the outcome may have an effect on the leader's psychology, particular in terms of cognitions. For example, according to research by Sam Robison (2006), George W. Bush showed significant change in beliefs (learning) as a result of the events of September 11, 2001. The outcome of a case may also provide feedback to the group regarding the effectiveness of the old structures and processes. For example, Janis (1982) argues that the negative feedback associated with the Bay of Pigs decision by the Kennedy administration contributed to significant changes in decision-making procedures by the administration. It may also be the case that the outcome changes things in the contextual environment. Some of the setbacks in the Vietnam War, for example, caused serious erosion of domestic support for that war.

Of course, to complicate our causal diagram further, once feedback has been processed and resulted in change, then these new sets of factors are likely to have an effect the next time around—essentially completing the feedback loop. George Bush's new beliefs certainly factored into many policies during the rest of his administration, Kennedy's improved decision-making apparatus showed its value during the Cuban Missile Crisis, and the United States pulled out of Vietnam in part due to situational domestic pressure. While we do not include these additional arrows in our diagram, understanding the possibility of feedback is important, and, where relevant in the case studies that follow, we note where such factors come into play. And since we measure all of our variables separately for each decision-making event, our data should reflect intra-administration changes that may result from such feedback loops.

Our framework also does not focus extensively on the actions of the opponent in our cases. Yet we recognize that the outcome of a case is dependent at least in part of the other side's behavior. Our framework does not ignore the role of the other, and indeed some of this is accounted for conceptually in our *Situation* variables. Nonetheless, our primary focus is on the internal decision making of our subject country. We argue, as Janis did so many years ago, that if proper internal procedures and mechanisms are followed, there is a higher probability of achieving a good outcome.

It is the internal components of decision making that can be most closely controlled by leaders and advisors, and therefore it is this area where prescriptive lessons can be learned and implemented. In our case studies, we discuss the posturing and actions of others where those are relevant, but our primary focus remains on internal decision making. It is true that Cuba's actions affected the outcome of the Bay of Pigs case; they fought back and stopped the exiles. However, had the Kennedy administration conducted better decision making—considered alternatives, questioned assumptions, and reduced out-group stereotypes—the case could have turned out much differently and significantly better than it did.

In the next part of the book, we investigate several U.S. foreign-policy cases over the last thirty years. Since Janis's work ended with the Nixon administration, we examine decision-making events from the Ford administration through the George W. Bush administration. Most of these cases are well-known and should be of interest for historical reasons. Indeed, part of our investigation of the decision making in each case covers the historical "unfolding" of the case. Our primary analytical purpose, however, is to get inside the "black box" of the decision-making process during each of these events. We look carefully at the human element: who said what to whom, what the actors were thinking and how they were behaving, and what procedures and processes were used in the case. In the case studies that follow, we include in our analysis a discussion of situational factors, components of group structure, and the nature of the decision processing.

We rely primarily on secondary source materials to conduct our case investigations. Using our analytical framework, we carefully read materials such as histories, writings by journalists, memoirs, and other sources that explain, as much as possible, what went on inside the process of decision making. Each type of source material has its limitations. For example, sometimes a memoir from someone who participated in the decision-making process may skew information for self-serving purposes, or perhaps a particular journalist or historian has a bias in the case. Yet, in spite of their limitations, each type of source also has much to add to the investigation. For instance, while a memoir may indeed have skewed information, there simply is no substitute for using the words of someone who was actually inside the process. Given these concerns, however, we use as many credible sources as possible for each case. Multiple sources not only provide a wide range of information and perspectives but also let us, as much as possible, "triangulate" the information, that is check for biases, confirm or refute accounts, and try to resolve contradictions.

As we read the materials for each case, we carefully considered each one of the variables listed above in the categories of *Situation, Group Structures,* and *Decision Processing*. This allowed us "code" each variable for each case, which means we specified the level or presence/absence of each variable.[1] As you will see in the case studies in the following chapters, after we present the history and story of the decision making in each case, we review the case in terms of the variables in these three categories. We conclude the discussion of each of these three categories by summing the number of problematic variables present in the category.

There are several advantages to pursuing case-based research in this manner. First, by looking at specifically defined variables in each case, it allows us to be systematic with the information we are considering across the set of cases. In other words, we looked for the exact same factors in every case we researched for the whole project. In addition, summing the number of problematic variables in each category in a case allows for direct and meaningful comparisons across cases. Because we have operationalized definitions for each set of variables, this allows us to note with confidence and consistency when one case has, say, many more decision-processing errors than another case. These sums are a type of measurement that form a scale. Finally, because our case studies yield scores for each variable and scales for each of the three sets of variables, these data allow us to run statistical models that look for broad patterns across the set of cases, something we return to in chapter 6.

You will also see in each of the case studies in chapters 4 and 5 that we present data on the two outcome (dependent) variables for each case. In this project in general, we are interested in explaining the effect of the decision-making process on the outcome of the decision, with the general hypothesis that better-quality decision making will result in more favorable outcomes. As we noted earlier, we specify two different kinds of outcomes: *National Interest* and the *Level of International Conflict*. Our approach to determining these dependent variables is very different from the approach used by Janis in his early work, which made the concept of groupthink famous (1972). Janis chose cases based upon whether he deemed them policy failures or policy successes. After selecting the cases in this way, he then evaluated the decision-making process in each case. This is problematic from a methodological perspective because it potentially confounds the analysis. When Janis was evaluating the quality of the decision-making process in each case, he already had a predetermined view of the outcome of the case, which could have had an influencing effect on the analysis.

To avoid this potential confounding, we separated the analysis of the dependent variables (the outcomes of the case) from the independent variables (the three sets of variables pertaining to decision making and the situation) using completely different methods. As noted above, we assessed the independent variables using operational definitions of each variable along with careful reading of case-study materials. This research was conducted strictly by the principal researchers in the project: the authors of this book. The dependent variables, on the other hand, were determined not by the principal investigators but by a panel of foreign-policy experts across the country who did not know about and were not involved with the assessment of the independent variables.

We contacted a pool of scholars who were experts in the area of foreign policy and asked them to participate in a study. The pool included scholars, both males and females, from a range of academic levels and with diverse methodological and ideological backgrounds. We gave them a questionnaire that included a short description of each case in the study, and we asked them to evaluate the outcome of each case in terms of national interests and the level of international conflict. We kept the experts blind to our research hypotheses, meaning they did not know we were separately investigating the quality of the decision making in each case. Here are the questions we asked them to use in judging each case:

(1) *National Interest.* During the days and weeks immediately following the foreign-policy decision in question, do you believe that the actor's national interests were significantly advanced, somewhat advanced, unaffected, somewhat hindered, or significantly hindered as a result of the decision? (Scale range 1 to 5, with 1 being significantly hindered and 5 being significantly advanced.)

(2) *Level of International Conflict.* During the days and weeks immediately following the foreign-policy decision in question, do you believe that the level of international conflict increased significantly, increased somewhat, remained about the same, decreased somewhat, or decreased significantly as a result of the decision? (Scale range 1 to 5, with 1 being significantly decreased and 5 being significantly increased.)

We also asked the respondents to assess their own confidence in rating each case as low, moderate, or high. If a respondent rated their confidence in a case as low, meaning the individual was not very familiar with the case, we did not include that respondent's ratings in the calculation of the outcome scores for that case. To determine the score for each variable for each case, we computed the average rating from all the experts who rated their own confidence in the case as medium or high. In all, twenty-eight experts provided ratings for the cases.

In the two chapters that follow, we have divided the case studies into two subsets. Chapter 4 includes four different cases where decision making was problematic. In many ways, the cases in this chapter represent how not to do decision making. They illustrate faults and point out where problems might arise. Chapter 5, on the other hand, presents three cases where the quality of decision making was much better, letting us look concretely at how leaders can conduct decision making more effectively. In each case, we report the results of our analysis of the independent variables in terms of situation/context, group structures, and decision processing, and we also report how our foreign-policy experts rated the outcomes of the case. The advantage of our analytical framework and methods is that they allow us to make consistent observations across cases, not only in terms of the various components of decision making but also in terms of judging the outcome. Because we have provided operational definitions for our specified independent variables, we are able to evaluate each one the same way across all cases. Likewise, the experts who rated the outcomes of the cases did so using the same outcome scales for each case, which makes it possible to compare the scores across cases. We are left with concrete comparisons of the quality of decision making in each case and its effect on the outcomes of the case.

PART II

Case Studies in American Foreign-Policy Decision Making

Four

CASE STUDIES IN LOW-QUALITY DECISION MAKING

In chapters 6 and 7, we will present our statistical analyses of the effects that group structure and process (chapter 6) and the personalities of decision makers (chapter 7) have on the quality of foreign-policy decision making. In those chapters, we analyze a diverse set of almost forty cases, spanning nine administrations in three countries. We are systematically investigating a larger and more diverse set of decisions than has been examined in a study of this sort before. Those chapters are the heart of our analysis, in that they provide the statistical support necessary for us to evaluate our model, clarify our understanding of the dynamics at the root of decision making, and settle specific, ongoing disputes in the field.

However, before getting to our statistical, cross-case analyses, it is useful to illustrate what our model suggests decision making should look like in practice, so that readers may enter those chapters with a clearer conception of the variables and dynamics being studied. Several of the decision events included in our analysis fit well with our expectations: flawed decision making led to poorly rated outcomes, while high-quality decision making led to higher-rated outcomes. Much as Janis illustrated his model with case studies of groupthink and case studies of vigilant decision making, in chapters 4 and 5 we review seven cases of decision making. We do this to show the real-world workings of the influences on decision making that we have discussed in the preceding chapters and to illustrate through real-world examples the types of connections that our model expects and that we will be testing across many cases in the statistical analyses that follow. We begin with four cases of poorly rated foreign-policy decisions that stemmed from decision groups whose structure and behavior featured numerous flaws.

The Carter Administration and the Shah

> Iran was the Carter administration's greatest setback.
> —Zbigniew Brzezinski, assistant to the president for national security affairs, 1983

By the fall of 1978, long-simmering opposition to the regime of the shah of Iran, Mohammed Reza Pahlavi, had gathered into a storm. But the senior officials of the U.S. government were slow to focus on these events. They were hemmed in by the shah's inaction and the splintered country he sought to continue to control. This was an unusually complicated case of decision making. By the time the Carter administration focused on these events, senior officials were increasingly not discussing Iran as if it were a coherent, functioning state. Instead, as the shah's hold on power disintegrated, the shah, the military, the religious bloc, and the secular nationalists were all seen as distinct actors, and some of these actors were seen as divided, or potentially divided, among themselves (particularly the military and the secular opponents of the shah's rule). One could not say with certainty how trustworthy and believable these parties were, and planning for contingencies involving Ayatollah Khomeini was complicated by him being in France during the final period of these policy debates.

U.S. decision makers faced logistical hurdles on top of the challenges already presented by the situation, and they often seemed to be dealing with a house of cards. If they took move x, policy option A would collapse. But if they took move y, policy option B would be blocked. And as events unfolded, the small number of options the United States had at hand steadily decreased. While facing this complex problem, the administration found itself distracted by a host of other pressing foreign-policy matters, and it was riven with internal disputes, some of which became acrimonious. Deeply divided, distracted, and with few if any appealing options at hand, it is perhaps not surprising that decision making on this issue has come in for considerable criticism, though of course it is debatable just how much the United States could have done to keep their long-time ally in power.

The shah ascended to his throne in 1941. British and Soviet forces had taken over the country and forced the shah's father to abdicate, as he was viewed as antagonistic to their interests. In 1953, the shah went into exile very briefly, but after a U.S.-backed coup brought down the prime minister, Mohammed Mossadegh, who had been his strongest challenger during the early years of his reign, he returned and proceeded to rule for another quarter century. His regime was marked by pervasive corruption, and as the country's GDP grew, many Iranians became embittered that the country's wealth seemed to accrue to only a select elite who lived fabulous lifestyles. The lavish celebration of the 2,500th anniversary of Iran's monarchy at Persepolis, where the shah hosted dozens of royals, presidents, and prime ministers from around the world, is perhaps the best-known example of this tendency toward excess. But while the shah might have been unpopular with many of his own people, especially late in his rule, he remained a key U.S. ally.

The U.S. relationship with the shah's Iran was of great importance. Iran was a buffer state in the cold war. The United States needed both to limit Iran's ties to the Soviets and to use Iran as a military ally and a source for intelligence. In addition to friendship with Iran being useful in terms of the global political and military balance, it was also a valuable ally given American interests in Middle Eastern politics and because of its natural resources. The shah's Iran balanced states that were viewed as more radical, such as Syria and Iraq. It was one of only two states in the area to extend diplomatic relations to Israel, and it openly supported the moves toward peace with Israel made by President Sadat of Egypt. Iran's immense oil reserves were important to the world economy generally and appeared all the more important in the wake of the oil embargo that followed the 1973 Arab-Israeli war. The governments of both countries benefited from the ties between their countries. And the United States had a long history of doing what it could to support the shah's rule, perhaps most obviously in the 1970s by approving huge arms sales to the country. The authoritarianism and abuses of the shah's state created difficulties for the relationship and would eventually lead to a revolution that would bring about a very different type of government ruling in Tehran. But even the Carter administration, which prioritized human-rights issues like no U.S. administration before it, was willing to focus on the advantages and overlook some of the shah's abuses, given his country's importance.

In 1978, Iran witnessed a level of political unrest not seen in many years. This included actions by opposition forces from across the political spectrum. But the U.S. intelligence agencies did not see a major threat to the shah's reign (Moens 1990), and in the fall of 1978, much of the senior levels of the U.S. government were focused instead on other events. This was the same period as the Camp David talks, key parts of the SALT negotiations, secret U.S.-Chinese negotiations, and a crisis in Nicaragua. And, of course, this list leaves out all the domestic political events that would require attention from the president and his top advisors during this period.

By late October, however, events had taken such a turn for the worse that some within the government thought it was time to reevaluate the U.S. approach to Iran. The State Department, while maintaining support for the shah's regime, produced a memo that argued that the shah needed to institute political reforms and that the United States should engage in a dialogue with the Iranian opposition groups, including Ayatollah Khomeini. NSC Advisor Brzezinski vehemently disagreed (Brzezinski 1983), and he blocked circulation of the memo. But events in Iran and a push from the U.S. embassy in Tehran pushed this issue higher on the administration's priority list, regardless.

On November 2, 1978, Ambassador Sullivan cabled Washington that the shah was considering changing his government and perhaps even stepping down. The shah wanted advice from the United States as to what he should do. In response, there was a special meeting of the Special Coordinating Committee of the National Security Council.

At the meeting, there was unanimous agreement that supporting the shah was the appropriate tack, but there was disagreement about which policies they should pursue to achieve that end. Ambassador Sullivan sent a second cable on November 9, titled "Thinking the Unthinkable," urging decision makers in Washington to start considering what should be done if the shah fell. But the leaders of the Carter administration held to their belief that the shah could survive. They remained focused on the question of what policy would be best to ensure that. It would be another month before core members of the decision-making group would begin to look at Iran through a different lens.

The administration commissioned an outside report on what to do about the situation, headed by George Ball, who had been a senior official at the Department of State in the 1960s. Ball delivered his report on December 13. It stated that the shah was "damaged beyond repair" (Moens 1990, 149). It was only at this point that some senior U.S. decision makers began to actively consider the possibility that the shah would lose power. And even at that late date, several of the principals refused to contemplate the situation through that perspective. This was barely a month before the shah and Empress Farah left their country. The result of this was a decision-making group that was deeply divided over the basic facts of the situation and fundamental U.S. objectives and needs but that had very little time to work through these differences and settle on a new course. While the administration was distracted by a host of other international activities and commitments, it remained stuck in terms of what to do regarding the shah, in no small part because group members approached this issue from very different perspectives. And, as those differences festered, these divisions led to an increasing level of intragroup conflict.

The senior leadership remained deeply divided, with some advocating a broad opposition coalition, perhaps even involving Ayatollah Khomeini. Others were supportive of the idea of a military coup. Over time the options offered seemed less and less in line with upholding the rule of the shah or the government of Prime Minister Bahktiar. But that only came to be the case as their ability to rule steadily declined. With a fractured political scene and deep divisions among the decision makers in Washington, the U.S. response was largely one of inaction. The Carter administration offered to allow the shah to come to the United States in January, but by the time he actually sought refuge in the United States, the offer had been rescinded due to fears of reprisals. On February 16, 1979, weeks after the shah had left for Egypt and after Khomeini's return from exile, the United States announced it would maintain diplomatic relations with the new Iranian government, even as the executions of some of Iran's generals, men who parts of the Carter administration had discussed helping to put in power, had begun. The Iranian Revolution would unfold over many months to come and result in the rise of a fundamentally anti-American government. The Carter administration had taken few concrete steps to block this from occurring.

Experts' Ratings

Given the results, which included the fall of a long-time U.S. ally, a state designed and led by Khomenei, and an increase in oil prices (though they had been rising while the shah still clung to power), it is not surprising that this case is rated very low in terms of the U.S. *National Interest*. In fact, this case was scored at 1.71 (out of 5) on our scale, the third-lowest score in our entire sample. Of course, the idea that the United States could have done much to prevent the fall of the shah's regime is highly debatable. But apart from the outcome of these events, it is also possible that this low score was influenced by unhappiness with the path chosen by the United States, which was largely one of inaction. On our scale measuring the *Level of International Conflict*, this case was scored at 3.81 (out of 5), which is higher than average. The instability caused by the Iranian revolution had immediate effects, and it reverberated across the region for years.

Situation

These events unfolded in a situational environment marked by few of the characteristics traditionally associated with groupthink, but some of them were present. The *Stress Level* of decision makers was not especially high. It was coded at 2 on our five-point scale. For much of this period, decision makers believed the shah could hold on. Beyond that, some believed that even if he was pushed out of power he might be replaced by a government that was not opposed to U.S. interests. It was often noted that Khomeini was strongly anticommunist, and some described the possibility of the religious forces forging an alliance with secular parties in the opposition. Decision makers did view the situation as a *Crisis*, however. It was unexpected, and by late December and January decision makers came to believe they faced a *Short Time Constraint*, since matters were moving quickly in Iran. The situation was a *Threat* to *Strategic Interests*, which ranks below *Vital Interests* in our coding system but was worrying to decision makers nonetheless.

Neither the views of *Allies*, nor those of *International Organizations*, nor those of domestic *Public Opinion* significantly factored into the decision-making process. There was no "sense of panic" among U.S. allies in the region (Vance 1983, 347). The *Military Differential* between the states was not relevant to the handling of this issue, as no direct U.S. military action was seriously contemplated.

As mentioned earlier, there were major *Situational Distractions* that may have impaired the quality of decision making in this case. A host of other international events were happening at the same time that demanded attention from top-level officials. With so little time being divided among major events involving key countries, such as the Soviet Union, China, Egypt, Israel, and Nicaragua, there was relatively little time to focus on Iran. The schedules of most top-level decision makers were spread thin. Secretary

Vance was out of the country a great deal. Secretary Brown was involved in battles over the defense budget. The president's direct involvement for much of this period could fairly be described as fitful. Brzezinski (1983, 358) described the era as "extraordinarily time-consuming, personally absorbing, and physically demanding." Adding this variable, the total number of *Situational* factors that may be anticipated to have a negative effect on decision making is three: *Crisis, Short Time,* and *Situational Distractions.*

Group Structure

In chapter 5, we consider another case involving the Carter administration, its response to the Ogaden war. In that case, we detail a particular set of *Group Structures,* structures that the literature on foreign-policy decision making predict would lead to a successful government. However, in this case, which occurred about a year later, the structure of the administration was different. The basic reason for this is touched on briefly late in that case study. A number of policy disputes in the first year or two of the Carter presidency, the response to the Ogaden war among them, led to strained relations between National Security Advisor Brzezinski and Secretary of State Cyrus Vance.

Carter's National Security Council had been designed in a way to encourage multiple voices in the policymaking process and to block the NSC advisor from assuming too much power, as some felt had happened a few years earlier, when the organization was run by Henry Kissinger. Brzezinski was only to directly run one of the council's two main committees, the Special Coordinating Committee. But that committee, which was aimed at overseeing complicated issues that involved multiple parts of the government's bureaucracy, naturally came to be the arena where many of the most important foreign and national-security issues were handled. And as Brzezinski became more distant from and contentious with the senior individuals from the Department of State, both the circle of decision makers with unfettered access to the White House and the openness of policy discussions began to contract. The divisions between State and the NSC also left little if any room for policy proposals favored by the senior staff of the NSC to be advocated by agents of the bureaucracy traditionally charged with leading foreign-policy discussions and debates. This led to NSC officials, particularly Brzezinski, stepping away from merely serving as adjudicators and evaluators and becoming advocates, and even in some cases implementers, of policy moves that they favored (Moens 1990). Taken together, these changes in institutional norms and structures meant that decision making involved fewer voices in the process and involved more inchoate channels of communication and authority than had existed only a year earlier.

That said, the decision-making group was not *Insulated*. Indeed, a broad array of voices had access to decision-making discussions, and, in fact, outside observers were brought into the process to ensure that a variety of perspectives were presented—George Ball's report, for example. But while the group was open, the leader had voiced a clear preference and held to it. President Carter made it clear that he wanted to maintain the rule of the shah. While he was open to a variety of tactics, he made it clear that he backed the continued reign of the current ruler. This *Biased Leadership* had the effect of keeping certain policy options on the table, perhaps after they were tenable, and whisking other options out of the mix. This was easier to accomplish given the lack of *Methodical Procedures* in place. We see this in Brzezinski's moves to cut off State's experts in the field and his attempt to get around Secretary Vance by bringing in George Ball. But more fundamentally it was true because he could use his position at the NSC to restructure decision-making venues and access in ways that would help promote his preferred option (support for the Iranian military). That the NSC advisor could, for example, hold talks with Iran's ambassador without the knowledge of anyone in the Department of State is a sign that the set channels of communication and authority between the various arms of the Carter administration had become crossed and that coordination was not occurring (Moens 1990). Ad hoc decision-making norms were fostered as the more firmly set structures that had been in place earlier in the Carter White House broke down.

The decision-making group was not *Homogeneous*, nor did it possess an *Illusion of Invulnerability*. Indeed, decision makers were well aware of the fact that they had few if any good options. The group included *Gatekeepers*. Zbigniew Brzezinski and his deputy, David Aaron, worked to sideline certain U.S. officials, most particularly the U.S. ambassador in Tehran, William Sullivan, and Henry Precht, the chief of the Iran desk at the Department of State. They also worked to limit discussion of engaging Khomeini. But nonetheless, on the whole the group still *Valued Disagreement*.

In this period, President Carter was *Interested in Foreign Policy*, though in this specific case he took a relatively distant role in setting it, and the decision-making team was composed of *Knowledgeable Experts*. However, there was a notable lack of *Teamwork*. By late 1978, battles between Brzezinski and Vance, while not seen in every situation, were far from uncommon. As Moens (1990, 157) noted, Carter "lacked a team that was united in its zeal to serve the President. They were working against one another instead of for Jimmy Carter. They left him torn." The *Unusual Structure* we see in this case is policy making being promoted by an expansive National Security Council, which was in practice advocating specific options more than evaluating them. All told, these structures created a situation rife with conflict and one where decision making may not have been as carefully constructed as it otherwise could have been. Combining these factors together, we see that number of problematic variables on the *Group-Structure* scale comes to 5.

Decision Processing

The manner in which policy was set during this case was problematic. We see instances of several negative process variables in this case. The general *Information Search* conducted by this group was good. Some of the data involved might have been inaccurate, but to the extent that was true, it often was not the fault of U.S. decision makers. The government collected data from a wide variety of sources, and to the extent that there were problems with the data it was either because it was exceedingly difficult to get reliable data (for example, Ayatollah Khomeini's plans or the likelihood a military coup would succeed) or because the sources themselves were poorly informed. Most notable among the latter were problems associated with information from the shah. As Secretary Vance (1983, 328) wrote, "none of us was fully aware of the extent to which the shah had lost touch with Iranian politics." Once these data were collected, this case saw much *Biased Information Processing*. Whether it was officials affiliated with the Department of State or the staff of the National Security Council, many held to their preexisting views. This was possibly most apparent regarding disputes about how wide an opposition alliance could be formed and whether or not it would be possible to successfully engage Khomeini. Competing factions in the Carter administration formed firm lines on these issues that did not change even as events on the ground moved along at a swift pace.

The group failed to *Survey Objectives* or to *Survey Alternatives* as effectively as it could have. President Carter and his government held on to their association with the shah for so long that one could question whether or not they were still holding onto what they believed the shah had provided them—security and access within the region. Both were imperiled by U.S. actions and inaction in this case. But nonetheless the question tended to be framed as "what can the United States do for the shah?" instead of "what should the United States be doing to secure its interests?" Similarly, certain options were not considered as deeply as they could have been, either because they appeared to be placing the United States too close to actors traditionally seen as opponents of U.S. interests in the region or because they could lead to a great deal of bloodshed. In addition, they *Stereotyped the Situation* in which they found themselves. At times the discussion veered into comparisons with and lessons learned from other crises in which traditional cold-war allies were threatened or in which U.S. action led to negative or bloody consequences. Brzezinski (1983) notes, for example, that the situation was compared to the events in Chile that led to the rise of General Pinochet. But while they stereotyped the situation, decision makers did not *Stereotype the Out-Group*. There was considerable discussion about the strengths, weaknesses, and motivations of virtually every major political actor involved in this crisis. Carter administration officials might have seen the event through a particular frame, but they did not see the individual political players through the same lens.

The group also did not *Suppress Dissent* within the administration. There was so much dissent between the principals, notably Brzezinski and Vance, that an "estrangement" (Vance 1983, 328) grew not only between the two men but between their aides. They tried to keep dissent within the administration. In fact, President Carter personally "castigated" (Brzezinski 1983, 389) midlevel Department of State employees for disloyalty in early February, after news reports stated they expected Iranian Prime Minister Bakhtiar to last only a few more days in office. But as long as disputes stayed within the administration, they were acceptable. There were not any *Unusual Process* characteristics that could have affected the quality of decision making. This means that the total number of variables for the *Decision-Processing* scale in this case is 4.

Conclusion

The Iranian Revolution can be seen as the low point of the Carter administration. An ally was eventually replaced by an enemy, and this event had grave consequences for both international and domestic politics. Not only did regional alliances change in the aftermath of these events, but the U.S. hostages held for 444 days in Iran became an enormous problem for the administration and helped sink the president's bid for reelection. Of course, the revolution cannot be laid squarely at the feet of the Carter administration. In Brzezinski's words (1983, 395), the shah "proved weak, vacillating, and suffered from a paralysis of will." When he finally made concessions, they were "too little too late" (Vance 1983, 331). As Vance noted, he failed to surround himself with enough power to hang on, and he failed to pit the opponents of his regime against one another. Partially because they assumed that a man who had reigned over a country for thirty-seven years knew his domestic position better than they did (Vance 1983), the United States put off considering options beyond supporting the shah until it was so late that the only options were "grim" (Brzezinski 1983, 397).

Brzezinski argued for supporting action by Iran's military—first to support the shah, and then after the shah's departure, military rule. The other side saw that as infeasible or highly problematic. The U.S. ambassador in Iran termed the military a "paper tiger" (Vance 1983, 338), and it was possible a coup would fail. And if it did not fail, it could have resulted in an extremely bloody conflict, something that President Carter feared would prove a boon for the Soviet bloc (Brzezinski 1983, 397). At one point or another during the final two months of meetings, Vance, Secretary of Defense Harold Brown, and President Carter all spoke positively regarding taking a military approach, should it come to that. But the longer they waited, the more unlikely it was to work. And Brown had deemed it unlikely to succeed even before the shah left the country. Being unwilling to risk a coup, but also having qualms about engaging Khomeini, the administration was torn. The president himself was torn, facing perhaps "a conflict between his reason and his emotions" (Brzezinski 1983, 355). So the actions the United States took were small cautious steps, as Iran fell into the midst of revolution.

This is perhaps not surprising. David Welch's (2005) theory of foreign-policy change expects that highly bureaucratized states will usually wait until there is an imminent catastrophe before altering their status quo position. The problem in this case was that once the United States was finally ready to move away from its status quo position on Iran, it was unable to do so, as the decision-making structure in place atop the national security policy apparatus was divided, unmethodical, and inefficient. And the competing strands of authority, combined with flashes of temper and ongoing personality disputes, led to inaction and an inability to chart a new course,

as the assumptions and perspectives participants brought to the table differed markedly, with no mechanism in place to force them to come together and hold to a new strategy.

Reagan Funding the Contras, 1981

The Reagan administration brought a number of changes to U.S. foreign
policy, but one idea was so centrally associated with the administration's
actions and approach to foreign policy that it came to be known as the
"Reagan Doctrine." This was the administration's active support for anticommunist insurgencies around the world. The political rhetoric used by
the administration was so broad that it was possible to apply the concept to
rebel groups the world over. Indeed, in his 1985 State of the Union Address
the president called for supporting "freedom fighters . . . on every continent." In practice, the administration's support for particular groups varied
widely. But while the administration may not have backed every rebellious
group fighting forces aligned with the Soviet bloc, their support for such
operations was widespread over the course of the 1980s and stretched across
many areas, from the mountains of Afghanistan to the tropical expanses of
Central America. This strategy would not be named until 1985, but it was
a feature of the administration's foreign policy from its first months in office and was indicative of both the worldview of the administration and its
operational preferences.

Prominent among these operations was U.S. support for the Contras in
Nicaragua. The first $19 million of this program was officially approved in
the fall of 1981. Once Anastasio Somoza Debayle, the last ruler in a dynasty
that had controlled Nicaragua since the 1930s, fled the country in 1979, the
U.S. government under both Carter and Reagan faced difficult decisions
relating to how to limit the new government's connections with communist countries and other revolutionary groups that were seeking to displace
in their own countries the sort of rule that the Sandinistas had displaced
when they ended the rule of the Somozas in Nicaragua. Under Somoza, the
country had been closely tied to the United States, but the new Nicaraguan
government relied heavily on assistance from Cuba. And as the civil war
in nearby El Salvador intensified, Nicaraguan aid to rebels there became a
more pressing concern of the United States.

The Carter administration's approach to this problem had fit, broadly
speaking, with the longstanding U.S. strategy of containment. But it also

kept the United States engaged in the country, trying to move the new regime in ways that fit with U.S. concerns and working with it on a broad set of issues. One prominent tool the Carter team used toward these ends was the dispersion of foreign aid to the Sandinista government. This was meant to keep them from becoming reliant upon, and thereby more strongly affected by, the Soviet bloc, and it provided the United States with a considerable threat to hang over Nicaragua. If the new government did not respond favorably to U.S. requests, it risked the loss of a considerable amount of money, and of course it was not a wealthy state. This approach kept the United States involved in Nicaragua and resulted in it staying engaged with the country on a variety of fronts. Under the Democratic administration, where the Sandinistas fit into the global political balance was a matter of great concern, but several prominent policymakers saw more behind Central America's troubles than simply the hand of Brezhnev or Castro.

A change in approach once Ronald Reagan took office was all but inevitable given Reagan's campaign, the frame through which the administration saw Nicaraguan politics, and the personnel in the administration who would come to have authority over decision making regarding the region. The rhetoric of the presidential campaign pushed the administration toward taking a much tougher line, in which any form of engagement with what were seen as revolutionary actors was close to impossible (Pastor 1987). Generally, the new administration saw Central America as little more than a "battleground with Moscow and Havana" (Oberdorfer 1983). To them, Nicaragua was on the wrong side of those battle lines, and those divides were what mattered politically, both locally and globally. Given this new decision-making context, it is not surprising that the U.S. approach to Nicaragua began to be reevaluated almost as soon as the new president was sworn into office. The shift would take months to unfold, given "the time-consuming transition process" (Pastor 1987, 231). But it was clear from the outset that Reagan would "not give Nicaragua time to consolidate its revolution" (Pastor 1987, 231) or tolerate "adventurism" (Pastor 1987, 232). Reagan was determined not to stand aside while the Caribbean became "a Communist lake in what should be an American pond" (Dugger 1983, 519).

Fitting with this harder line, U.S. Ambassador Pezzullo was ordered to convey to the Sandinistas that the United States would pull its aid from Nicaragua if they did not cease their support of rebels in El Salvador. Fearing the loss of $75 million, Nicaragua changed its policy as requested. U.S. intelligence confirmed this. But on April 1, 1981, the White House canceled U.S. aid to Nicaragua nonetheless. Ambassador Pezzullo argued that this removed the only leverage the United States had over the state, leverage that had been used effectively to get what it sought regarding El Salvador. But most voices in the administration viewed the Nicaraguan regime as fundamentally untrustworthy and likely to resume its support of the rebels at some point. The Reagan administration wanted changes in Nicaragua's foreign and economic policies, and it wanted its military to be cut by nearly 50 percent, from 23,000 to 15,000 troops (Pastor 1987, 234). Given the scope of the changes it sought, many in the administration believed that regime change was necessary. They did not believe that diplomacy and economic influence could accomplish the level of change they sought in the country. And as they watched Nicaragua's behavior in the wake of the end of U.S. aid, they saw it dealing more with states they distrusted, receiving monetary aid from Libya, tanks from Algeria, and wheat from the Soviets—who, of course, were getting it from the United States (Dickey 1985)—which reaffirmed their belief in the need to see significant change in the country.

A major policy change in a key trouble spot had occurred quickly, even though the plans for what to do next regarding Nicaragua were not yet in place. The new administration was pushing U.S. policy in new directions. More and more officials were appointed who believed containment was not enough. These individuals wanted communist governments and revolutionary actors defeated. As containment ideas were put aside, so were public servants who had supported them (Scott 1996). As the administration took shape, it became noted for its "ideological purity" (Destler et al. 1984, 109). It housed a collection of true believers united in supporting activism and confrontation in an international world defined along the lines of Washington and Moscow, where often all one needed to know about specific political actors were their allegiances in the cold war.

These beliefs were personified in the two principals who were arguably the most engaged in leading a change in U.S. policy in Central America in 1981, Secretary of State Alexander Haig and Director of Central Intelligence William Casey. Haig had risen rapidly during the Nixon administration. He started as National Security Advisor Henry Kissinger's military assistant in 1969, later became his deputy, was promoted over hundreds of others to become vice chief of staff of the Army but was back in the White House after a few months, assuming the position of chief of staff in the spring of 1973. When it came to foreign policy, Haig supported using direct, forceful measures to weaken members of the Soviet bloc. Given his prioritization of the cold-war balance above all else, it is not surprising that matters in the Western hemisphere were not his top concern. He "knew nothing about Latin America and generally couldn't care less" (Dickey 1985, 103). But when matters in Latin America were implicated by cold-war conflicts he did care, so it is perhaps not surprising that in the Americas his attention quickly gravitated toward Cuba. He wanted high-visibility moves undertaken by the U.S. military to show Cuba that the United States was serious about using overwhelming force to secure a change in its government.

William Casey had spent his career both in and out of government service. He had worked in the OSS during World War II, become a successful corporate attorney, held top jobs under Nixon (chairman of the Security and Exchange Commission, undersecretary of state), and served as campaign manager of Reagan's victorious run for the White House in 1980. He had greatly wanted to be secretary of state, and when he was offered the job of DCI instead he made it clear that he would be a policymaker, not simply an analyst and advisor. Like Haig, he pushed for active moves against communist forces and their allies from the start of the administration, though, as one might predict given his position in the administration, he was much more supportive of covert action as a means to achieve his desired ends. As early as March 1981, Casey was pushing for covert aid "to pro-U.S. elements in Afghanistan, Cambodia, Cuba, Grenada, Iran, Laos, Libya, and Nicaragua" (Persico 1990, 264).

In 1981, both men were pushing for active moves in Central America and the Caribbean, but they were arguing for strikingly different policies. Haig sought the direct application of military pressure and of showing a willingness to employ massive levels of resources toward the cause of ending the communists' reign in Cuba. He talked often of the Korean War, the Cuban Missile Crisis, and the need to send a direct message to Moscow. Casey advocated covert action against multiple countries. As was the case with Haig, for Casey the fundamental target was Moscow. And the surreptitious support of rebel groups in several countries was often discussed more as an intensification of the fight against the Soviet menace than as operations to alter the makeup of various developing-world governments.

Casey's position won out. The White House had no interest in engaging in a costly conflict with Cuba that would take the focus off of the domestic and economic initiatives that the administration was trying to prioritize in 1981. They doubted that either Congress or the public would stand for such a risky and costly proposal. And they were supported by veteran staff at the Department of State who doubted that Haig's plan would prove successful at changing Cuba. In contrast, Casey's proposal put a lower level of U.S. prestige and resources on the line, and it could be more easily defended as simply a natural ratcheting up of decisions to which the United States was already committed. On March 9, 1981, just six weeks into the Reagan administration, a presidential finding had been issued that increased the level of covert action in Central America. Director Casey had notified the congressional intelligence committees of this increase and had "left with the committees' blessing" (Persico 1990, 265). Also earlier in the year, the United States had declined to "enforce the neutrality laws against the Nicaraguan and Cuban exiles who were training in Florida and California to overthrow the Nicaraguan government" (Pastor 1987, 236). And there was a preexisting covert program active in Nicaragua that had been undertaken by the junta ruling Argentina. One response to critics who decried U.S. support of the Contras because it increased violence in the region was to note that the covert operation was already underway and that the United States was merely stepping into a preexisting conflict to assist the more pro-American side.

Much like Haig's organization was not united behind his Cuba plan, neither was Casey's organization united in support for his plan for covert action in Nicaragua, regardless of the preexisting situation, which made it relatively less costly. Questions over its scope and its chances of success lingered. Haig remained the most prominent opponent of this covert proposal. He had several problems with the plan (Pastor 1987, 237). First, "covert action was a contradiction in terms." It was highly unlikely that this would remain secret. Second, Cuba was a much more important venue for action, especially if the overall point was to send a message to Moscow. But even if one did want to focus on Nicaragua, Casey's solution was a "cop-out." The support provided was "inadequate to the nature of the problem" and would simply increase the level of violence in the region. It would not solve anything. The Contras were a weak organization "almost entirely dependent" on American support (Scott 1996, 155–156). Haig did not believe they could displace the Sandinistas. But centering policy on such a goal was perhaps Haig's most fundamental problem with this plan. Haig believed the fundamental matter at stake was foreign policy. The Contra strategy would point the administration toward prioritizing changing the government of Nicaragua. Haig believed another country's form of government was of secondary importance to how it behaved in the international arena. Haig cared about international relations, not comparative government—and should the latter be one's top concern, he believed the Contra strategy to be wholly inadequate to accomplishing that end.

But the White House was determined to block foreign-policy initiatives on the scale favored by Haig. And most expert voices on the region that would have objected to Casey's plans were sidelined. Partially, this was a matter of how and where the decision was made. Casey's leadership on the issue, and placing so much of it under the control of the CIA, blocked a number of would-be policymakers from becoming involved. Fitting with this, the national security advisor, Richard Allen, was the least powerful person to hold the position in many years. This further enabled Casey, a decision maker who had a great deal of influence within the White House and enjoyed the confidence of the president (Dickey 107), to pull policy-making into his own organization and away from 1600 Pennsylvania Avenue and the Department of State. Haig's repeated conflicts with the Reagan White House, which would eventually lead to his dismissal in 1982, made it clear that his ties and influence there were not as strong as Casey's. Furthermore, the staffing of the new administration had gone forward in a way that marginalized area experts who would possibly have raised further qualms about the Contra plan. Neither Reagan's first assistant secretary of state for the region, the first two ambassadors he named to the country, nor the CIA operations director who would oversee implementation of the plan had experience in the region. But all were "action oriented" (Dickey 1985, 103) and seen to possess the right ideological beliefs. And where some saw "cowboyism" (Dickey 1985, 107), the administration saw people willing to press forward against communists and those who sympathized with them. As Pastor (1987, 235) put it: "After the fall of 1981, the covert and overt warriors replaced the diplomats."

This program went forward and was greatly expanded over the course of the Reagan administration. Funding the Contras damaged relations between the United States and numerous Latin American countries and contributed to a negative view of U.S. foreign policy that has been held by many across the globe. If one subscribes to the theory that aggressive action against Soviet allies and potential Soviet allies, especially in our own hemisphere, was necessary to bring down the other superpower, it is conceivable that one might rate this decision somewhat favorably in terms of U.S. interests. But then again, Sandinista leader Daniel Ortega did not lose the presidency of

Nicaragua until after the Berlin Wall had fallen, and he would be elected president once again in 2006. The Contras proved to be disorganized and corrupt, and they created a host of political problems for the Reagan administration, both domestically and internationally. Administration support for such a program might seem somewhat predictable given its dominant ideology, the emergence of William Casey as a major policymaker, and the lack of a strong National Security Council or other mechanisms to more fully consider the risks, costs, and objectives involved.

Experts' Ratings

Regarding *National Interest*, our foreign-policy experts gave this decision a low score, 2.10 on a five-point scale. That is, they believed that this decision was not in the overall national interest. While our survey instrument did not quiz them on the reasons behind their rating, one reason may stem from the relative costs and gains involved in the operation. The short-term gains were negligible, and the operation created a host of political difficulties for the United States. The other outcome measure we investigate is the effect of the decision on the *Level of International Conflict*. Since the purpose of supporting the Contras was to increase international conflict as a means of affecting political change, it is not surprising that our expert coders gave this decision one of the highest ratings in our sample.

Situation

This decision was made in an environment where concerns over timing and threat were minor. This event evidenced almost none of the situational characteristics that have been associated with poor performance in the small-group literature. The *Stress Level* was low, and was rated as a 1 on the five-point scale. This was not a *Crisis* situation. While the Reagan administration was generally distressed over trends in Central America and in the global cold war, their policy did not stem from a specific *Recent Failure*. There was no *Short Time Constraint* driving U.S. action. In fact, Nicaragua had appeared to respond positively to U.S. pressure earlier in the year.

Since U.S. action on this topic was frequently framed through the lens of the cold war and U.S. relations with Cuba, decision makers believed that *Strategic Interests* but not *Vital Interests* were at stake. In fact, the secretary of state believed the focus on Nicaragua was misplaced. The opinions of

Allies and *International Organizations* had neither an overall positive nor an overall negative impact on U.S. decision makers. International actors were divided along predictable lines, reflecting systemic international divides, and some of the countries and leaders who had at first been friendly to the Sandinistas were cooling on them by the time the Reagan administration acted. While *Public Opinion* would eventually turn against the Reagan administration's support for the Contras, such opposition did not exist when decision makers were making their fateful choices in the autumn of 1981. Similarly, while *Legislative Opinion* would later turn strongly against this operation, when the decision was made it was something of an afterthought. The following year, the Boland Amendment would pass the House without opposition. Neither the House Intelligence Committee nor Senator Barry Goldwater (R-AZ), the chairman of the Senate Intelligence Committee, was on good terms with Director of Central Intelligence Casey (Dickey 1985). But when the funding program was initiated, it was not clear that it would have such negative repercussions for the administration (Persico 1990, 265), and at least for a time the Congress was willing to defer to the administration, as was seen when the presidential finding was presented to them in March.

The *Military-Capabilities Differential* between the United States and Nicaragua was not relevant in this situation, as the United States was not pursuing a policy that involved the overt, direct involvement of its military forces. There was, however, a negative *Situational Distraction* that affected decision making in this case. In late October and November 1981, the news was dominated by a string of stories on how bad the economy was. Unemployment was higher than it had ever been during the Carter presidency, the national debt was crossing a prominent mark, and Budget Director David Stockman was attracting a great deal of criticism. This resulted in the White House focusing heavily on economic concerns and not paying a great deal of attention to foreign policy in Latin America at the time when the decision to initiate this program was being made.

When summed, we see that the total number of negative *Situational Factors* is 1.

Group Structure

The decision-making group was not *Insulated*. Policymakers from across the administration were involved in setting this decision, and the National

Security Council was not working in a way that excluded particular voices. However, it was led by a *Biased Leader*. What was discussed was arguably less what to do and more how and when to do it. Reagan wanted communists and friends of communists in Central and South America actively threatened and undermined. And it had been made clear from staffing and promotion decisions that a failure to support such actions would hurt one's career. This is a case where there was a lack of *Methodical Procedures* in place. In an effort to avoid some of the problems that had occurred in foreign-policy making in 1970s, the Reagan administration had planned to have a relatively weak National Security Council. But this did not fit well with Reagan's hands-off leadership style. That, combined with a weak NSC advisor and a weak NSC staff, resulted in a poorly organized decision-making environment, where decisions could often be avoided, competing ideas ignored, and fights allowed to fester.

This is a case where the decision-making group was *Homogeneous*. It was more ideologically unified than the preceding presidential administrations (Kowert 2002). All the key decision makers held similar perspectives about the nature of foreign policy and the notable international players. There was an unusually high level of concordance between the political orientations of the principals during the first year of the Reagan administration. Likewise, during the first year of the administration there was an *Illusion of Invulnerability* present. Simply consider the favored options of Haig and Casey in this case. Either in intensity or in scope they could be considered grandiose. And given that Reagan's objectives were "activist and ambitious" (Kowert 2002, 52), at this early stage the administration had great faith in its ability to move others at a low cost.

There were no *Gatekeepers*. However, it is clear that the administration did not *Value Disagreement*. Reagan's personality was such that he disliked interpersonal conflict, and his learning style was such that he associated consensus with validity (Kowert 2002, 93). This led him and those around him to limit policy debates. This is a case where the decision was made by neither an *Interested Leader* nor a *Knowledgeable Team*. President Reagan himself was barely involved in policymaking of this sort. He was an extreme delegator. And the decision-making team knew little of Central America, much less of Nicaragua specifically. This was a decision-making group largely devoid of *Teamwork*. "Serious conflict emerged in the system almost immediately as a result of personal and political rivalries" (George and Stern 1998, 226). Allen's National Security Council was not strong enough to limit this. Some of the principals continually fought with the rest. It was said, for example, that Haig was "succeeding mainly in starting pitched battles with other members of the cabinet and advisors to the president" (Dickey 1985, 103). There was also an *Unusual Structural Characteristic* that would have an effect on this case: the unusual degree to which the CIA would organize and oversee foreign policy in the administration, including this particular event. Director Casey was unusually influential and successful. He became a skilled policymaking principal and was able to greatly expand his influence and that of his agency. Given that this fell outside of the usual channels of decision making, and that the organization's operations made it difficult to monitor and oversee, this definitely had the potential to complicate careful, considered decision making involving all the relevant policymaking actors.

In this period, we see an administration that was filled with antagonistic principals, nonexperts with authority, and where vigorous debates and careful procedures were not encouraged. The *Group-Structure* scale totals 9, one of the highest numbers in the sample.

Decision Processing

This case involved a *Poor Information Search*. It was not thorough, and the Reagan administration processed the information it did receive in a *Biased* way. Its members came into office with a particular worldview regarding a variety of actors and actions in Central America. New information that came to top U.S. officials was continually viewed through this preexisting perceptual prism. Information was not used to refine their understanding of the region but was instead used to bolster their preexisting views and the righteousness of their course of action. The administration did not thoroughly *Survey Objectives*, nor did it carefully *Survey Alternatives*. There was little consideration of the specific desired end state they were pursuing, and there was no careful weighing of competing alternatives.

There was extensive *Stereotyping of the Situation* and *Stereotyping of the Out-Group*. The policymaking principals saw this Nicaraguan situation as being a part of the cold war, and they tended to view the competing groups involved as primarily surrogates for the United States or the Soviet Union. They did not see the conflicts at issue as indigenous, nor did they view much variation in the parties beyond where they fit into the cold-war calculus.

However, while decision making during this case was clearly shaped by the ideological prisms of those leading the government of the United States to such a degree that a careful weighing of objectives and alternatives was dispensed with, these leaders did *Not Suppress Dissent*. While as a structural matter the administration was set up in a way that curtailed disagreement, when there was some in this case, the principals allowed it in the venues where it emerged.

Therefore the *Decision-Processing* scale totals 6 faults, all of the possible variables in the scale apart from suppressing dissent.

Conclusion

This is a case in which an administration was determined to do something, anything, to make clear that it was vigorously confronting the threat of communist expansion in the Western hemisphere. A new administration had come in determined to implement new ideas. Their agenda put them on a path toward greater conflict, and their worldview and the manner in which the decision was made, with few checks demanded of policy proposals, biased information processing, and few critiques presented to question dominant stereotypes, pushed them further toward escalation.

The divisions within the administration, the infighting, and the fluid and sometimes chaotic set of decision-making procedures, when combined with a lack regional expertise or oversight by the president or even a stronger national security advisor, was a recipe for a creating policies that were not thoroughly considered, that could conflict with others, or were at the very least suboptimal. There was less a decision-making process than there was simply a core set of goals, and whoever could win authority over dealing with an issue varied depending upon the time, the topic, and the relevant resources involved. While things would change in Reagan's second term, in his first there was a great deal of almost ad hoc decision making on important foreign-policy issues, given the president's tendency to delegate, the weak National Security Council, the high levels of secrecy involved in certain decisions, and the frequently warring principals. This was a setting in which it is easy to see how policies that might best meet the national interest could be blocked, delayed, inadequately funded, or the like. Without better coordination or more careful and detailed planning, policymaking suffered and led to a number of initiatives that either failed or brought about unexpected negatives. While the line of subsequent actions begun with this initial funding certainly led the Reagan administration to experience the latter, this case is also an example of how a poorly functioning group can lead to the adoption of a major policy even when the principals know it is not likely to successfully achieve its targeted end through the means provided.

Reagan's Strategic Defense Initiative

Ronald Reagan had a dream. Actually, there were multiple parts to the dream: the first was to protect Americans and U.S. military installations from nuclear weapons; the second was to move away from the policy of mutually assured destruction (MAD) as the core deterrence strategy for the United States; and the third—his ultimate dream—was to rid the world of nuclear weapons.[1] These were lofty dreams indeed and, one can argue, dreams that were idealistic and peaceful in their intentions. And yet, dreams—even idealistic ones—cannot substitute for high-quality, rigorous decision making that evaluates the implications of the decision, the feasibility of the project, the costs and benefits involved, and the effect on allies and opponents.

Perhaps the most critical policy decision geared toward these dreams was to propose the development of an antiballistic missile system based in space. The Reagan administration called the proposal the Strategic Defense Initiative (SDI), but the media pejoratively dubbed it "Star Wars." As idealistic as was Reagan's dream regarding SDI, the administration failed terribly in conducting an effective decision-making process in this case and made no real attempts to assess even rudimentary questions before Reagan announced his idea regarding missile defense to the world on March 23, 1983. Indeed, there was virtually no decision-making process in this case at all. The case achieves notoriety in our database as having one of the most unusual structural factors among our cases: although this was one of the most important strategic-policy changes made by the United States during the cold war, the secretary of defense and the secretary of state (structurally the two most important foreign-policy advisors to the president) were not involved in the decision-making process—in fact, they were not even informed of the decision until two days before the announcement was made.

If there was little or no decision-making process, then how was the decision made? In this case, perhaps more than any other we have investigated, the decision was made by the president—nearly exclusively—based almost entirely on his own views and dreams. Its origins for Reagan may go back more than forty years. In 1940, Reagan starred in a movie entitled *Mur-*

der in the Air. He played a secret-service agent charged with protecting a new, secret weapon called the Inertia Projector, which could destroy enemy aircraft before they reached the United States. A quote from the movie is eerily close to Reagan's dreams noted earlier: the Inertia Projector "not only makes the United States invincible in war, but in so doing promises to become the greatest force for world peace ever discovered."

Over the years, other nonfictitious sources certainly contributed to Reagan's beliefs about the value of a possible missile defense system. In 1967, Reagan attended a briefing in California with Edward Teller, a member of the Manhattan Project and perhaps the key contributor to the development of the hydrogen bomb. The briefing centered on missile defense, and Teller seems certain that Reagan paid close attention and understood the implications of the topic (Teller and Shoolery 2001).

In his 1976 campaign for the presidency, Reagan was already voicing strong opposition to MAD as the key deterrence policy of the cold war. He likened it to two individuals sitting in a room pointing loaded guns at each other, with each individual knowing that a wrong move or a wrong word would result in quick death for both (Cannon 1991, 318; Talbott 1988, 189).

Perhaps the most significant contribution to Reagan's beliefs about the necessity of missile defense came when he visited the North American Aerospace Defense Command (NORAD) in Wyoming on July 31, 1979, during the early stages of Reagan's presidential campaign (Cannon 1991; Shultz 1993; Talbott 1988). After touring the impressive facilities, Reagan asked Air Force General James Hill what could be done if the radar systems detected an incoming Soviet missile. Hill's answer, that nothing could be done except to track the missile and perhaps provide some warning to the target area (and, of course, retaliate), seems to have left a deep and lasting impression on Reagan. Martin Anderson, an advisor to Reagan who was with him for the tour, later reported to George Shultz that "Reagan shook his head (at the news from Hill), deeply disturbed that America had no means of defense against nuclear attack. He was clearly stunned. 'There must be something better than this,' he said. The impression this experience made on him was indelible" (Shultz 1993, 262). Shortly thereafter, Reagan asked Anderson to write a policy memorandum for the campaign arguing for a missile-defense system, though other campaign officials perceived the topic as too controversial, so it never became a notable subject on the campaign trail (Cannon 1991; Shultz 1993; Talbott 1988).

Shortly after Reagan's election, a small working group formed in the White House to consider missile defense. Participants included Ed Meese, who was then serving as counselor to the president; Richard Allen, Reagan's first national security advisor; George Keyworth, Reagan's science advisor, who was recommended for the position by Teller; and Anderson, who was then serving as assistant to the president for policy development. In September 1981, two others joined the group, both with military backgrounds: Karl Bendetsen, former undersecretary of the Army; and Daniel Graham, former head of the Defense Intelligence Agency and then current head of High Frontier, a private organization devoted to missile defense. Bill Clark replaced Allen as national security advisor in 1982, and on January 8 of that year, this working group, along with three conservative fundraisers for the president, met with Reagan to discuss missile defense (Cannon 1991, 320).

Notable about this working group is that it consisted primarily of people working in the White House. While some had ties to the major foreign-policy bureaucracies (Clark came over to NSA from State; Graham and Bendetsen had past connections to Defense), no one then in the departments of State or Defense participated. Though nothing concrete came from this group, Anderson describes the meeting with Reagan as an important moment for the development of missile defense (Anderson 1988). However, as Cannon (1991, 323) describes it, this group "lacked the background and the Pentagon support necessary to fashion a strategic defense proposal," and the group discontinued its work when Anderson left the White House to return to the Hoover Institution.

Several sources note that momentum for missile defense returned in 1983 not because of any great technological breakthroughs or more vigorous decision-making processes but rather because defense policy in the administration came off the tracks in another area, specifically regarding the MX missile and the "Dense Pack" proposal (Cannon 1991; Shultz 1993; Talbott 1988). Dense Pack was a proposal to cluster MX missiles closely together in Wyoming so that, theoretically speaking, when the first Soviet warhead detonated, it would have the effect of destroying all other incoming missiles and warheads, thus allowing up to 70 percent of the remaining U.S. MX missiles to survive in their hardened silos. But many in Congress had significant questions and concerns about the idea, and it was voted down on December 8, 1982, handing the administration a major defense-policy defeat.

While several in the administration were smarting from the setback and wondering what might be next for the agenda, the effect among the joint chiefs of staff appears to be the most salient in the causal chain that resulted in SDI. The setback caused the chiefs to reconsider strategic policy in general; this led the issue of missile defense to resurface among them, and it did so in a very timely way, as we discuss below. The chief of naval operations, Admiral James Watkins, was the clearest voice among the joint chiefs in favor of missile defense. He based his position, similar to Reagan's, on moral concerns about MAD; the defeat of the MX proposal provided a timely reason for him to revisit the issue (Cannon 1991, 327). Importantly, Watkins shared his views with Vice Admiral John Poindexter, who was serving in the NSA at the time, and Poindexter relayed the information to Robert "Bud" McFarlane, who had recently become deputy national security advisor. McFarlane, perhaps more than anyone except for Reagan himself, became the key mover and manipulator in the process from that point on—and things happened extraordinarily quickly after that.

McFarlane encouraged Watkins to have the joint chiefs raise the issue of missile defense with Reagan at their regularly scheduled quarterly meeting on February 11, 1983. Toward that end, Watkins prepared a short report on the topic and shared it in a meeting of the joint chiefs on February 2. Much to Watkins's surprise, the other chiefs, who were also concerned about the failure of the MX in Congress, were quick to voice their support for Watkins's report. According to Cannon (1991), they unanimously agreed to present the report to Reagan on February 11.

During the meeting with the president, missile defense was discussed near the end of General John Vessey's report (Vessey was chairman of the joint chiefs at the time). According to multiple accounts, what the chiefs said and what Reagan heard were not the same thing. Part of the reason for this may lie with McFarlane, who manipulated the interpretation of the chiefs' report in the most favorable terms possible for missile defense (Cannon 1991; Talbott 1988), and part of it is surely that Reagan heard what he wanted to hear. The chiefs apparently talked about the idea in broad brushstroke terms, as one part of the strategic balance between offensive and defensive capabilities and philosophies. The president (with McFarlane's prompting) heard that "with the technology of today there can be such a screen" that protects Americans from incoming ballistic missiles (Cannon 1991, 285). Watkins later explicitly stated that he gave no such direct impression to the president, saying "We never believed in the umbrella" (Cannon 1991, 285). But frequently in the decision process what is actually said or implied is not what is heard or understood. Reagan and McFarlane heard what they wanted to hear, and that was that the chiefs agreed that missile defense was a real possibility based on the technology of the day.

McFarlane briefed Clark on the meeting. Clark, though he was serving as national security advisor, had virtually no experience in foreign policy or national security and knew nothing about military technology. He had come to the administration from the California Supreme Court; in the White House he was referred to as "Judge Clark." But Clark knew Ronald Reagan well and he knew what Ronald Reagan wanted; he also knew politics. Once McFarlane briefed Clark, he, along with McFarlane, orchestrated tight control of the process until Reagan announced the proposal only six weeks later. Clark knew how passionate Reagan was about the subject, and he either knew or strongly suspected that Secretary of State George Shultz and Secretary of Defense Caspar Weinberger would be opposed to the dramatic policy change. According to Cannon (1991), Clark deliberately kept Shultz and Weinberger out of the loop until two days before the announcement. This is a classic example of Janis's (1982) concept of a "mindguard"—someone within the decision-making group who knowingly keeps information from others for the purpose of moving the preferred policy forward.

Separate from McFarlane's and Clark's control and total circumvention of normal foreign-policy decision-making procedures, the key influence behind the decision and the rate at which it was adopted was clearly Reagan himself. Several accounts note that once Reagan heard what he wanted to hear from the joint chiefs, he wanted to make the announcement as soon as possible (Cannon 1991; Talbott 1988). The administration had already requested network time for the president to speak on defense issues on March 23, and, when discussing it with Clark, Reagan simply said "Let's do it" (Cannon 1991, 331). That was the extent of and the end to the decision-making process for perhaps the most dramatic change in U.S. strategic thinking during the cold war.

Experts' Ratings

Clearly the decision-making process in this case was highly unusual. By any standards, normal decision-making procedures were not followed. However, before analyzing the case more specifically using the variables in our framework, let us look at how our foreign-policy experts rated the short-term outcomes of the case in terms of national interests and the level of international conflict. On a scale from 1 to 5, with 1 indicating the lowest possible score and 5 the highest in terms of national interests, the SDI case was rated 2.05 by our experts, well below the average for our cases of 3.05. Clearly the experts thought that the proposal for missile defense was not advantageous to the U.S. short-term *National Interest*. The costs incurred by pursuing the program were astronomical, it hurt relations with allies, and it significantly hindered cooperative discussions with the Soviet Union. The experts also rated the case negatively in terms of the *Level of International Conflict*. On the conflict scale, with possible scores ranging from 1 on the low end to 5 on the conflict end, the experts averaged 4.10, which is above the average for our cases. They saw the decision as increasing the level of international conflict and heightening tensions with the Soviet Union. Let us turn now to a more thorough analysis of the specific independent variables in our framework.

Situation

There were very few situational pressures affecting Reagan and the decision-making process in this case. *Stress Levels* were low, it was not a *Crisis*, and there were no *Time Constraints* forcing a quick decision. Given that this was a cold-war related case, we coded the *Threat Level* as moderate and the *Military Balance* (between the United States and the Soviet Union) as relatively even. The *Views of Allies, International Organizations*, and *Congress* were either never considered or deemed irrelevant. (George Shultz, once he was involved, expressed concerns about the views of allies, but by that point the decision had already been made by Reagan.) *Public Opinion* in the United States turned out to be supportive, something that Clark, Mc-Farlane, or even Reagan may well have anticipated.

When considering cases that our experts judged as having a negative outcome, we are looking to see if our situation variables created an adverse environment that hindered the decision-making process. In the SDI case, we coded only one of the situation variables as being detrimental: the administration had suffered a *Recent Failure*—Congress's rejection of funding for the MX missile. That failure affected the decision-making process, because Clark, MacFarlane, and the joint chiefs all had it on their minds. However, taken as a set, out of the eleven possible *Situational Factors* that could constrain the administration, only one was present in this case. This indicates that situational pressures were minimal. It was not the case with SDI that the situational variables created an adverse environmental context that inherently limited the quality of decision making.

Group Structures

The number of group structural faults in the SDI case that we coded is the highest of any of our cases. In fact, we found evidence for all eleven of our possible structural faults. The group[2] was quintessentially *Insulated* and intentionally kept that way by Clark. There was no reaching out to or soliciting input from others in the foreign-policy advisory system, security or technical experts outside of the administration, or allies. Not only was the decision a major departure from existing strategic thinking, but the decision-making process also involved massive technological and scientific issues. George Keyworth, as science advisor for the administration, was involved in the informal meetings in the White House early in the administration, but he had no expertise in missile defense; in addition, there is no evidence that he was involved in providing advice during the actual decision-making with Reagan, Clark, and MacFarlane. While the joint chiefs raised the issue with Reagan during their February 11, 1983, meeting, it certainly was not the case that they provided technical information, data, or insights. As George Shultz (1993, 250) pointed out, "Why place so much confidence in the Joint Chiefs of Staff? They are in no position to make what amounts to a scientific judgment."

The case demonstrates clearly the presence of a *Biased Leader*. Reagan not only liked the idea well before he became president and was personally quite invested in it, but two key players around him (MacFarlane and Clark) knew he liked the idea, and this fueled their actions to keep control over this initiative in the White House. *Methodical Procedures* were not followed in this case; indeed virtually none of our cases are so far outside of the norm in terms of standard procedures for a major foreign-policy decision as this one. We coded the group as being *Homogenous*. The only real "advice" Reagan received for SDI came from security-oriented personnel who were all preoccupied with the defeat of the Dense Pack plan, namely MacFarlane and the joint chiefs. After that, the process was controlled strictly within the Reagan White House—and really only among two individuals whose primary focus was advocating for Reagan, not critically evaluating policy.

Those involved in the process, namely MacFarlane, Clark, and Reagan, had a strong *Illusion of Invulnerability*. Reagan's seemed to flow from his idealistic vision regarding nuclear doctrine—that creating missile defense had to be right to make the world a safer place. MacFarlane's and Clark's had more to do with their own knowledge of and closeness to Reagan; what was right for Ronald Reagan simply had to be right. Clark's actions to keep out other normal participants in the foreign-policy process are an extreme example of *Gatekeeping*. It is also clear in the administration that there was little room for *Dissent* in the decision-making process, particularly in this case. While Reagan was intensely interested in this particular policy, he was by no means generally an expert in or particularly *Interested in Foreign Policy* in general. As a structural variable, we code this at the general level, as opposed to the level of the specific case, and this instance is a good example of why. There was a long history in U.S. foreign policy pertaining to the potential dangers of developing a missile defense system (by either side). These concerns led to the signing of the Anti-Ballistic Missile Treaty many years before. If Reagan had a strong foreign-policy background, he would have been better versed in those concerns and might have been more likely to seek out more information on international and scientific complications associated with the possible policy change.

The group, as it existed in its limited form in this case, did not *Have Broad Foreign-Policy Knowledge or Experience*. Clearly this was the case for Reagan himself, but it was also the case for Clark, who, as noted earlier, came to the administration with virtually no experience in security or foreign-policy matters. *Teamwork* was simply not present in this case at all. Teamwork was frequently lacking in the Reagan administration's broader foreign-policy group, which often featured battles between the National Security Council, Secretary Shultz, and Secretary Weinberger. This general tendency may have facilitated the lack of teamwork in the SDI case because Clark may not have wanted to open that Pandora's box. But in this case, teamwork was never given a chance because Clark systematically excluded everyone else on the normal foreign-policy team. Finally, we coded the case as having an *Unusual Structural Problem*, namely that Shultz and Weinberger (and therefore the rest of the advisory systems of the departments of State and Defense) were shut out of the decision-making process, clearly a highly unusual occurrence.

Decision Processing

Moving beyond the structures of the decision-making group, here we turn to the processing of the decision during the case. Not surprisingly based on our discussion thus far, we found many faults in the administration's decision processing during the SDI case. For example, our first variable in this category is *Information Search*, which was woefully lacking in this case. Critical information that should have been sought included such things as technical and scientific information regarding the prospects for establishing a missile defense system, input on the strategic implications of a defense shield in light of the existing MAD doctrine on each side of the cold war, possible time projections for the project, cost analysis, input from allies, and others. While these would seem like basic areas within which to search for information, none of them were investigated prior to the decision.

This case also demonstrates a high level of *Biased Information Processing*, in this case led directly by Reagan himself. Reagan appears to have become enamored with the idea during his visit to NORAD in 1979, and his bias from then on was clear and unequivocal. We also coded the process as one that failed to *Survey Objectives* adequately and as one that failed to *Survey Alternatives* adequately. Though Reagan had broad goals of protecting the United States and moving away from the policy of MAD, it is much less clear that he and the others involved in this case were able to make explicit links between Reagan's idealized goals and SDI. In addition, no one considered the range of foreign-policy objectives that could be helped or hindered by the policy. No meetings ever took place where decision makers sat down and systematically talked about objectives in foreign policy that would reduce nuclear tensions in the world. In addition, no other alternative policy options were considered. Instead, Reagan had an idea that he liked very much, and, rather than considering a set of possible objectives and alternatives, the administration simply went with Reagan's idea.

We also found that Reagan and his close advisors in this case *Stereotyped the Out-Group*. This case took place fairly early in the Reagan presidency, and during this time he and others in the administration held very strong views of the Soviet Union, made manifest by Reagan's now famous description of the country as the "evil empire." Finally, we coded the case as having elements of *Pressures for Uniformity*. MacFarlane and Clark both knew well how much Reagan wanted to move forward with a missile-defense proposal. Clark also suspected that Shultz and Weinberger would have concerns about the dramatic policy shift, so, rather than allow for their concerns to come out, he closed the process down and kept them completely out of the loop, a classic example of suppressing dissent and maintaining uniformity.

There are two decision-processing variables we did not identify as being problematic in this case. First, we saw no example of decision makers *Stereotyping the Situation*, that is comparing it to another situation in the past and drawing false conclusions about the present situation. The notion of missile defense was unique, and though some tied it into the general policy area of defensive (versus offensive) policy, the specific situation of ballistic-missile defense was not compared to past situations. We also saw no evidence for any *Other Unusual Decision Processes* in this case. In all, we found six of the eight *Decision-Processing* variables to be problematic in the SDI decision, well above average (2.84) among our cases.

Conclusion

Here again we see a case where an ill-structured decision-making group engaged in poor decision-making processes. We should note at this point that the aftermath of this decision was not entirely negative. This program became useful as the impetus for arms-control negotiations later in the Reagan years. The administration believed that without the threat of the program and the bargaining chip it became, the Soviets would not have come to the table. But our outcome variables have to do with short-term national interest and international conflict. And on those measures it is not surprising that the foreign-policy experts scored this decision so poorly. In the near term, it had a starkly negative effect on U.S.-USSR relations. While the Reagan administration sought alterations in Soviet behavior, the Soviets highly prioritized this program immediately. Given that the Soviet ambassador in Washington termed it "the most dangerously destabilizing factor in our relationship" (Shultz 1993, 474), it is evident that it made a bad relationship even worse and complicated any attempts that the United States was making to change Soviet policies. And it destabilized the United States' relationship with other countries, complicated several U.S. international strategies and commitments (most obviously certain treaty obligations), and it created domestic political problems as well. The program was expensive, stoked battles both within the administration and with Congress, and raised national debates that were difficult for the administration to win. Popular discussion of the program quickly described it as "an impenetrable shield" (Shultz 1993, 259)—something it was not, and could not have been, even if its technological ambitions eventually met every hoped-for objective. The expectations for the program were set so high that living up to them proved politically costly and contentious.

Could these problems have been fixed if the administration had functioned differently when it made this decision? Not entirely. Any program that looked like SDI was likely to create a host of political difficulties and escalate international conflict, at least in the short term. But keep in mind why this case stands out. It is an example of strikingly flawed decision making from the standpoint of the structures through which it flowed and the processes through which it moved forward. Policy was set by an unsystematic organization through which warring parties twisted information and excluded opponents who would have brought needed perspectives into the process. Secretary Shultz has stated that he became a supporter of SDI and saw "potential greatness" (Shultz 1993, 263) in the concept. But Shultz also confessed in his memoir that decision making in this case proceeded poorly and created a number of problems due to the president's style and his being poorly served by some of his aides. Reagan had "a tendency to rely on his staff and friends to the point of accepting uncritically—even wishfully—advice that was sometimes amateurish and even irresponsible" (Shultz 1993, 263). If Reagan had been functioning within a decision-making system that demanded more careful, systematic consideration of foreign-policy topics, and if he had been receiving better information that was handled in an unbiased way, it may well have been possible to limit the negative outcomes that stemmed from this decision.

George W. Bush and the 2002 Steel Tariffs

In 2002, the Bush White House found itself confronting a situation in which holding fast to principles the United States government had pushed for decades, and which the Republican Party purported to embrace, had the potential to cause serious electoral harm to the president and other Republicans. The U.S. International Trade Commission issued a ruling in response to a surge in steel imports that determined that U.S. firms were suffering from these changes in the industry, and this merited government action to protect them. In choosing how to act on this ruling, the federal government faced a choice. Should it act in line with longstanding arguments and policies supporting free trade? Or should it impose protectionist tariffs that would violate the government's commitment to free trade but which could provide political benefits to the administration?

This was a stark difference over policy. While those advocating tariffs differed over their appropriate level, the divide between those in favor of tariffs and those opposed to tariffs reflected fundamentally different approaches to how this issue should be framed. They differed over basic assumptions about how one could most effectively deal with one of the leading issues in international economics. They also differed over the extent to which domestic political concerns should affect policymaking.

Given the importance of the issue in terms of both domestic politics and the signals the administration's choice would send to the international community, it is not surprising that it soon engaged some of the most prominent people in the administration. These included Vice President Cheney; Deputy White House Chief of Staff Karl Rove, who was the president's top political advisor; United States Trade Representative Robert Zoellick; and Secretary of the Treasury Paul O'Neill. This was a topic O'Neill knew well, because for a dozen years he had been the chairman and CEO of Alcoa. Being familiar with industry issues and having commissioned his own research on the topic, O'Neill believed tariffs were not the answer. He did not think those would truly help the U.S. steel industry. He believed that tariffs would give companies an excuse not to engage in needed retooling, and he had taken on the industry directly regarding their need for reform. O'Neill saw a need for change both domestically and internationally and that U.S. companies needed to be reformed and international talks on steel issues pushed forward, and he believed he could successfully move U.S. policy on both matters.

However, a number of people in the White House, particularly Karl Rove, saw this less as an economic issue than a political one. And with those opinions finding favor in the hallways in the White House, Vice President Cheney helped shape the decision-making process in a way that limited the ability of tariff opponents to make their case, even though he, personally, thought the tariffs were a bad idea (Gellman 2008, 270). Cheney's unprecedented role as the most powerful vice president in the history of the office has been well documented (Gellman 2008). He had unusual access to both the president and to information. Many of the top figures in the administration had worked with or for him in the preceding decades, and he had the largest staff in the history of the office. His top aides were immensely powerful in their own right (Mayer 2006). Additionally, Rove's role in the policymaking process made it easier for political concerns to affect policy. He was one of the "most influential staff members ever to advise a president" (Carney 2002), and he had a powerful role in both setting and selling policy, whether the issue at hand was judicial nominations, stem-cell research, or steel tariffs (Cannon and Simendinger 2002). The White House was concerned that not instituting tariffs could hurt President Bush and the Republicans in places such as Pennsylvania, West Virginia, and Ohio. Administration officials also saw other types of political gain that the president might be able to reap if he proceeded with tariffs. The White House could make a trade with certain senators: if Bush instituted tariffs, those senators could then vote to give him trade-promotion authority. Beyond that, Zoellick believed that if tariffs were instituted they could then be a valuable bargaining chip at the World Trade Organization's upcoming talks on eliminating farm subsidies (Allen and Weisman 2003).

The administration came to consider five policy options: (1) reject the ITC-recommended tariffs; (2) set tariffs triggered only by surges; (3) set a limited, rolling tariff schedule; (4) impose tariffs of 20 percent on certain products; or (5) set tariffs of up to 40 percent on all products, which was what the steel companies and their various allies in electorally precious rust-belt states were pushing for (Suskind 2004, 218–219).

When it came time to settle on a policy, the president's most senior advisors remained divided. The clash between ideology and politics made this "one of the most excruciating decisions of Mr. Bush's" term (Kahn and Sanger 2002). On February 10, 2002, Cheney met with O'Neill and Federal Reserve Chairman Alan Greenspan, both of whom were opposed to tariffs, ostensibly to give them a first crack at the policy debate, though perhaps also to try to curtail what they would say the following day at the meeting of the policymaking principals. Cheney said their opinions "would be duly noted; there would be little more that they needed to say" (Suskind 2004, 218).

The following day, the principals met in a meeting that included the vice president; the attorney general; the secretaries of State, Treasury, Commerce, and Labor; the director of the Office of Management and Budget; the U.S. trade representative; the national security advisor; and the heads of the National Economic Council and the Council of Economic Advisors. President Bush was not in attendance. Most voices in the administration agreed with the view that Greenspan had conveyed to Cheney a day earlier: tariffs would break a bipartisan free-trade consensus, violate WTO agree-

ments, and weaken the hand of the United States in future trade negotiations. Whether their arguments were ideological, economic, or a mixture
of the two, most of the foreign policy–making principals spoke up in favor
of a free-trade, free-market response and opposed tariffs. Secretary O'Neill
said they wouldn't help the steel industry. Like Greenspan, he was worried
about breaking the bipartisan free-trade consensus. National Security Advisor Rice noted the importance of protecting Mexico and Canada because of
the government's NAFTA commitments. Commerce Secretary Don Evans
noted that steel prices had already increased by 6 percent, so the need for
punitive action had lessened and that it was important to stay true to free-
trade principles. OMB Director Mitch Daniels questioned why others felt
it was necessary to bend their principles for political expediency when they
were at 85 percent in the polls. As the meeting went on, Secretary of State
Colin Powell complained that he had yet to hear a single good reason to
institute tariffs (Suskind 2004).

But while a "single good reason" might not have been forthcoming at the
meeting of the principals, the final decision rested with the White House.
And the White House contained people who were more favorably disposed
toward imposing tariffs. Vice President Cheney had not "wanted to end
up in open debate with O'Neill, whose stance on steel was well-informed"
(Suskind 2004, 217). He did not want the administration to become even
more deeply divided. He seems to have known which way President Bush
was likely to go on the issue, and a debate involving the president could be
damaging. If in avoiding such a clash the principals were left isolated from
the president and lacking a substantive reason to use to explain the policy,
so be it. The White House's decision-making structure allowed for Cheney
and a few to others to exist as a "praetorian guard" around the president,
which left Bush "in an echo chamber of his own making" (Suskind 2004,
293). As Christopher DeMuth, president of the influential American Enterprise Institute, put it, the "circle around this President is smaller and tighter
than any we've seen in recent times . . . and I was in Nixon's" (Suskind
2004, 321). With those closest to the president keeping their circle tight and
pressing for a pro-tariff decision, Bush chose to apply tariffs. In the end, this
choice was made despite opposition from most of the heads of the relevant
cabinet departments. It was a decision that was "largely driven by his [the
president's] political advisors" (Allen and Weisman 2003).

This case, then, is another that is marked by *Unusual Structural Conditions* in the decision-making process. On the one hand, the February 11

NSC meeting was attended by appropriate advisors, allowed open and extensive discussion of the topic, and included a large range of comments on the merits and limitations of various policy options; in other words, that particular meeting looked like a part of a rational, generally beneficial decision-making process. On the other hand, however, in many ways that meeting had little relevance for the actual decision making that took place later. Recall that President Bush did not attend the February 11 meeting and so was not privy to the full range of discussions that took place there. Instead, as those framing the decision-making process knew all along, the final word in advising the president would come from a tightly knit ring of advisors whose perspective was focused on domestic politics and thus supported the imposition of tariffs. In many other cases we have analyzed, there is a strong correlation between structural elements of decision making and the quality of information processing during policy consideration: poor structures generally beget poor information processing and vice versa. In this case, however, that correlation was not present. The February 11 meeting appears to have featured good information processing and a good discussion of policy limits and merits. But in this case, the structural problems in the Bush administration trumped the good decision processing. Those closest to the president wanted tariffs, and they structured the process to make sure that policy was adopted.

Experts' Ratings

The World Trade Organization ruled in late 2003 that the tariffs were illegal (Becker 2003). The following month, the president decided to remove them, though they had been scheduled to be in place until 2005. As they were in place for less than two years, it is not surprising that any benefits they might have provided were minor. But their negative consequences were considerable. Domestically, they caused an uproar with U.S. businesses that consumed steel. Senator Lamar Alexander (R-TN) stated they "shifted more steel-consuming jobs overseas than exist in the steel-producing industry in the United States" (Allen and Weisman 2003). Internationally, the response was arguably even more negative, with accusations of double standards and hypocrisy. Retaliatory measures were taken against U.S. businesses in response. Even "key administration officials" believed that the episode "turned into a debacle" (Allen and Weisman 2003). Given these reactions, it is not surprising that our expert coders ranked this decision as one that was very poor from the standpoint of the *National Interest*. In fact, at 2.0 on the five-point scale, this is one of the lowest ranked decisions in our sample of thirty-nine events. It was ranked near the middle of the cases in terms of the *Level of International Conflict* that resulted from the action. It was coded at 3.5 on that five-point scale.

Situation

This decision was made in a situational environment in which pressures for action were low and where, apart from domestic political concerns, the influences that might affect decision makers were pushing in a direction opposed to the policy option that the Bush administration chose to pursue. Decision makers' *Stress Level* was low. There was no *Crisis* at hand. The administration was not responding to a *Recent Failure* on its part. In fact, its approval ratings were high. There was no *Short Time Constraint* that was pushing the administration's hand. The *Level of Interests* at stake was peripheral. While certain companies were suffering, no one in the administration saw this as a matter of strategic interest, and some in the administration doubted whether or not this decision would have much of an effect at all on the health of U.S. steel firms.

International opinion on the matter was overwhelmingly negative. Both U.S. *Allies* and relevant *International Organizations* made loud cries against U.S. tariffs. Tariffs flew in the face of decades of U.S. economic policy and a host of agreements the United States had promised to uphold with members of the international community. Of course, eventually President Bush would face punitive action in response to his move. And in the face of the WTO ruling and actions taken to punish certain segments of the U.S. economy in response to his decision, Bush would choose to lift the steel tariffs early. But in 2002, he was willing to break with the international community.

This was largely due to domestic political situational variables. Much of the U.S. population was not paying close attention to this issue. But the activated publics that were following it, in places such as Pennsylvania and West Virginia, were highly supportive of the president's action. This favorable *Public Opinion* played a role in creating largely favorable *Legislative Opinion* for the policy. As to other situational factors, the *Military-Capabilities Differential* is irrelevant in this case, and there were no *Unusual Situational Distractions* that decision makers had to deal with. Therefore the total number of problematic *Situational Variables* during this case was 2: the opinions of allies and international organizations.

Group Structures

Moving on to the structures and set norms of the decision-making group, we see that this group was not *Insulated*. This coding might surprise some, given the extensive literature on the Bush White House that describes it as an isolated echo chamber where few people had direct access to the president. It appears true that President Bush existed in something of a cocoon. He certainly could have heard a wider variety of voices and policy arguments had he widened his policymaking circle. Nevertheless, those advocating policy options that were not in line with the administration's eventual position were in the White House and made their views known in the appropriate forums. On these economic questions dissent was permitted and the policymaking principals heard it. This was, however, a situation where the group's *Leader* (whether one considers that leader to be Bush or Cheney, the latter of whom appears to be driving decision making in Suskind's 2004 account in *The Price of Loyalty*) was at least somewhat *Biased* toward a certain outcome. Neither the president nor the vice president appeared interested in engaging arguments against the tariffs that were being raised by their senior economic and foreign-policy advisors. Both men appear to have been perfectly comfortable with adjusting the views of their government and party to meet short-term political exigencies.

This was a decision-making group that lacked *Methodical Procedures*. As is mentioned elsewhere in this text and in a host of volumes on decision making in the Bush administration, the Bush White House was notably dysfunctional, especially during the first term. Information was shared—or not—through peculiar channels, and there was an unusual elasticity in the pattern of meetings and who was invited to them. The lack of stable procedures and norms was evident throughout this time period.

On the whole, this was not a *Homogenous Group*. A wide variety of advisors had their voice heard at some point during the decision-making process. And this is not a group that was operating under an *Illusion of Invulnerability*. Group members were well aware of the potential negative effects of instituting tariffs, and some group members clearly had a deep grasp of how these issues fit into larger policy topics.

There were *Gatekeepers* in this decision-making environment, Vice President Cheney being the most obvious one. He repeatedly sought to curtail information and debate (Suskind 2004) and systematically tried to keep certain actors from interacting with other actors and specific information from being spread. Likewise, this was not a group that *Valued Disagreement*. The norm of coming to President Bush with a preset policy proposal, and the example of Vice President Cheney seeking to silence voices opposed to tariffs, indicate that this White House was not one where multiple opinions were desired.

This happened at a time when the *Leader Was Interested in Foreign Policy*. Of course, whether or not George W. Bush was particularly interested in international economic policy is perhaps debatable. But this variable is coded to mark a president's general interest in foreign policy. This is done because various domains of foreign policy often bleed into each other, and if a president is activated toward one, he or she may take a more direct role in setting foreign policy more generally. Of course this may not occur in every case, and here we see an instance where the president was not especially engaged, but the variable is coded as a structural characteristic that is likely to reflect presidential tendencies more broadly.

This decision was also made at a time when the foreign-policy decision-making team was *Knowledgeable*. Some of the decision makers involved here were not new to these issues, and of course there was a general feeling among many that this decision-making team had the right resumes and experience for their respective jobs. That being said, there was strikingly little *Teamwork* among them. Again and again, infighting marked attempts to set policy within the Bush White House, and this case of decision fits that pattern as well, though perhaps not quite as spectacularly as the disputes among Cheney, Powell, and Rumsfeld over issues of international security.

There was one *Unusual Structural Factor* that we are coding for this case, and that is the lack of a clear leader driving administration decision making. President Bush may well have been "the decider," as he famously called himself, but on many issues his involvement came extremely late in the decision-making process. It was a common practice in the Bush White House for his top advisors to meet outside his presence and come up with a policy proposal for him to sign off on (Woodward 2002). This left some who sought to manipulate his decision in a fairly strong position. A great deal of the decision making went on without the president's knowledge or direction. It was also a convenient way to keep certain views from the president, as the president would usually hear the recommendation of the principals more than their particular arguments. And in this case one could argue that the president was even more removed from the process than was usual.

This system meant that decisions could be put off for long periods of time if there was not agreement among the president's advisors, and that they might be made on the basis of skewed or incomplete information. It also meant that those who were in a position to drive group discussions (something that varied by issue topic) and those closest to the president were in a particularly strong position to shape policy options and even essentially the choice itself before the president was involved. When fitted with the lack of methodical procedures in the decision-making group, this structural hole led the administration to make a number of decisions in a rather haphazard manner. Sometimes it was unclear who was pushing what. Sometimes it was even unclear whether or not a decision had been made. The record in this case suggests that while the "decider" was Bush, in many ways the "leader" on this issue was Cheney. Coding of this extra group-structure variable puts the number of negative structural characteristics at 6, well above average for our sample of cases.

Decision Processing

While the structure of the decision-making group was quite problematic, the decision-making process in this case was largely what one would hope for. In this case it is clear that the group conducted a thorough *Information Search*, and it did not process the information it received in a *Biased* manner.

However, there was an instance of poor planning when it came to whether or not decision makers thoroughly *Surveyed Objectives*. Those who were framing this in traditional policy terms and those who were seeing the choice through a more political lens were often talking past each other or simply not bringing matters up. Secretary Powell asking "why do this?" was indicative of the fact that there was no settled-upon endgame. Different decision makers were pointing policy toward quite different ends, and they did not engage each other. This led to a policy whose desired goal was never clearly articulated and agreed upon during the decision-making process.

Nevertheless, the decision makers did *Survey Alternative* policy options. And they avoided relying upon *Stereotypes in Framing the Situation*. For the most part, they also avoided *Stereotyping the Out-Groups* they were dealing with. While certainly some members of the group hoped that their colleagues would support their own preferred policy proposals, excessive *Pressures Toward Uniformity* were not pushed in this case. And there were *No Unusual Process Variables* that made this case unique from other instances of similar decision making.

On the whole, this was not an example of a decision-making process that featured low-quality *Decision Processing*. In fact, we only coded one processing error in this case. It is probably worth noting that the variable on which we saw that one error, a thorough *Survey of Objectives*, is an important matter. If decision makers did an incomplete job of thinking through the goal of their policymaking, it is not surprising that actions they took in pursuit of such a hazy end result might fail to achieve it or cause other problems.

In the steel-tariffs case, we see that the problems in the functioning of the decision-making group stem more from enduring structural issues tied to the patterns of communication and authority that existed in the Bush administration. And given those problems, which were considerable, lacking a clearly agreed upon objective could make the administration even more dysfunctional.

Five

CASE STUDIES IN HIGH-QUALITY
DECISION MAKING

In the preceding chapter, we saw how flawed decision making can lead to policy outcomes that are harmful to the national interest and increase the level of international conflict. We also saw that flawed group structures can in certain cases lead to flawed decision processing. In this chapter, we examine the same connection between policymaking and outcome quality. However, here we see examples of groups judged to have performed ably. We note that their highly rated performance emerges from decision units that lacked many of the negative characteristics associated with the policy-making teams discussed in chapter 4. In these cases, high-quality decision making produced positive results.

The Carter Administration and the Ogaden Crisis

The late 1970s were a tumultuous time for international politics. Détente between the United States and the Soviet Union was on its last legs. New actors were emerging on the world stage, particularly in light of the era's oil shocks and economic upheaval. And a new U.S. president had come to power, a president who was committed to approaching foreign policy in a new way—including setting aside Henry Kissinger's overarching focus on cold-war calculus and placing a new emphasis on human rights. These shifts in global, regional, and U.S. politics all affected politics in the Horn of Africa in 1977 and 1978. Traditional alliances were dropped, different frames for viewing international politics were adopted, and the U.S. government elected to back away from the sort of tit-for-tat actions and superpower bluffs that so often marked its involvement in the developing world, both before and after these events occurred. There was not unanimity in the executive branch about this change, of course. There were, however, extended discussions and debates over whether the United States should carry through with such a change.

As we begin to consider this case, it is important to note from the outset that almost no one in government thought the Horn of Africa was very important strategically (Drew 1978). The development of Diego Garcia had lessened our need for military bases in the area. Nonetheless, instability in the Horn was a matter that grabbed the attention of several senior decision makers in the U.S. government. Why? The most basic answer is that this was an area of great international instability, and there was a real prospect that the fighting there would intensify, perhaps greatly. Second, there was the prospect of major gain by forces allied with the Soviet bloc. Third, and related to the preceding point, major U.S. allies in the Middle East and Europe were seeking U.S. action that would stabilize the region and block gains by the Soviet bloc. Finally, President Carter was himself very much determined to put Africa on the international agenda. However, he did not want Africa to be seen as merely a pawn to be pushed in various directions or sacrificed at the whim of the great powers. Carter was the first president since Kennedy to visit the continent, and he was greatly interested in African issues. When the situation demanded it and the plans were appropriate, Carter was willing to expend U.S. resources on the continent in a traditional, cold war–focused manner (for example, when aid was provided to quash a coup in Zaire). But Carter also hoped to open up new connections with the continent and approach it in a new way (Moens 1990).

At the global level, in the mid-1970s, Soviet-aligned forces were finding success in and near various parts of Africa. The Soviets, with the assistance of Cuban troops, had been fighting for influence in Angola. Across the Gulf of Aden, Soviet allies ruled the People's Democratic Republic of Yemen. In 1977, as instability racked Ethiopia, Fidel Castro carried out a diplomatic mission aimed at creating a Marxist federation involving Ethiopia, Djibouti, and Somalia. That mission failed, but it was evidence of both growing instability in the Horn and the growing friendship between the Soviets and Ethiopia.

This was a major change from the status quo that had existed in the region for most of the preceding quarter century. In 1953, the United States and Ethiopia signed a twenty-five-year deal granting the Americans use of naval and air facilities in Ethiopia. During that era, Ethiopia received $279 million in military aid from the United States, and the Americans trained thousands of members of Ethiopia's military (Selassie 1984, 260). But changes within Ethiopia had weakened that alignment. In 1974, the country's long-time leader, Haile Selassie, was ousted, and the country fell into factional fighting. The Ford administration cut U.S. aid to Ethiopia in 1976. Ethiopia was considered to be of declining strategic importance, given the construction of the military base on Diego Garcia, and a growing number of human-rights violations in Ethiopia made it harder for the Americans to openly side with their traditional ally. This growing distance from the United States led Ethiopia to sign an arms deal with the Soviets in December 1976. Two months later, Cyrus Vance, the new secretary of state, announced a further cut in U.S. aid to Ethiopia (Halliday 1977).

The instability in Ethiopia was particularly acute in the Ogaden region. The pro-Somalia Western Somali Liberation Front (WSLF) was attacking Ethiopian forces and offices in the Somali-inhabited Ogaden. In 1976, the Somali government began providing the WSLF with arms and other aid, and in July 1977, tens of thousands of troops of the Somali National Army invaded their neighbor to the north. While the Soviets had ties to both Somalia and Ethiopia's new government, this move led the Soviets to cut their ties to Somalia, and Soviet military aid and advisors and thousands of Cuban troops flooded into Ethiopia. Somalia then expelled the Soviets from within its borders and called on the United States for assistance.

This intensification of the conflict led many voices to rise up and call for a peaceful solution. It also led to pressure on the United States from several international actors. A number of African states called out for U.S. assistance in light of the increasing instability in the region. France and Iran encouraged the United States to take action. The Saudis were becoming a more important actor in the region, especially as the price of oil rose. They already had a record of affecting the cold-war alliances of states near them, as witnessed by their pressure on Egypt to expel its Soviet advisors in 1971 (Halliday 1977). Now they intensified their longstanding pressure on Somalia to do the same thing and hoped that U.S. actions would further that goal and, more generally, contain Soviet influence throughout the region. The Saudis were "petrified" by the prospect of a Soviet presence across the Red

Sea (Brzezinski 1983, 179). There were also international voices opposed to a strong U.S. intervention on the side of Somalia. The Organization of African Unity had deemed Somalia the aggressor and called on it to withdraw from Ogaden. Until that was done, they opposed aiding Somalia.

Similarly, within the Carter administration there were both voices advocating U.S. action in the dispute and voices advocating caution and opposition to rewarding Somalia for its aggressive behavior, even if it had broken from the Soviet bloc. The push for U.S. action in the region was led by National Security Advisor Zbigniew Brzezinski. He saw this conflict as part of a global fight against the communist bloc, and he believed that some U.S. response had to occur; otherwise the United States risked losing credibility in the world's eyes. Brzezinski's most contentious rival for influence over foreign policy among President Carter's top aides, Secretary of State Cyrus Vance, saw the conflict through a completely different frame. Vance noted that the Carter administration had come to office promising to see Africa as its own world, not simply as a chessboard on which the superpowers made moves and countermoves. He believed that this was fundamentally a local conflict centered on Somali irredentism. Seeing it as an essential cold-war struggle was "short-sighted and somewhat naïve" (Vance 1983, 72). The core issues were not matters of concern to either Washington or Moscow, and the international allegiances of the governments in the region were weak. Vance was not alone in asserting that this was a local African issue. Similar comments were made by Vice President Walter Mondale and UN Ambassador Andrew Young (Moens 1990, 90–91). Young and Assistant Secretary of State for African Affairs Richard Moose believed that eventually Ethiopia would expel the Soviets of their own accord, as Egypt and Sudan had done (Moens 1990, 99).

Possible responses to the situation were discussed at a series of meetings of the National Security Council and its Special Coordinating Committee. These started in December 1977 and stretched on for months, with perhaps the most consequential meetings occurring in February 1978. Brzezinski and David Aaron, the deputy national security advisor, continued to push for some level of a military response. Among the policy options proposed were "large-scale U.S. naval deployments to the area; providing U.S. air cover for Somali forces if the Ethiopians and Cubans crossed the border in pursuit; and funneling military aid to Somalia (and even the Eritrean rebels) through proxies, to tie down the Soviets and Cubans in a bloody and inconclusive struggle" (Vance 1983, 86). However, most military responses were deemed infeasible by many policymakers inside the administration, including Secretary of Defense Harold Brown. But Brzezinski and Aaron continued to make their case that given the context of the cold war, some show of military might was called for even if it was "only for the record" (Brzezinski 1983, 182).

By February, a specific military option was the focus of discussion. Brzezinski argued for sending U.S. and French aircraft carriers to the region. He believed it was essential to demonstrate U.S. resolve to check the Soviets and their allies and to show that the U.S. respected the concerns of key allies who were important in helping contain the Soviet bloc. Secretary Brown countered that a carrier task force should not be sent without a clear plan for what it would do once it was in the region. And both Brown and Secretary Vance raised the issue of what would happen if, after the carrier arrived, Somalia then intensified the conflict. That would in practice result in a bluff being called against the United States, and if the whole purpose of deploying the ships was to enhance U.S. credibility, the move would then be a failure. As Vance put it, "we are getting sucked in. The Somalis brought this on themselves. They are no great friends of ours, and they are reaping the fruits of their actions. For us to put our prestige on the line and to take military steps is a risk we should not take" (Brzezinski 1983, 182). In his memoir, Brzezinski notes that Brown had more positive things to say about the proposal once the president said some favorable words about it and that Vice President Mondale leaned toward the plan but was reluctant to recommend it.

In the end, on the carrier option, it came down to Brzezinski on one side and Secretary Vance, Secretary Brown, and the joint chiefs on the other. Ultimately, President Carter decided against deploying the carrier group. While this decision was in part based on seeing the conflict as more of a local dispute in which cold-war interests were weak, it was likely also based, at least in part, on a fear of antagonizing the Soviets at a time when the United States was attempting to make progress on a variety of issues with the other superpower, including SALT, the CTB treaty, and chemical warfare and nuclear proliferation. The extended discussions over the potential implications of a more hawkish move made clear that other administration priorities could be imperiled if the United States countered instability in the region with a show of force. President Carter did order other actions that were either direct or indirect responses to the war in the Horn and the Soviet buildup in the region. He approved an increase in support for the governments of Sudan and Kenya. Diplomacy was carried out to try to organize the African states against the presence of Cuban troops in Africa. And he postponed the Indian Ocean Demilitarization Talks. But options that were centered on a direct U.S. military presence in the region were put aside. Brzezinski attributes this, at least in part, to U.S. decision makers having been "bitten by the Vietnam bug" (Brzezinski 1983, 183). But it is clear that there were reasons behind this policy choice based on a coherent, substantive perspective regarding this conflict that simply differed from that put forward by Brzezinski.

Brzezinski argues that U.S. inaction emboldened the Soviets and contributed to them taking a more active and aggressive line against the United States in the late 1970s. The anti-Brzezinski side would likely note that they kept the United States out of a lengthy, costly, and bitter battle in which the United States did not have a clear ally. While Somalia soon pulled its own troops out of Ogaden, they continued to support the rebels in the region (Selassie 1984). And, as instability continued, the Soviets sank more and more resources into the fight: advisors, tens of thousands of Cuban troops, and a billion dollars in aid. Keeping the U.S. military uninvolved saved the United States from expending such resources and allowed it to avoid the wrath of African actors who were opposed to a U.S. military intervention. Nevertheless, the United States was still able to work with Somalia as a cold-war ally and gain access to Somali military installations.

Experts' Ratings

When considering these events, our experts judged the path that U.S. decision makers took to be one that was generally positive. The 3.28 rating on the five-point scale measuring the *National Interest* shows that this decision is rated as somewhat above average regarding the U.S. short-term position in international politics. The 2.33 rating on the five-point scale measuring the *Level of International Conflict* is one of the lowest measurements among all the cases included in our analyses. The expert coders believed that the U.S. decision in this situation notably reduced the level of conflict in the international system.

Situation

This was a decision in which there were few situational factors either demanding or constraining U.S. action and few such influences that would be expected to produce low-quality decision making. The *Stress Level* among those participating in the debates was very low. They did not see the event as a *Crisis*.[1] While it could certainly be argued that the Carter administration had seen a *Recent Failure* in terms of aspects of its relations with the Soviet Union, the events in the Horn of Africa were *not* viewed by most decision makers through that frame. Most decision makers did not see the U.S.-USSR relationship as necessarily determining what should be done regarding the events at hand. The decision makers did not feel pressed to act quickly. They did not perceive a *Short Time Constraint*. They calmly evaluated alternatives and listened to a variety of pleas and voices over a period of months. The *Threat Level* was generally considered to be low, with only peripheral interests at stake. As mentioned earlier (Drew 1978, 114), few in government thought that the Horn was very important strategically. And few felt strong ties to the countries involved. Ethiopia had only recently become a Soviet ally, and Somalia's move away from the Soviet bloc and its attempts to win favor with the United States were quite new as well.

Other international actors created specific pressures for action, but at least to a degree, these balanced each other out. The United States heard pressure from Middle Eastern *Allies* such as Egypt and Iran, who were worried about growing instability in the region. But while these may have proved a negative pressure (pushing the United States toward more active involvement in the dispute than the Carter administration apparently wished to engage), it was balanced by the helpful role played by *International Organizations*. The United States sided with the OAU in this conflict and worked within its frame of the situation.

Domestic political pressures did not come into play. There was no discernible interest in the dispute evident in *Public Opinion*. And perhaps relatedly, *Legislative Opinion* on the matter was largely absent. If the United States had become involved in the conflict, its relative military strength could potentially have been an important matter. But even though the *Military-Capabilities Differential* between the parties could have been strongly in favor of the United States, it chose not to get directly involved in that way. There were no *Unusual Situational Factors* that appeared to have an

influence on decision making in this case. Therefore the number of problematic situational variables in this case is only 1, that one coming from the
influence *Allies'* views had on decision makers.

Group Structure

The structure of decision making in the Carter administration at this point
during that presidency was largely devoid of negative group-structural characteristics that may potentially impair decision making. Here the group was
Not Insulated, the group leader was generally *Not Biased*, and *Methodical Procedures* were well established by the decision-making group. Many
decision makers routinely participated in foreign-policy making in the administration, including President Carter, Vice President Mondale, National Security Advisor Zbigniew Brzezinski, UN Ambassador Andrew Young,
Secretary of Defense Harold Brown, Secretary of State Cyrus Vance, and
Assistant Secretary of State Richard Moose. The National Security Council
and the Council's special Coordinating Committee met regularly, often on
a weekly basis. This meant that the principals had forums for discussion
and planning, run in a systematic way, and decision makers weighed options and objectives in some settings where the president was present and
some where he was absent. This decision-making environment included
people from a variety of perspectives, and the goal of this administrative
structure was to keep discussions open to a variety of views that would be
discussed in a careful, deliberate manner. The decision-making group was
not *Homogeneous*. There was no *Illusion of Invulnerability* apparent in the
administration. There were no *Gatekeepers* working to quash dissent and
the exchange of ideas. The group traditionally *Valued Disagreement*. Only
Brzezinski was disagreeing with the general consensus in this case, but he
was in no way silenced. In fact, he had multiple venues and meetings in
which to air his concerns. And President Carter, who was conflicted over
the appropriate course of action in this case (Moens 1990), as a rule wanted
to hear differing views.

The *Leader Was Interested in Foreign Policy*. As has been noted, Carter
was particularly interested in foreign policy involving Africa. The group was
Knowledgeable and Experienced. Participants had decades of experience in
foreign policy, and the group involved experts on both regional and global
politics. There was also good *Teamwork* among the decision makers. While
Moens's account of the decision making in this case notes the "growing divi-

sion" (Moens 1990, 102) between Vance and Brzezinski that would eventually become much remarked upon, at this point in the team's history it still functioned appropriately and cohesively, even if Vance was upset by some of Brzezinski's remarks and even though their disputes in this case likely contributed to the growing disagreements between them. Thus the total number of negative structural characteristics in this case then is 0.

Decision Processing

This is a case in which the process of decision making was exemplary by the standards of the group decision-making literature. The participants carried out a detailed *Information Search* and heard a broad set of information on the dispute from a number of sources and perspectives. The processing of that information was not *Biased* or skewed toward particular goals or tactics. The *Survey of Objectives* was arguably unusually thorough, given that the different views of the participants led to detailed discussions of what the conflict meant, both regionally and globally. Similarly, the *Survey of Alternatives* was thorough, with probing questions being asked about the utility and feasibility of a variety of possible policy options. The limitations on the potential scope and impact of U.S. action were remarked upon explicitly, and the focus moved to the carrier group option only after other possible moves had been carefully winnowed down. Decision makers did not *Stereotype the Situation*. Indeed, they presented starkly different descriptions of it. Similarly, they did not *Stereotype the Out-Group*, apart from a brief mention of Ethiopia being where World War II began and one side of the debate seeing certain actors as Soviet stooges. But an alternate view of the actors was also very much in evidence, and a wide range of interpretations of the actors and their motives makes it clear that there were no prevailing stereotypes within the decision-making group. There were no *Pressures Toward Uniformity*, nor were there any *Unusual Process* factors. As was the case with the *Group-Structure* scale, the *Decision-Processing* scale is also coded as 0. None of the problematic processes that we expect may impair group decision making were major influences in this case.

Conclusion

The outcome of this case was coded positively by our experts. The level of international conflict was contained, and the United States saw at least limited gains in terms of its national interests, with little in the way of costs expended. In addition, it is possible that a more pro-Somali action could have led that country to delay removing its army from Ogaden, leaving U.S. military forces near a war zone that showed no sign of stabilizing in the immediate future. In other words, while the path the Carter administration took saw it accrue small gains at little cost, that path may have been further beneficial in that it kept the United States from becoming exposed in what could have become a costly conflict.

This positive outcome resulted from a decision-making process that was careful, deliberate, and allowed for detailed discussions and evaluations of competing policy prescriptions—both at the strategic and tactical levels. Alternative conceptions of the conflict, the stakes, the opportunities, and the costs were considered. Senior decision makers, both principals and top staff, were allowed to take part. Debate was encouraged. A group structure was in place to allow for carefully considered decision making to be carried out. Such analysis was evident in the decision processes observed in this case, and the situational environment did not contain elements that would push the decision unit out of its careful and deliberate routine. This resulted in the sort of favorable policy outcome that our model would expect.

The Reagan Administration and Easing Ferdinand Marcos Out of Power

This is a case in which events beyond U.S. borders and initiated by non-Americans led to a fundamental change in government in one of the most populous countries on Earth. The increasing corruption of the Marcos regime, its growing unpopularity, and the (at least perceived) increasing fortunes of communist rebels raised deep concerns among many U.S. officials. Several American decision makers came to see Marcos's behavior as endangering both his ability to fight off the growing opposition and, relatedly, the ability of the United States to maintain control of its military bases in the country. But while certain U.S. officials came to view ditching U.S. ties to Marcos as in the country's best interest, the Reagan White House dragged its heels before the president himself was eventually brought to that position as well. In this case, we see how the president went against his own personal preferences, responding to the advice of his advisors and changing events on the ground. In so doing, he helped produce a positive outcome for U.S. national interests and helped lower the level of conflict in the region.

Over its many years in office, the Marcos regime had become insular and corrupt. It left many in the country feeling that they had no opportunity to affect the actions of their government. This led to a great deal of internal opposition within the political system (to the degree that was possible given how the Marcoses corrupted and manipulated that system, and of course opposition activities were nearly impossible after Marcos started ruling under martial law in 1972) and to rebellions both by Islamic groups like the Moro National Liberation Front and the Moro Islamic Liberation Front and by the armed wing of the Communist Party, the New People's Army (NPA). The imposition of martial law stoked further opposition to the ruling elite, and as the recession of the 1980s "floored" (Brands 1992, 322) the economy of the Philippines, the stability and control of the political system came into further doubt.

Many consider the assassination of Benigno Aquino to be the tipping point that marks the final phase of the Marcos era. Aquino had long been one of Marcos's most prominent critics. He was exiled in 1980, and when he attempted to return to the Philippines in 1983, he was shot in the head as he tried to disembark from his plane. The killing of Aquino aroused immense outrage and pressure on Marcos. This pressure, from both domestic and international sources, including the U.S. government, led Marcos to name an independent panel to investigate the assassination, the Agrava Commission. And when that commission issued its findings, a year to the day after the assassination, most of its members reported that there had been a conspiracy behind the assassination, involving General Fabian Ver, the commander in chief of the Philippines' armed forces and a close friend of Marcos. In the wake of these events, opposition to the Marcos regime intensified. The Catholic Church continually criticized the government. Cardinal Sin, the head of the church in the Philippines, became one of Marcos's leading critics. And the military began to split, with opponents of General Ver organizing around General Fidel Ramos.

As the situation unfolded, some U.S. officials began to have second thoughts about their ties to the Filipino powers that be. While for the Reagan administration, "human rights in the Philippines hardly existed as an item worthy of discussion" (Brands 1992, 320–321), U.S. officials were greatly concerned with the ability to maintain control over their military bases. They were increasingly worried about the strength of the communist resistance in the country, and feared that its growth might lead to further instability both within the Philippines and in the surrounding region. And some U.S. officials were disenchanted with supporting what they saw as an anti–free market elite. For many years, the United States had viewed Marcos as an important cold-war ally, and U.S. officials were reluctant to criticize his actions for fear of weakening his hold on power. But as he continued to grasp power through means that stoked internal opposition, some U.S. officials altered their view of whether backing Marcos was in the interest of the United States. Secretary of State George Shultz wrote that as 1985 progressed, he "became increasingly convinced that Marcos was the problem, not the solution" (Shultz 1993, 613).

That view came to be held throughout the U.S. Department of State and stemmed in no small measure from U.S. Ambassador Stephen Bosworth sending a string of cables from Manila pointing out Marcos's weaknesses and the behind-the-scenes scheming by some in his court, including General Ver and Marcos's wife Imelda, to take power. This view was also gaining support among some of the U.S. military's senior brass, particularly those who were closest to the events, such as Admiral William Crowe, the head of the U.S. Pacific Command. Be they diplomats or military men (or both), many top U.S. officials were coming to see several U.S. priorities imperiled by Marcos's mismanagement, particularly as more and more cables were sent from the Pacific region to Washington about the deteriorating state of affairs. But early on the Reagan White House remained committed to backing its old friend's reign and worked to contain criticisms of Marcos.

Events on the ground, both in the Philippines and in Washington, continued to push matters forward. Congress continually pushed for harsher action against the Marcos government. It altered policy and took public stands decrying the lack of freedom in the country. For example, in 1984 Congress transferred almost half of the Reagan administration's budget request for military aid to the Philippines to economic assistance.

But the primary movement was being pushed forward by the Filipinos themselves. On November 3, 1985, Marcos announced he was calling early elections. Corazon Aquino, the widow of the slain opposition leader, announced she would run for president, and the opposition leader Salvador Laurel announced he would run on a ticket with Aquino in order to avoid splitting the opposition vote. While Marcos impeded their campaign (by keeping them off national television, for example), their movement continued to grow.

The White House was not among Aquino's fans. President Reagan continued to support his longtime friend. In addition, he was heavily affected by a conversation he, Mrs. Reagan, and White House Chief of Staff Don Regan had with *The New York Times*'s Abe Rosenthal, in which Rosenthal labeled Aquino a "dazed, vacant woman." That conversation had a "deep and lasting impact" (Shultz 1993, 617) on the Reagans and the White House staff and contributed to the fact that "the White House desired a Marcos victory" (Brands 1992, 332). In fact, Reagan was greatly upset by newspaper stories that he saw as attacks by the U.S. Department of State on President Marcos (State officials were saying that they would be happy to work with a democratically elected government). But regardless, Aquino proved popular.

When the election was held, there were reports of a great deal of electoral fraud by the government. Outside observers, including prominent members of Congress, believed the counting of the votes was unfair. Senator Richard Lugar (R-IN), the respected chairman of the Senate Foreign Relations Committee, was interviewed across major American media outlets and played a powerful role in shaping the perception that Marcos had stolen the election. That perception was the dominant understanding of the election's outcome. Nonetheless, the line from the White House was that Marcos had been reelected, and Reagan himself publicly stated that Aquino's forces may have been committing voter fraud as well (though there was no evidence of that).

But the aftermath of the election made it very difficult for the Reagan White House to continue to support Marcos. After Aquino claimed victory, General Ramos and Defense Minister Enrile resigned and holed up at Camp Aguinaldo with anti-Marcos parts of the Filipino military. Aquino went to an island to try to protect herself. In the United States, Lugar called on Marcos to step aside, and on February 19, the Senate voted 85 to 9 in favor of a resolution stating that the elections were too marred by improprieties to be considered fair. Masses of Filipinos rose up and blocked General Ver's troops from moving against the forces at Camp Aguinaldo on February 23, but it seemed likely that Ver would try again.

In this environment there was a major meeting of decision makers, mostly high-ranking people from the departments of State and Defense, at Secretary Shultz's home, on February 23. Ambassador Bosworth had informed Shultz that Marcos would only step aside if Reagan personally urged him to leave. Those present agreed that Marcos had lost the ability to rule, and whether or not they liked Aquino, losing her would mean losing the only nonleftist alternative to a man they thought had already lost control of the country. The mood that day was affected by the reigning worldview of cold-war concerns. They wanted to protect American control over key military bases and block the spread of communism.

Later that day, as tensions continued to mount in Manila, the U.S. National Security Planning Group met to discuss what to do. Chief of Staff Regan was strongly opposed to pushing Marcos out of power. But given the earlier meeting (which Regan had not attended), Shultz was able to say that all the other officials present were united in believing that Marcos was going to lose power, and if he was vainly allowed to hold on to it much longer, the consequences would be worse (Shultz 1993). With his national security advisors united, President Reagan agreed to send Marcos a message that night stating that the time had come for a transition of power.

On February 25, both Marcos and Aquino staged inaugurals, but Marcos left the Philippines for the United States. The gravity of events on the ground, combined with the surprising unanimity among his senior national security advisors (Secretaries Shultz and Weinberger regularly warred against one another), put Reagan in a position where his hand was forced. As H. W. Brands (1992, 336) put it, "the people of the Philippines presented the Reagan administration with a stunning fait accompli . . . Marcos had so disgraced himself with the Filipino people that even Reagan could no longer support him." Of course, that did not mean that Reagan had necessarily come around to supporting Aquino. He "felt aggrieved that his former friend and ally had gone down the drain" (Shultz 1993, 639) and harbored doubts about Aquino's legitimacy. But even if he was not happy about it, he helped ease Marcos out of power more quickly than might have otherwise been the case. Because of that, many lives may have been saved, and a new government came to power that was friendlier than the leftist opposition group that the Reagan administration feared most.

Experts' Ratings

Before we examine the specific variables used in our model, we should note how the expert coders rated U.S. decision making in this case. On the measure of *National Interest*, where 1 represents the lowest possible score and 5 the highest possible score, this case was rated 4.14, meaning it is considered a situation in which the decision benefited U.S. national interests. On the scale measuring the *Level of International Conflict*, where 1 is the lowest score and 5 is the highest score, this decision is rated 2.33. That is one of the lowest scores in the entire sample of decisions, and it shows that this decision is considered to have lowered the level of international conflict.

Situation

How did the environment outside the executive branch affect this process? Here the decision did not involve an imminent military threat to the United States, which may have allowed a relatively calm and measured analysis of the issues at hand. However, the topic did involve very important security assets (Anderson et al. 1985a), so it quickly attracted attention and rose high on the list of national priorities. This is key, as achieving and maintaining the focus of the pertinent decision-making team is often vital to ensuring that a coherent national policy is developed and carried through to fruition. And while excessive stress can lead to a breakdown in the personal performance of key decision makers (Thomson 1968), a heightened awareness and prioritization of an issue can lead one to think more clearly about it (Schafer and Crichlow 2002) and act to prevent it from festering.

While many of the key movements underlying the change in U.S. policy occurred prior to February 1986, the final decision to dump Marcos was made in a very tense situation, during which it was feared he was about to launch an assault on the opposition. The *Stress Level* was coded as a 4 (on a five-point scale). The prospect of Marcos taking imminent violent action might have made President Reagan agree to a harder line against him earlier than he otherwise would have. There is no firm evidence for that, however, and anti-Marcos opinions had swept so broadly across the U.S. government by that point that the time-constraint issue may have only affected the timing of the change in policy, not whether or not it would occur. While the *Threat to Strategic Interests* was real, and the decision makers did believe that they were operating under a *Short Time Constraint*, the course of events was not surprising in February 1986, so this decision did not occur during a *Crisis*, according to the established definition.

The group was also not operating in the wake of a *Recent Failure*. While the situation was often compared to that of Iran in 1980, an event that many in the Reagan administration believed had been poorly handled, that had occurred over six years earlier and under the preceding administration. The *Military-Capabilities Differential* between the countries was not important to decision making. At no time was a clash between the two countries' militaries envisaged.

What were the views and activities of the public, the legislature, allied governments, and international governmental organizations? In this case, these forces had an important role in shaping U.S. foreign policy for a number of reasons, not the least of which was the fact that all were largely united in favoring change in the Philippines. There were several *International Organizations* pressing for reform. Some, like the IMF, were actually blocking financial assistance to Marcos (Anderson et al. 1985b). The Catholic Church was, of course, one of the most important players involved in building, promoting, and protecting the anti-Marcos movement inside the Philippines, and their actions moved U.S. officials as well (Branigin and Burgess 1986). *Allies* in the region, such as Lee Kuan Yew of Singapore, felt that Marcos's fall was only a matter of time (Anderson et al. 1985a). Support for the reformists in U.S. *Public Opinion* was enormous, and, no doubt related to this, opposition to Marcos was high in Congress in the years preceding the transfer of power. This opposition was bipartisan, and the administration, which was much slower than Congress to side with the opposition in the Philippines (Wallace and Kaylor 1986), faced hostile questions before a host of panels for years before it eventually urged Marcos to leave. The lead role taken by Senator Lugar is well known, but other senators repeatedly pressed the administration to back change when they had the opportunity to do so. Resolutions supporting the opposition were passed, and legislation aimed at cutting off Marcos's remaining U.S. aid attracted broad support (White 1986). Once the election was seen as stolen, even staunch Republican senators such as Thad Cochran of Mississippi gave up on the Marcos cause. Cochran famously wore his yellow golf pants—yellow being the color of the Aquino campaign—to a postelection press conference to make that point clear (Bonner 1987). *Legislative Opinion* was, thus, highly favorable to the cause being spearheaded by many in the administration, easing Marcos out of power. Marcos understood the role Congress played in the U.S. decision-making structure, and Congress was reliably providing "the 'sticks' that strengthened the credibility of the administration's reformist stance" (Weissman 1995, 152).

This activation and confluence of elite opinion likely had a positive effect on U.S. decision making in this case. The growing unanimity of opinion likely made it easier for policymakers in the executive branch to resolve any competing beliefs they had over their views on this issue. And, as the preferences of these actors were in tune with the views held by much of the policymaking apparatus, they did not serve as the basis for challenging the emerging U.S. policy. Instead, they helped set it by reconciling wavering officials to the cause and helped enforce it through their united views and high level of activity on this matter.

The total number of problematic *Situation* variables for this case is only 2. While there was a high stress level and a short time constraint, the rest of the situational environment did not contain factors often associated with impairing the quality of decision making.

Group Structure

President Reagan's first term was marred by a level of intra-administration infighting that was remarkable even by the standards of Washington, D.C. Continual turnover at the NSC, Secretary Haig pursuing his own foreign policy, and a lengthy series of fights (which often festered) between the departments of State and Defense (often backed by DCI William Casey and the CIA) produced several policies that were poorly planned or not thought through—policies that, unsurprisingly, ended in failure and unachieved aims.

The second Reagan term saw these fights dissipate and a more coherent and orderly policy process take hold. Both the departments of State and Defense had successfully defended their access to the decision-making group. The roles of group members had been more clearly delineated. A rough pecking order had been established, and the group was working more like a team than it had been in the early 1980s. It was in this latter environment, one more conducive to vigilant decision making, that the Philippines crisis occurred.

Decision makers in this case were not *Insulating* themselves from a variety of voices. They took in information from a wide variety of sources, including diplomats in the field, military advisors, members of the media, and private citizens with knowledge of the region, such as Robert Trent Jones Jr. (Bonner 1987, 395–398). They did not rely on their own counsel. This was the case even though the president and his White House advisors were clearly biased about what path to take. Secretary Shultz's memoirs are filled with warnings from National Security Advisor Poindexter not to go too far in advocating change, and White House Chief of Staff Donald Regan never came around to the idea of dropping support for Marcos, much less supporting Corazon Aquino in his place. In fact, according to Shultz (1993, 639), he was "wildly upset" at the decision to support her. And these moves, while perhaps reflecting their own personal feelings, clearly reflected those of the president, who repeatedly stressed his desire to support Marcos. Reagan was reluctant to view the results of the stolen election as illegitimate (Shultz 1993, 641). Reagan hoped that Marcos "would change, not leave" (Shultz 1993, 618). Nonetheless, even in the face of this *Biased Leadership, Methodical Procedures* were still followed. People were allowed to do their assigned jobs without being removed, even if they disagreed with the president's assumptions, and meetings were largely conducted in an orderly and informed manner that was aimed toward building a coherent policy for the country.

The decision-making group was not excessively *Homogeneous*. People from a variety of backgrounds and viewpoints were heard. The group did not believe it could control events. It did not operate under an *Illusion of Invulnerability*. In the wake of the fall of the shah and what many saw as failed attempts to force Marcos to alter his policies, few overestimated their power over the situation, particularly as street protests and a mass movement opposed to Marcos gained strength inside the Philippines. And they saw themselves at some risk of losing control over what many of them valued most of all—an anticommunist ally and their military bases.

Evaluating whether or not there were *Gatekeepers* involved in this process is somewhat tricky. There were certainly voices who sought to temper some specific comments. Poindexter's warnings to Shultz come to mind, as does Shultz's meeting with Morton Abramowitz (the head of the intelligence shop within the State Department). Shultz was afraid that Abramowitz had lost his objectivity and that his negative views of the Marcos regime might have tainted his analysis (Shultz 1993). Nevertheless, we do not think these actions fully match the definition of gatekeeping. Neither Poindexter nor Shultz blocked specific information from reaching the president or other decision makers. They both were interested in keeping the process running and ensuring that it featured information that decision makers could use. Reagan still got negative information on the Marcos regime, and Abramowitz kept writing his analyses. Relatedly, at this point in the administration, the Reagan team clearly *Valued Disagreement*. The president heard a great deal that he would rather not have heard, and he did not cut off this negative information, nor did he fire or ignore those who had different views on this topic than he did. This hearing of dissenting viewpoints and respect for those who shared them fostered a level of *Teamwork* at this point in the administration that had not been prevalent at the start of Reagan's term in office.

Finally, in this case the relatively uninformed president was not driving foreign policy. While there were foreign-policy issues that interested him, he was not broadly or personally *Interested in Foreign Policy*. Secretary Shultz noted his disinterest in many reports and briefing papers on the Philippines (Shultz 1993, 614). Policy was being formulated at lower levels by government officials who had a much deeper understanding of the Philippine situation—both in terms of its past and its present. That an *Experienced and Knowledgeable* team of individuals who had an appreciation for the region's history and complexities were driving policy change likely had a positive impact on the resulting policies.

Overall, the structural variables show a governmental system designed and often working as policy analysts would hope. Methodical procedures were in place, officials were allowed to do their jobs without excessive political intervention, the bureaucracies were getting along reasonably well (perhaps partially because both military leaders and diplomats were broadly in agreement on what was at risk and what was creating the risk), informed people were making decisions and did not have an inflated sense of their power over the situation at hand, and pressure points that could subvert careful and vigilant processes were not a common feature of the system. The president's clearly stated desires could have had a heavy, negative impact on vigilant decision making, but his allowance for dissent, the fact that the dissenters were still (at least to a degree) trusted team members, and the increased level of teamwork that existed late in the Reagan years limited the effect of his biases. The number of negative structural factors seen in this case then was only 2—a leader who was biased yet disinterested in foreign policy in general.

Decision Processing

In this case, there were group structures and norms that facilitated careful, systematic analysis, and these led to a decision-making process in which almost all the traditional "symptoms of groupthink" were avoided. The decision-making group heard from a variety of voices and conducted a wide-ranging *Information Search*. They did not let their longstanding ideological affinities with the Marcos regime *Bias* how they interpreted information on the situation. They were careful to develop a clear understanding of their ultimate *Objectives*, and over the months preceding the change of power they weighed a variety of policy *Alternatives* that might take them there. Dissenters were not blocked or expelled during the decision-making process. While the participants in the decision-making process were made well aware of the views of the White House, there were no undue *Pressures for Uniformity*. And for the most part there was no *Stereotyping of the Out-Group*. While some in the White House quite clearly did stereotype Aquino and her allies in the opposition, most U.S. decision makers were not dead set against her. In fact, some viewed her quite favorably.

The only "symptom" that was present was, perhaps predictably, *Stereotyping the Situation*. For decades, U.S. governments had faced a difficult decision. Should they back oppressive anticommunist regimes or should they risk communists coming to power? Given the priority that the fight against communism had across U.S. governments, and certainly in the Reagan administration, the United States often opted for dictatorships over instability. This was a familiar framework, and most international events were seen and judged, in large part, by how they were perceived to relate to the relative power of the United States in the fight against communism. It is therefore no great surprise that many decision makers continually compared this situation to others that involved whether or not to prop up a fading cold-war ally, regardless of distinct dissimilarities between the cases. In particular, there were frequent comparisons between the Philippines situation and the fall of the shah of Iran. As this was the only process variable coded negatively, the total *Decision-Processing* score for this case is 1.

Conclusion

The outcome of this case was coded positively by our panel of experts. A bloody showdown in Manila may very well have been averted. The communist threat was not strengthened. The United States maintained its military bases. U.S. goals were met, and the costs appear to have been minimal.

This positive outcome was achieved in a decision-making environment that fits with our expectations about what sort of setting should produce more favorable outcomes. The scores on the structural and process scales were low, indicating that and these factors were designed and working in a way that should have ameliorated negative norms and processes that might otherwise impair decision making. This success was a result of high-quality decision processes, as one would expect given our model.

The Clinton Administration and South Asia: Nuclear Capabilities and Another War Over Kashmir

Background

On May 11 and 13, 1998, India successfully tested nuclear devices. Her frequent enemy, Pakistan, followed with its own tests two weeks later, on May 28 and 30. Matters escalated significantly during the winter of 1999, when Pakistani militants, backed by the Pakistani army, crossed the Line of Control in Kashmir, leading to the Kargil conflict in the spring of that year. The world held its collective breath as these two countries in South Asia, long one of the world's most dangerous regions, became nuclear armed and approached what could be their fourth major war since 1948.

There were several phases of decision making for the Clinton administration in this case. The first was the attempt to stop Pakistan from conducting retaliatory tests. Though this was unsuccessful, it was followed quickly by the development of a number of punitive sanctions against both countries designed to inflict major costs on each and move them in the direction of de-escalation. There was indeed progress along these lines throughout 1998 and early 1999, marked most notably during the Lahore Summit, initiated by Pakistan's Prime Minister Nawaz Sharif as an attempt to normalize relations with India. However, during this same time, Pakistan's military was secretly planning the intrusion across the Line of Control and began implementing it soon after the summit. India detected the incursion in early May, and the Kargil conflict began.

The United States and the Clinton administration were uniquely placed at the time to play an important role in South Asia. The United States was solidly established as the preeminent global power and leader. This was a decade after the end of the cold war and seven years since the U.S.-led collective-security action successfully removed Iraqi forces from Kuwait. In addition, the United States had a longstanding strategic relationship with Pakistan, due mostly to cold-war politics but continuing on through this time period. The U.S. relationship with India during the cold war was different, with India sometimes tilting to the Soviet Union and sometimes playing a major independent role through the Non-Aligned Movement. However, relations between the United States and India had improved since the end of the cold war. U.S. foreign policy was emphasizing spreading democracy, and India is the world's largest democracy and an important emerging market.

Shock and Concern in May 1998

On Monday, May 11, 1998, the Clinton administration was already very busy handling several major international issues: the peace process in Northern Ireland; events in Kosovo; Middle East negotiations; the Taliban and al Qaeda in Afghanistan; the upcoming G-8 meeting in the United Kingdom, which included Russia for the first time; and a special private meeting between Clinton and President Yeltsin. But, as Strobe Talbott noted, none of these "quite qualified as a crisis" (2006, 1). A crisis, however, is exactly what developed for the administration that day, as information about India's nuclear tests surfaced.

The administration was caught completely off guard regarding the Indian tests (Bidwai and Vanaik 2000, 46; Harris 2005, 409; Hyland 1999, 192). The State Department, CIA, National Security Advisor Sandy Berger, and Secretary of State Madeleine Albright all first learned of the tests, much to their chagrin, from CNN (Talbott 2006, 2–3). Indeed, the administration has been criticized for being caught by surprise (Hyland 1999, 192) and for the "downgrading of the monitoring level" of India's nuclear ambitions prior to the tests (Bidwai and Vanaik 2000, 47). Nonetheless, once the tests came to light, the administration acted quickly and directly to implement punitive measures toward India and to try to keep Pakistan from testing also.

The administration felt deceived, perhaps even betrayed, by India's nuclear tests. In February 1998, a Hindu-nationalist Indian party, the Bharatiiya Janata Party (BJP), came to power, and their platform called for moving India's nuclear program forward, so the Clinton administration had reason to be concerned. Nonetheless, the BJP had taken active steps to reassure the United States and others that it had no intention of making any radical changes in policy, specifically telling Bill Richardson, the special envoy sent by Clinton to India after the BJP's election, that the government would "maintain a high degree of continuity with the core policies of its predecessor regimes" (Bidwai and Vanaik 2000, 46). Prime Minister Atal Bihari Vajpayee said publicly in April 1998 that India would undertake an escalation of its nuclear program only "if it was considered absolutely necessary" (Bidwai and Vanaik 2000, 45).

Perhaps because of this active deception on the part of the BJP, when Clinton learned of the tests he became very angry and reportedly said, "We're going to come down on those guys like a ton of bricks" (Talbott 2004, 52). And, indeed, in short order the United States took a number of punitive policies toward India, including ending defense sales and other military support, denying government credit and loan guarantees, opposing loans and other assistance from the World Bank and the IMF, prohibiting U.S. banks from granting credit, and terminating most U.S. assistance programs (Talbott 2004, 53). The administration also contacted major international organizations, including the United Nations, NATO, the Organization of American States, the Gulf Cooperation Council, and the G-8, to urge each of them to condemn India's actions.

Regarding Pakistan, Clinton personally called Sharif, urging restraint by Pakistan and offering "huge amounts" of aid, warplanes, and even a visit to Washington. In addition, Clinton sent Deputy Secretary of State Strobe Talbott to meet with the Pakistanis (Bidwai and Vanaik 2000, 53; Clinton 2005, 786; Harris 2005, 409; Hyland 1999, 193; Talbott 2004, 57). Of course, there was tremendous domestic political pressure on Sharif for Pakistan to counter with its own tests, with some of the most powerful pressure no doubt coming from the military, headed by Pervez Musharraf. Clinton himself states that Sharif "couldn't resist the political pressure" (Clinton 2005, 786). But Bidwai and Vanaik (2000, 53) point out that the offers made by the Clinton administration tempted Sharif as much as possible. It was also clear to Sharif that the international political and economic costs of testing would be devastating. Despite the tremendous domestic pressure on Sharif to conduct the tests, he did not rush into them and "carefully weighed his options" (Bidwai and Vanaik 2000, 53).

This valiant set of actions by the United States might well have kept Sharif from testing, but India, ironically, had other things in mind. Bidwai and Vanaik (2000) argue that India coaxed and bullied Pakistan into testing, which gave India the post hoc excuse that its own tests were therefore justified (2000, 52). Certainly in the ensuing two weeks following India's tests, rather than deescalating with Pakistan, India did exactly the opposite, boasting of its new capabilities, "chiding Pakistan," and even threatening to take the part of Kashmir from Pakistan that had long been settled by the Shimla Agreement in 1972 (Bidwai and Vanaik 2000, 54).

Once Pakistan did test, the United States and others imposed harsh sanctions on Pakistan as well, and there was near unanimity in the international community reprimanding both countries, calling on them to deescalate and urging them to sign the Nuclear Non-Proliferation Treaty (NPT) and the Comprehensive Test Ban Treaty (CTBT). The sanctions had a major and immediate effect on both countries, causing their currencies to decline significantly, foreign investment to disappear, and diminishing foreign credit and aid, which led to effects ranging from sharply raising the cost of infrastructure projects to far-reaching social and humanitarian problems (Bidwai and Vanaik 2000, 55–56).

Prior to the events of May 1998, Deputy Secretary of State Talbott had established a team of advisors and area experts to deal with South Asia. By the summer of that year, the team was meeting regularly, often daily, and would continue to do so for the next two years (Talbott 2004, 92). The team consisted of representatives from the State Department; National Security Council; Treasury Department; others from the departments of Defense, Justice, Commerce, and Energy; and members of the intelligence community. Talbott describes these meetings as "extraordinarily collegial," allowing for all parties to "talk through the disparate and often competing goals" associated with the volatile region and keeping "to a minimum the personal backbiting, bureaucratic warfare, and mischievous leaks that too often accompany policymaking" (Talbott 2004, 92).

By summer 1998, India had sent feelers to Washington to see if improvements in relations could begin. The Indian ambassador to the United States, Naresh Chandra, working through indirect channels, requested the opportunity for India to send Minister of External Affairs Jaswant Singh as a special envoy to Washington. And they signaled that India might be willing to sign the CTBT (Talbott 2004, 76–77). The United States kept pressure on India through the summer, including harsh, direct words by Secretary Albright to Singh when they met in conjunction with meetings of ASEAN countries in Manila in July (Talbott 2004, 114–115). But there were also a series of meetings between Singh and Talbott that helped improve relations between the two countries, and there was even talk of a possible visit by Clinton to India (Talbott 2004, 115). However, stunning events in Africa and Washington in August 1998 suddenly took center stage.

On August 7, U.S. embassies in Tanzania and Kenya were simultaneously bombed, killing hundreds of people. On August 17, President Clinton admitted to having a relationship with Monica Lewinsky. And, three days later, in retaliation for the bombings in Tanzania and Kenya, the U.S. attacked al Qaeda training camps in Afghanistan with sixty cruise missiles. Besides turning attention away from de-escalation discussions in South Asia, the latter action specifically had implications for U.S.-Pakistani relations, because the cruise missiles had to pass over Pakistani territory without Pakistani permission, given the close ties between their intelligence services and the Taliban in Afghanistan. General Joe Ralston, vice chairman of the joint chiefs of staff, arranged to be with the Pakistani Army chief, General Jehangir Karamat, in Islamabad at the time of the flyover, to assure him that the missiles were not an attack by anyone on Pakistan. Afterward, according to Talbott (2004, 116), "Karamat felt humiliated and betrayed." In addition, several Pakistani intelligence officers in the al Qaeda camps at the time were killed in the attack, and one of the cruise missiles went down in Pakistani territory.

The Kargil Conflict

It is unclear why Pakistan initiated the Lahore Summit, which was intended to reduce hostilities and move in the direction of normalizing relations with India, while simultaneously preparing for the military crossing of the Line of Control at Kargil. Talbott (2004, 59) speculates that even in mid-May 1998, the military in Pakistan was calling more shots than the civilian government. Certainly Musharraf was a prominent force in the country at the time, perhaps even more powerful than Sharif. The Lahore Summit may have been primarily Sharif's initiative, but the Kargil action had Musharraf's and the military's fingerprints all over it (Harris 2005, 410). But it is difficult to imagine that Musharraf was able to initiate the Kargil action without at least some type of acquiescence by Sharif. Regardless, once India discovered the Pakistani presence in Kargil, there was little doubt that a counteroffensive would be forthcoming.

The preceding war between India and Pakistan happened twenty-eight years earlier, in 1971. The destruction wrought by that war was astronomical, with millions of fatalities and refugees, the division of Pakistan into two countries (Pakistan and Bangladesh), and significantly heightened tensions between the United States and the Soviet Union. While the cold war between the United States and the Soviets was long over by 1999, many of the other points of conflict between India and Pakistan remained well in place when Pakistan took the Kargil action, and this time both sides had demonstrated nuclear capabilities.

Pakistan immediately lost the public-relations battle, as they were seen universally as the aggressor. President Clinton was direct and clear with Sharif about this and promised to hold up a $100 million IMF loan, which the country needed desperately, if Pakistan did not withdraw. Sharif travelled to China, another long-term Pakistani friend—and rival of India—hoping for support, but found none (Talbott 2004, 159). Pakistan was politically isolated, and India was massing troops. Fighting went on between the two sides, with Pakistan holding the better strategic positions on some of the ridgelines and heights in Kargil, but India was in the process of mobilizing nearly 750,000 troops. Sharif knew Pakistan was in trouble and began desperately seeking assistance from Clinton and the United States.

After both sides had tested their nuclear devices the previous year, Clinton pushed his administration hard in pursuing alternative policy options for the region. Talbott (2004, 78–79) reports Clinton saying, "we can't give up trying. I'd like to find a way in on this one. . . . I want us to be bold and in the lead on this one." Even though the United States had historically been closer to Pakistan, and even though India initiated the nuclear component of the crisis, the Clinton administration thought that improved relations with India were crucial to any solution. A major component of the administration's diplomatic efforts, therefore, was to significantly engage and reassure India. Nowhere did this matter more than when Pakistan became desperate over the Kargil war. India knew Pakistan was desperate and was certain that Pakistan would cajole the United States into becoming involved on their side or into making intolerable demands on India, such as reopening discussions on Kashmir before Pakistan withdrew. As a result, throughout the Kargil conflict the administration maintained very close and open contacts with its counterparts in India, even at times communicating with the Indians about specific contacts and requests made by the Pakistanis. India correctly and appreciatively understood these communications as confidence-building measures by the United States. As Talbott notes, "this time the United States was tilting in India's direction rather than Pakistan's" (Talbott 2004, 158), and India felt reassured.

By late June, Sharif was desperate to try to get help from the United States (Harris 2005, 410). On July 2, he personally called Clinton to ask for U.S. intervention. Clinton was clear that while he was happy to try to play the role of peacemaker in the conflict, the first move needed to be made by Pakistan in the form of withdrawal (Harris 2005, 410; Talbott 2004, 160). The following day Sharif called Clinton again, this time requesting an opportunity to come to Washington to meet directly with Clinton. Clinton again said that the first move would have to be made by Pakistan in the form of withdrawing their troops. Before Pakistan took that action, it would be awkward at best to invite Pakistan, the perceived aggressor, to Washington. Without committing to withdrawal and without an official state invitation, Sharif announced that he was coming to Washington anyway (Harris 2005, 410; Talbott 2004, 160).

During the administration's preparation for Sharif's visit, Sandy Berger said that the meeting might be the most important one of the Clinton presidency (Harris 2005, 411). Long preparations were held in Berger's office. Talbott describes that among those in the meetings, "There was . . . a sense of vast and nearly unprecedented peril" (Talbott 2004, 161). Sharif was desperate. He brought his wife and children with him on the trip, raising issues about the safety of his family back in Pakistan and leading the administration to wonder if perhaps he was planning to seek political asylum (Talbott 2004, 161). And Pakistan as a country was desperate. U.S. intelligence services reported to the administration the night before Sharif arrived that they had indications that Pakistan was preparing its nuclear arsenal for possible use (Harris 2005, 411; Talbott 2004, 161).

Advisors told Clinton that a delicate balance had to be maintained. The United States needed to be clear and forceful with Sharif, mandating that Pakistan withdraw from their positions on the wrong side of the Line of Control before anything else could happen. And yet, the United States also had an interest in making sure that Sharif was able to return to Pakistan and survive politically, at least long enough to end the crisis. The administration had excellent information on who would be in Sharif's entourage, their ties to the Pakistani intelligence services, and their likely gamesmanship tactics while meeting with the president (Harris 2005; Talbott 2004). Clinton was well prepared for the meeting and was effective and forceful with Sharif.

The administration had prepared two possible statements that could be released to the press after the meeting between Clinton and Sharif. The first he showed to Sharif after becoming frustrated with the intransigence of the Pakistani leader. The statement was devastating. It blamed Pakistan entirely for the crisis, clearly not the kind of outcome that Sharif had hoped for or could tolerate as a result of his trip to Washington. After a break, Clinton showed the second possible statement to Sharif that praised him as a peacemaker for withdrawing, called for a ceasefire if the Pakistanis withdrew to their side of the Line of Control, and recommitted Clinton to a visit to

South Asia. After some hesitation, Sharif accepted the second statement with one addition, a promise by Clinton to encourage the resumption of the Lahore process after the original Line of Control had been fully restored, a commitment that was easy for Clinton to agree to because of his interest in the region and because the promise mandated that Pakistan withdraw as a prerequisite (Talbott 2004, 161–168). The Kargil conflict had come to a peaceful end.

Experts' Ratings

The foreign-policy experts in our study rated the outcome of this case as 4.0 on our five-point scale measuring *National Interest*. This is nearly a full standard deviation above the mean score of the cases in our sample, meaning that the experts thought the outcome of this case advanced U.S. national interests. The United States certainly had interests in seeing a non-nuclear, peaceful resolution to the events in South Asia between 1998 and 1999, but the experts also probably saw the value in the United States developing more positive relations with India as a developing global power and a stable democracy.

The experts rated the outcome of the case in terms of the *Level of International Conflict* as 2.60, which is more than a standard deviation below the sample mean on this variable. The experts saw U.S. action in this case as contributing to a reduction in the level of conflict. Though the history of the region since World War II is one laden with major conflicts involving huge numbers of casualties, this time the conflict ended with relatively few casualties, no nuclear explosions, and a general de-escalation of hostilities by each side.

Situation

This is a case where several *Situation* variables played a potentially problematic role in the decision-making process. The *Stress Level* was very high, perhaps the highest of any international situation faced by the Clinton administration. The situation was clearly a *Crisis*. There were great *Time Constraints* on the administration during this case, both in trying to keep Pakistan from testing nuclear devices and in trying to prevent further escalation in the Kargil conflict. *Legislative Opinion* was problematic for the administration on one important point: Jesse Helms and other Senate

Republicans used the South Asian nuclear tests to argue that the CTBT was a failure and that the United States ought not ratify it. This hurt the administration's leadership and credibility in asking for India and Pakistan to ratify the treaty as part of the conflict-resolution process (Clinton 2005, 186; Talbott 2004, 56). There was also a very high level of *Situational Distractions* faced by the administration during this case. The G-8 meeting was scheduled to take place shortly after India tested in May 1998; the Northern Ireland peace process was at a critical stage; the conflict in Kosovo was heating up; negotiations were taking place in the Middle East; that summer al Qaeda bombed the U.S. embassies in Tanzania and Kenya, and the United States launched cruise missiles into Afghanistan in retaliation; and, during that same time period, President Clinton admitted his involvement with Monica Lewinsky.

Some of the other situation variables, however, were not problematic for the administration. They had not had a significant *Recent Failure. Allies* and *International Organizations* were ready partners with the United States throughout the case, including such disparate international actors as the G-8, United Nations, NATO, ASEAN, NAM, and others. Even though the crisis was a dangerous one, the *Level of Interests* at stake for the United States was only *Strategic*, not vital, as there were no threats to the blood or treasure of the United States directly. In addition, the United States had a *Favorable Military Differential* over both India and Pakistan. Finally, while the U.S. public was no doubt aware of the crisis in South Asia and as concerned as many others throughout the world, *Public Opinion* was not problematic for the administration's decision making. Thus, we coded a total of 5 problematic situational factors in this case: *Stress, Crisis, Short Time Constraint, Legislative Opinion*, and *Situational Distractions*, which is well above the average number for our cases.

Group Structure

At this point in the Clinton administration, the foreign policy–making structures were sound and well established. The group was not *Insulated*. Top advisors relied extensively on area experts for information and input, and the administration had regular, effective, and extensive contacts with others throughout the international system. A clear pattern of *Methodical Procedures* was in place. The National Security Council, headed by Sandy Berger, functioned well, particularly in the area of South Asia. In addition, the State Department was particularly active in this case, most notably in the regularly meeting team on South Asia headed by Strobe Talbott. The group was not *Homogenous* and included such diverse individuals as Madeleine Albright, Sandy Berger, William Cohen, Strobe Talbott, Bruce Reidel, Don Camp, Gary Samore, and Karen Mathiasen. There was no *Illusion of Invulnerability* in the administration. There were no signs of any *Gatekeepers*, quite the contrary—the administration sought maximum information throughout and involved many disparate advisors and bureaucrats. The group *Valued Disagreement*. Though when Clinton was first elected president, his primary focus was on domestic and economic matters,[2] by 1998 Clinton had personally become quite active and broadly *Interested in Foreign Policy*. The decision-making team was clearly *Knowledgeable and Experienced*, and there was extensive and effective *Teamwork* throughout the administration (see Talbott 2004, 92, for an excellent description of teamwork in the administration's foreign-policy making). There were no *Unusual Structural Factors* in the decision-making apparatus at this time.

Of the 11 possible *Group-Structure* variables, 10 of them indicate good structures in the Clinton administration for this case. The only problematic structural variable we coded was *Biased Leader*. Clinton was known for his directness and hot temper at times behind closed doors. His advisors often knew early in a situation where he stood, and in this case, that's exactly what happened with his "ton of bricks" comment the day after India first tested.

Decision Processing

As with *Group Structures*, we found that the Clinton administration's *Decision Processing* in this case was very good, with only 1 coded fault. We coded this case as having a *Poor Information Search*. This fault really applies only to the early part of the case, when the administration was blindsided by the Indian nuclear tests. The administration was broadly criticized for this (Bidwai and Vanaik 2000, 47; Hyland 1999, 192), and they readily acknowledged their shortcomings in this regard (Harris 2005; Talbott 2004). Later in the crisis, the information search by the administration was very good, involving extensive international contacts, heavy involvement of area experts in the process, and excellent intelligence activities.

There were no signs of *Biased Information Processing* in the case. Indeed, Clinton pushed his advisors for new and creative approaches for resolving the conflict. There was a thorough *Survey of Objectives* and *Survey of Alternatives*. The decision-making group did not *Stereotype* either the *Situation* or the *Out-Group*. There were no *Pressures Toward Uniformity*, and no *Unusual Process Factors* emerged in this case. In all, then, only one *Decision-Processing Fault* is noted in this case.

Conclusion

From the start, this case had the potential for disaster. India and Pakistan had been through three earlier major wars, and their enmity continued to run very deep in the late 1990s. Though the possibility of the two countries having nuclear weapons was hardly a secret, after the two tested them in 1998, the escalation of tensions was tremendous. While one part of Pakistan's leadership initiated de-escalation with the Lahore Summit, apparently another part of their leadership was emboldened by the nuclear tests and perceived that it might change India's calculus regarding the Line of Control. And this adventurism by Pakistan in early 1999 raised tensions to new levels, as the now clearly nuclear-capable enemies faced off once again.

As noted earlier, the United States was uniquely positioned to play an important role in this South Asian conflict. But there were very dangerous waters that the administration had to navigate. This was a case where the situational environment could have played a very damaging role. It is easy to imagine that the level of situational hazards could have caused great distractions and wrong turns by the administration. Yet the administration moved in highly nuanced, effective directions, ultimately playing a crucial and central role in ending the conflict. Though the situational hazards were real and significant, they were managed by an administration that was effectively structured and conducted good decision processes.

These good decision-making structures and processes served the administration well as they undertook careful but deliberate confidence-building measures with India and put cautious yet appropriate pressure on Pakistan. Jaswant Singh telephoned Strobe Talbott the evening of Sharif's acquiescence and said the following: "Something terrible has happened these past several months between us and our neighbors. But something quite new and good has happened this weekend between our own countries, yours and mine—something related to the matter of trust. My prime minister and I thank your president for that" (Talbott 2004, 169).

PART III

Statistical Analyses

Six

THE EFFECT OF GROUPTHINK VERSUS HIGH-QUALITY DECISION MAKING ON OUTCOMES

Overview

In the previous two chapters, we have discussed a set of cases that demonstrate general support for our hypothesis: in those cases where poor structures and decision-making processes were used, the outcomes were quite poor; where better structures and processes were in place, the outcomes tended to be much more positive. Case studies are helpful for getting inside the decision process and seeing better and worse decision making at work in real episodes. Each case is a unique story, and it is important to look carefully inside the process of each. However, there are limitations to relying only on individual case studies to investigate our hypothesis. Our main interest is to better understand general *patterns* in decision making rather than the particulars of any one case. Put somewhat differently, an in-depth case study can tell us much about a particular case but relatively little about general patterns across a broad set of historical cases or about expected patterns in future cases.

Let us make this argument even more strongly and while doing so point out an important limitation of our own work thus far in the book. The cases we presented in the two previous chapters were not "randomly" chosen. We selected cases based upon two general criteria: (1) they were important historical cases that included typical components of foreign-policy decisions, such as security challenges or ally relationships and (2) they exemplified the general pattern of the relationship between process and outcome that we have found in our research. In social-science terminology, that makes these cases a "purposive sample": they were chosen for specific purposes rather than randomly. This also means that we cannot assume they are representative of a larger sample of cases, and we are limited in drawing generalizable conclusions from them. This does not mean that they are not instructive. On the contrary, as noted above, getting inside a case is always instructive, especially a case that helps exemplify certain dimensions of decision making. But if we want to know whether the patterns in these cases are generalizable to a larger universe of cases, then we need a different type of analysis.

Statistical analysis allows us to look for such patterns. By comparing the same kind of information—translated into data—across many cases, we can assess the probability that one or more variables affect the process or outcome of a case. So far our case studies have suggested that the quality of decision making is related to the quality of the outcome. Here we more systematically analyze that proposition (and others) by using data and statistics involving a much larger number of cases. Another result of statistical analysis can be the discovery of patterns that are not seen in an analysis of a handful of cases. This can increase the confidence in our findings.

In order to conduct statistical analysis, we need data. And in the present project, this means converting the information we gathered from all of our case studies into numerical representations. Readers have already seen some of these data presented in individual case studies in the previous chapters, and chapter 3 presented the complete set of variables in our model and provided a description of how we converted the case-study materials to numerical representations. Here we provide a brief recapitulation of that description.

The outcome (dependent) variables were ascertained using expert-coding methods. We surveyed a panel of foreign-policy experts and asked them to rate the outcome of each case in terms of whether the decision helped or hindered national interests and whether it increased or decreased the level of international conflict; each outcome variable ranged from one to five. Using their responses, we computed average scores for each of these variables for every case in our study. For the variable *National Interests*, case scores ranged from 1.71 to 4.57, with higher scores representing advances in national interests. The mean of this variable across all our cases is 3.09, with a standard deviation of .92.[1] *Level of International Conflict* ranged from 2.17 to 4.71, with higher scores indicating higher levels of conflict. The mean for the conflict variable is 3.48, with a standard deviation of .68.

The explanatory (independent) variables were derived from case-study methods conducted by the principal investigators in the project (the authors of this book). We gathered secondary-source materials for each case: memoirs, biographies, journalistic investigations, and historical accounts. As we read through the case-study materials, we coded all of the process variables in three categories: *Situation/Context*, *Group Structures*, and *Decision Processing*. These methods resulted in an analysis for each case very much like the case studies presented in chapters 4 and 5, although we did not produce full narrative treatments of each case. As noted in chapter 3, each variable in the three process categories has specific coding values. For example, in the category of decision processing, our first variable is *Poor Information Search*. Based on the coding criteria specified in advance (and presented in chapter 3 of this book), we assessed whether or not the administration failed to search for readily available information. If this was the case, we coded the variable 1, meaning that their search for information was poor. If, however, the administration conducted a thorough search for information, we coded the variable 0, meaning the information search was good. Based on the operational definitions for the variables in our three categories discussed in chapter 3, we were able to assign a numerical representation to each variable in this way.

These data allow us to run statistical models that investigate the causal effect of the independent variables on the dependent variables. The statistical model we use here is called ordinary least squares (OLS) regression. The general idea with OLS is that it finds the best-fitting linear relationship between two variables. Imagine a graph with the independent variable on the horizontal axis and the dependent variable on the vertical axis. Any case may be plotted on the graph by first moving along the horizontal axis to the value for the independent variable and then up the vertical axis to the value for the independent variable. Conceptually speaking, OLS regression does this task for every case in the dataset and then looks for a pattern among the plotted cases in the form of the best-fitting line. The linear relationship may be *positive*, meaning that an increase in the level of the independent variable leads on average to an increase in the level of the dependent variable, or *negative*, meaning that an increase in the level of the independent variable leads on average to a decrease in the level of the dependent variable.[2]

The direction of the relationship is indicated by the B coefficient in the tables in this chapter: a positive value on the coefficient indicates a positive relationship, while a negative value indicates a negative relationship. It is also possible that the relationship between the variables is *not significant*, meaning generally that the data are so dispersed that we cannot be confident there is any linear relationship. This is indicated by the p (for probability) value in the tables. Smaller p values indicate a higher probability that there is a relationship as indicated by the B coefficient. In this study, the p value generally used to indicate if a relationship is significant is $p \leq .05$.

In the tables in this chapter, we also include two additional statistics. The first is the Beta, which is the standardized version of the B coefficient. The sign (positive or negative) of the Beta will always be the same as the sign of the B coefficient, and the sign has the same meaning in terms of the direction of the relationship between the independent and dependent variable. However, because the Beta is standardized, the relative effect of different independent variables may be compared even if the units of the independent variable are significantly different. In other words, the Beta statistic is helpful in looking comparatively at the effect of different independent variables; if the value of the Beta for one variable is higher than for another, it means the effect of the first is greater on the dependent variable than the effect of the second. The other statistic in our tables is the R-squared (R^2). This is the proportion of variance in the dependent variable that is explained by the independent variable(s) in the model. This means that if we enter the values for the independent variable(s), the R^2 statistic tells us what proportion of values for the dependent variable would be correctly predicted. Higher values on this statistic tell us that our independent variables do a good job of explaining outcomes.

As discussed above, statistics allow us to look for patterns in the data and test hypotheses. Our general hypothesis is that components of the decision-making process will affect the quality of outcome in a decision episode. This general hypothesis can be applied to each of our three categories of independent variables: we expect that situation variables, structural variables, and decision-processing variables will each have an effect on outcomes. In chapter 3, we provided a figure that modeled these possible relationships; here we present a slightly different version of that figure that deals just with the variables covered in this chapter.[3]

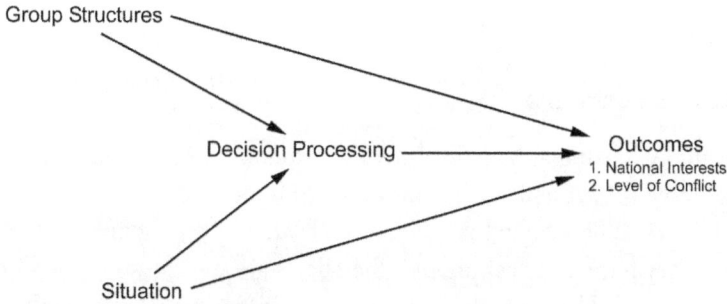

FIGURE 6.1   A model of foreign-policy decision making

Think of each of the arrows in this figure as a directional hypothesis. We hypothesize that each of the three sets of independent variables will have a causal effect on *Outcomes*: a more positive *Situational* context and better *Group Structures* and *Decision Processing* should have positive effects on *Outcomes* in terms of *National Interests* and a reduction in the *Level of International Conflict*. In addition, we expect the quality of *Group Structures* and the nature of the *Situation* to have an effect on the quality of *Decision Processing*: better *Group Structures* should lead to more effective *Decision Processing*, while a more adverse *Situational* context should lead to more problematic *Decision Processing*.

In our analyses below, we first look at the effect of each individual variable within the three sets to consider independent effects on the dependent variables in the model. This allows us to analyze the effect of each specific variable separately. However, we are also interested in the aggregate effect of the individual variables within each set. While some individual variables within a set may matter more than others, we wonder how the set—as a whole—affects the dependent variables. In order to assess this, we have constructed additive scales that sum up the number of problematic occurrences of the separate variables within each set for each case. These scales tell us when one case has more *Structural* faults or *Decision-Processing* errors or a more adverse *Situational* context than other cases. These scales comprise the heart of our statistical analysis about how process variables affect outcomes.

Analysis

Situation Variables

We begin by looking at the effect that the *Situation* variables have on *Outcomes*. Table 6.1 presents the results of the *Situation* variables on *National Interests*. As can be seen in the table, several variables are significant, meaning that they have an effect, though the effects are not always in the direction anticipated. Three variables that would seem to contribute to a difficult decision-making environment actually resulted in better outcomes in terms of *National Interests*: *Stress*, *Crisis*, and *Short Time Constraint*. Higher levels of each of these variables, instead of causing adverse effects, correlated with higher levels of *National Interests*. Of these three, *Stress* is the best predictor. Knowing the level of *Stress* in a case accounts for nearly 25 percent of the variance in the dependent variable ($R^2 = .248$) in a bivariate test.

Two other variables also correlated with better outcomes in terms of *National Interests*: the *Views of Allies* and the *Views of International Organizations*. When decision makers' preferences coincided with these international actors, the outcome was more likely to enhance national interests than when these views diverged. One other variable approaches significance in table 6.1: the more favorable the *Military-Capabilities Differential*, the

TABLE 6.1   Bivariate regression models: Situation variables explaining national-interest outcomes

Situation variables	b (SE)	Beta	p	R^2
Stress level	.326 (.093)	.498	.001	.248
Crisis	.688 (.296)	.357	.026	.127
Recent failure	−.295 (.300)	−.160	.332	.025
Short time constraint	.851 (.264)	.468	.003	.219
Level of interests	.108 (.202)	.087	.597	.008
Allies' views	.358 (.170)	.328	.042	.107
International organizations' views	.666 (.215)	.454	.004	.206
Public opinion	−.045 (.239)	−.031	.852	.001
Legislative opinion	.134 (.209)	.105	.525	.011
Military-capability differential	.808 (.460)	.321	.090	.103
Other situation distraction	.305 (.313)	.158	.337	.025
Adverse-situation scale	.081 (.080)	.165	.314	.027

Note: $n = 39$ (except for *Military-Capability Differential*, where $n = 29$). All p values are two-tailed significance tests.

more likely it is that the decision will enhance *National Interests*; however, because this only approaches significance, we have less confidence in the relationship. None of the other *Situation* variables approach significance in explaining the *National-Interest* outcome.

Overall, these results are hardly robust, as only a few of the *Situation* variables were significant in the expected direction. This seems to suggest that contextual factors may not be crucial in affecting the outcome of a case. This is even more apparent when looking at the results in table 6.2, which shows the effect of the *Situation* variables on the *Level of International Conflict*. In this case, none of the variables are significant or even approach significance, yet several should have potential for correlating with conflict, such as *Crisis*, *Recent Failure*, and the *Level of Interests* at stake in the case.

It is possible that there is an aggregate effect of these situational variables. Indeed, Janis refers to a "provocative situational context" (Janis 1982, 244) to talk about how combinations of adverse situational factors can be problematic for decision making. To assess this, as we noted above, we have created an aggregate scale that sums the number of problematic situational variables in each case.[4] The results of the regression analyses for this *Adverse-Situation* scale can also be seen in tables 6.1 and 6.2 as the last variable in each table. In neither case, however, is the scale significant.

TABLE 6.2   Bivariate regression models: Situation variables explaining level of international conflict

Situation variables	b (SE)	Beta	p	R^2
Stress level	−.023 (.079)	−.498	.772	.002
Crisis	−.183 (.231)	−.129	.434	.017
Recent failure	.225 (.220)	.166	.313	.028
Short time constraint	−.172 (.218)	−.129	.435	.017
Level of interests	.118 (.148)	.130	.432	.017
Allies' views	−.069 (132)	−.085	.604	.007
International organizations' views	−.201 (.174)	−.187	.255	.035
Public opinion	.168 (.174)	.157	.339	.025
Legislative opinion	.114 (.153)	.121	.462	.015
Military-capability differential	.046 (.365)	.024	.900	.001
Other situation distraction	−.083 (.233)	−.058	.724	.003
Adverse-situation scale	.008 (.059)	.023	.888	.001

Note: $n = 39$ (except for *Military-Capability Differential*, where $n = 29$). All p values are two-tailed significance tests.

TABLE 6.3   Bivariate regression models: Situation variables explaining decision-processing faults

Situation variables	b (SE)	Beta	p	R^2
Stress level	−.295 (.269)	−.178	.279	.032
Crisis	−.769 (.793)	−.157	.339	.025
Recent failure	.043 (.770)	.009	.955	.000
Short time constraint	−1.387 (.723)	−.301	.063	.091
Level of interest	.150 (.515)	.048	.773	.002
Allies' views	.518 (.447)	.187	.254	.035
International organizations' views	−.202 (.610)	−.054	.742	.003
Public opinion	.288 (.604)	.078	.637	.006
Legislative opinion	−.396 (.528)	−.122	.458	.015
Military-capability differential	−.160 (1.250)	−.025	.899	.001
Other situation distraction	−1.308 (.774)	−.268	.100	.072
Adverse-situation scale	−.126 (.204)	−.102	.538	.010

Note: n = 39 (except for *Military-Capabililty Differential*, where n = 29). All p values are two-tailed significance tests.

It is simply not the case that a more adverse situational environment has an effect on outcomes in terms of either *National Interests* or the *Level of International Conflict*.

As seen in figure 6.1, based upon Janis's theoretical work, we also speculate that *Situation* variables may have an effect on the quality of decision making in the episode. This is marked by the arrow going from *Situation* to *Decision Processing* in the figure. To assess this possibility using regression analysis, our dependent variable is an additive scale composed of dichotomous versions of all of the *Decision-Processing* variables. We sum the number of problematic *Decision-Processing* variables in each case to create a scale, with higher numbers representing poorer decision processing in the case. Using this scale as the dependent variable, we ran regression models testing the effect of each of the *Situation* variables along with the *Adverse-Situation* scale. The results can be seen in table 6.3.

Once again, it appears that there is virtually no negative effect of the *Situation* variables on decision making. Only two variables even approach significance, and in neither case are they in the direction anticipated. *Short Time Constraints* actually correlate with fewer *Decision-Processing* problems. Similarly, when decision makers face *Unusual Distractions* in the decision environment, they tend to have fewer *Decision-Processing* faults. None of the other *Situation* variables approach significance. In addition, the *Adverse-Situation* scale is also not significant, and, in fact, the sign for the B coefficient is the opposite of the one anticipated. It is clearly not the case that as the situation becomes more provocative the average decision-making group commits more errors.

Many years ago, Janis expected that these situational factors would adversely affect decision-making episodes. However, taken together, the results suggest that these factors do not play a major role in affecting the outcomes or the quality of decision making. These are average effects, of course, and certainly it seems possible that an adverse environment may affect a particular case. But the data here demonstrate that these contextual factors are not significantly problematic on average. In fact, some of the factors investigated here seem to result in more positives than negatives for decision makers. It may be that in some cases as the situation becomes more provocative, decision makers become more vigilant. While the data suggest that effect is also limited, we can say with some certainty that problematic *Situation* variables do not have the adverse sort of effect anticipated by Janis.

Group Structures

We turn now to an analysis of the effects of *Group-Structural* factors. These structures include the staffing, norms, precedents, and organizational patterns that are set up by the leader and his or her advisors. In our model, these structures generally exist prior to the commencement of policymaking in any particular case. They pertain to the way the group has set itself up and structured their decision-making apparatus. The hypothesized effects of these group structures, represented by two arrows, can be seen in figure 6.1. One arrow, pointing to *Outcomes*, indicates that better decision-making structures should result in better outcomes. The second arrow, pointing to *Decision Processing*, means that we expect better structures to correlate with better decision-making processes during the actual episode. Regression analyses let us test these hypotheses.

We begin with the effect that each individual structural variable has on outcomes. The results for *National Interests* can be seen in table 6.4. As seen in the table, nearly all of these structural variables have a significant effect on outcomes in terms of *National Interests*. Several factors result in more negative national interests. Groups that are *Insulated* produce less favorable outcomes than groups that are not. Groups that feature an *Illusion of Invulnerability* tend to produce poor national-interest outcomes.

When *Gatekeeping* is present in the group, national interests are not served well. And if a group has an *Unusual Structural Fault*, it is likely to have a worse outcome in terms of national interests. On the other hand, several structural factors enhance national interests. If the group follows *Methodical Procedures* and *Values Disagreement*, the outcome is more likely to be favorable. In addition, if the decision-making team is *Knowledgeable and Experienced* and features *Teamwork*, better national interests are likely to come about. Only three of the structural variables are not significant: *Biased Leader, Group Homogeneity,* and *Foreign-Policy Interest of the Leader* (though even these three nonsignificant variables have coefficients in the expected direction).

This area is the one that decision makers seemingly have the most control over. Before any situational stresses of a specific case come into play, before any decision making occurs, the leader and his or her advisors exist within a particular decision-making apparatus that is, at least in part, a product of their own design. It is up to them if a diversified, experienced set of advisors is in place; if procedures exist to keep the group from being isolated; if methodical routines are established; if gatekeepers are prohibited; and if clear signals have been sent that disagreement is valued. These data suggest, rather strongly, that such structural arrangements—set in advance of any specific decision episode—are likely to have positive effects on *National Interests.* On the other hand, when staffing, structures, and precedents are

TABLE 6.4   Bivariate regression models: Group-structural variables explaining national-interest outcomes

Group-structural variables	b (SE)	Beta	p	R^2
Group insulation	−1.060 (.411)	−.390	.014	.152
Biased leader	−.464 (.315)	−.236	.148	.056
Methodical procedures	1.110 (.238)	.609	.000	.371
Group homogeneity	−.619 (.551)	−.181	.269	.033
Illusion of invulnerability	−.682 (.336)	−.316	.050	.100
Gatekeepers	−1.115 (.267)	−.566	.000	.321
Group values disagreement	1.172 (.252)	.608	.000	.370
Foreign-policy interest of leader	.352 (.294)	.193	.239	.037
Team knowledge/experience	1.182 (.526)	.347	.031	.120
Teamwork	.945 (.258)	.516	.001	.266
Unusual structural factor	−.579 (293)	−.319	.048	.102
Structural-faults scale	−.213 (.040)	−.663	.000	.439

Note: $n = 39$. All p values are two-tailed significance tests.

in place that impair systematic, diligent, and careful decision making, the effect is likely to be negative for *National Interests*.

We assess the aggregate effect of problematic structures by creating an additive scale where we sum the number of structural faults in each case.[5] The results of the regression model assessing the scale's effect on *National Interests* are seen in the last variable listed in table 6.4. The more *Group-Structural* faults in a case, the poorer the outcome will be in terms of *National Interests*. Remembering that there are eleven possible structural faults in the scale, interpreting the *B* coefficient (.213) in the model is interesting: each additional structural fault in a case is likely to reduce the *National-Interest* outcome (as rated by the foreign-policy experts) by .213. In addition, nearly 44 percent of the variance in *National Interests* is explained by the *Structural-Faults* scale. Put somewhat differently, these data show that higher numbers of structural faults in the decision-making apparatus of an administration go a long way toward explaining problematic outcomes in terms of national interests. Given that decision makers have ample opportunity and wide latitude to put together these structures, the prescription here is clear: by creating better decision-making structures, they are likely to achieve better decision outcomes.

Similar patterns can be seen when looking at the effect of *Group Structures* on the *Level of International Conflict*, the results of which are in table 6.5. Several structural variables contribute to outcomes marked by an in-

TABLE 6.5   Bivariate regression models: Group-structural variables explaining level of international conflict

Group-structural variables	*b* (SE)	Beta	*p*	R^2
Group insulation	.281 (.326)	.140	.394	.020
Biased leader	.506 (.223)	.349	.029	.122
Methodical procedures	−.624 (.195)	−.466	.003	.217
Group homogeneity	.516 (.405)	.206	.208	.042
Illusion of invulnerability	.524 (.246)	.331	.040	.109
Gatekeepers	.721 (.206)	.498	.001	.248
Group values disagreement	−.551 (.215)	−.388	.014	.151
Foreign-policy interest of leader	−.036 (.220)	−.027	.871	.001
Team knowledge/experience	−.488 (.404)	−.195	.235	.038
Teamwork	−.389 (.212)	−.289	.074	.084
Unusual structural factor	.194 (.217)	.145	.377	.021
Structural-faults scale	.111 (.034)	.470	.003	.221

Note: $n = 39$. All p values are two-tailed significance tests.

crease in international conflict. If traditionally the leader is *Biased*, if the group has an *Illusion of Invulnerability*, or if there is one or more *Gatekeepers* in the system, decision outcomes are more likely to demonstrate higher conflict levels. On the other hand, if the group has a tradition of using *Methodical Procedures* or if it *Values Disagreement*, outcomes are likely to have lower conflict levels. The same pattern can be seen when there is good *Teamwork*: it appears that may decrease international conflict, though this variable only approaches significance ($p = .074$).

The last variable listed at the bottom of table 6.5 is the aggregated *Structural-Faults* scale. It indicates that as the group has more *Group-Structural* faults, there is an increased likelihood of more international conflict in a decision episode. While the scale is significant ($p = .003$), it does not have as strong an effect on *Conflict* outcomes as it does on *National-Interest* outcomes. *Group-Structural* faults are a good predictor of both types of outcomes, but they matter more in explaining *National Interests*.

As seen in figure 6.1, we also expect that *Group Structures* will have an effect on the quality of *Decision Processing* during the episode: better structures should result in fewer *Decision-Processing* faults. The results of these tests are in table 6.6. The B coefficients are easily interpreted in this table. All of the structural variables (except the *Structural-Faults* scale) are dichotomous (coded as 0 or 1), and the dependent variable is the scale composed of faults in decision processing during the case. So each B value indicates

TABLE 6.6   Bivariate regression models: Group-structural variables explaining decision-processing faults

Group-structural variables	b (SE)	Beta	p	R^2
Group insulation	3.241 (1.000)	.470	.003	.221
Biased leader	2.852 (.673)	.571	.000	.326
Methodical procedures	−2.635 (.624)	−.570	.000	.325
Group homogeneity	1.833 (1.389)	.212	.195	.045
Illusion of invulnerability	2.922 (.760)	.534	.000	.286
Gatekeepers	2.806 (.679)	.562	.000	.316
Group values disagreement	−3.269 (.597)	−.669	.000	.448
Foreign-policy interest of leader	−.667 (.752)	−.144	.381	.021
Team knowledge/experience	−3.639 (1.289)	−.421	.008	.177
Teamwork	−2.027 (.687)	−.436	.005	.190
Unusual structural factor	1.695 (.705)	.368	.021	.135
Structural-Faults Scale	.617 (.087)	.758	.000	.575

Note: $n = 39$. All p values are two-tailed significance tests.

how many additional *Decision-Processing* faults there will be on average when that particular *Group-Structure* variable is present. For example, the B coefficient for *Group Insulation* is 3.241, which means that if the group has a pattern of being insulated, there will be on average more than three additional decision-processing problems in the case. By way of reminder, the scale ranking *Decision-Processing* faults ranges from 0 to 8 and averages 2.97 faults across our set of cases. With this information, it is apparent from even a quick glance at table 6.6 that many of the *Group-Structure* variables are important predictors of the level of faults in the decision processing of a case.

If the group is *Insulated*, has a *Biased Leader*, has an *Illusion of Invulnerability*, has *Gatekeepers*, or has another *Unusual Structural Fault*, it is likely to have more *Decision-Processing* faults in any particular case. Factors that work to reduce *Decision-Processing* faults include having *Methodical Procedures*, *Valuing Disagreement*, having a *Knowledgeable and Experienced* team, and having a tradition of good *Teamwork*. All of these variables are significant, and all result in a notable increase in the number of processing faults, ranging from 1.7 to 3.6. In addition, several of these individual variables, by themselves, explain a significant amount of variance in the level of *Decision-Processing* faults. For instance, if the group values disagreement, this explains nearly 45 percent of the variance in the dependent variable ($R^2 = .448$).[6] Three other variables explain over 30 percent of the variance, and several others have high R^2s as well. Clearly these data demonstrate that good decision-making structures by the group will have a positive effect on the quality of decision processing during a typical case.

This point is made even clearer when looking at the effect of the *Structural-Faults* scale. When we aggregate the number of structural faults in a case and use that in a regression model to explain the number of faults in decision processing, the results are very strong (see the last variable listed in table 6.6). For each additional structural fault in place before a case begins, the model predicts an average increase in the number of decision-processing faults of .617. Put a bit differently, if one group has only two structural faults and another one has seven, the second group is likely to have three more decision-processing faults during a typical case than the first group—a very costly effect. This model explains nearly 60 percent of the variance in decision-processing faults, which means that the number of structural faults in an administration is an excellent predictor of the quality of decision making during a foreign-policy case. If leaders want good-quality decision making when a specific decision event or crisis comes along, they would be very well advised, based upon the data here, to carefully set up good group structures in advance.

Decision Processing

This is our third category of independent variables. These variables consider what goes on while the group is engaged in the actual decision making for each case. They look at such things as rationally weighing competing policy options, processing information, suppressing dissent, and developing problematic stereotypes. As can be seen in figure 6.1, we expect that better-quality decision processing will result in better outcomes in terms of *National Interests* and the *Level of International Conflict*. Let us look at how each of these variables has an effect on the two different dependent variables.

Table 6.7 presents the results of the *Decision-Processing* variables on *National Interests*. Several of the variables have an effect in the expected direction on national interests. When *Biased Information Processing* happens in a case, it tends to have an adverse effect on *National-Interest* outcomes. The same is true when groups *Stereotype the Situation*. On the other hand, when the decision-making group carefully *Surveys Alternatives*, it is much more likely to have a beneficial outcome in terms of *National Interests*. All three of these variables are statistically significant and explain a fair amount of variance in the dependent variable. One other decision-processing variable approaches significance: when groups are clear in *Surveying Objec-*

TABLE 6.7   Bivariate regression models: Decision-processing variables explaining national-interest outcomes

Decision-processing variables	b (SE)	Beta	p	R^2
Poor information search	.462 (.334)	.222	.174	.049
Biased information processing	−.847 (.264)	−.966	.003	.217
Survey objectives	.515 (.292)	.279	.085	.078
Survey alternatives	.931 (.271)	.492	.001	.242
Stereotype situation	−.587 (.284)	−.322	.046	.104
Stereotype out-group	−.009 (.299)	−.005	.977	.000
Uniformity pressures	−.317 (.358)	−.152	.355	.023
Unusual process factors	−.269 (.352)	−.125	.450	.016
Decision processing–faults scale	−.169 (.059)	−.428	.007	.183

Note: $n = 39$. All p values are two-tailed significance tests.

tives, the pattern suggests they may have better outcomes. None of the other variables approach significance, though most of them have *B* values with signs we would anticipate, meaning that the direction of the correlation is as expected even though the models did not reach significance. One variable, however, is far from being significant. At least in this set of cases, *Stereotyping the Out-Group* has no patterned effect on *National Interests*.

The last variable listed in table 6.7 is the *Decision-Processing* scale, which aggregates the number of problematic variables in this category. We expect that higher numbers of *Decision-Processing* faults will correlate with worse outcomes in terms of *National Interests*, and indeed that is the case. Each additional decision-processing problem results in an average decrease in the *National-Interest* score of .169. The scale is significant ($p = .007$) and explains nearly 20 percent of the variance in *National Interests* ($R^2 = .183$). In other words, the number of *Decision-Processing* faults in a case is a good predictor of how well the case turns out in terms of *National Interests*: more decision-processing faults typically leads to poorer national-interests outcome.

The effect of the *Decision-Processing* variables on the *Level of International Conflict* is even more dramatic, as seen in table 6.8. Six of the individual variables are significant, all of them in the expected direction. *Biased Information Processing, Stereotyping the Situation, Stereotyping the Out-Group*, and *Pressure for Uniformity* during a decision event all result in higher conflict levels. However, conflict levels are likely to be lower when the decision group does a careful job of *Surveying Objectives* and *Surveying Alternatives*. All of these variables are highly significant and explain between

TABLE 6.8   Bivariate regression models: Decision-processing variables explaining level of international conflict

Decision-processing variables	b (SE)	Beta	p	R^2
Poor information search	−.018 (.251)	−.012	.942	.000
Biased information processing	.608 (.196)	.455	.004	.207
Survey objectives	−.727 (.189)	−.535	.000	.286
Survey alternatives	−.628 (.204)ᵃ	−.451	.004	.203
Stereotype situation	.579 (.199)	.432	.006	.187
Stereotype out-group	.837 (.171)	.626	.000	.392
Uniformity pressures	.519 (.237)	.339	.035	.115
Unusual process factors	.133 (.260)	.084	.612	.007
Decision processing–faults scale	.179 (.037)	.618	.000	.382

Note: n = 39. All p values are two-tailed significance tests.

11 and 39 percent of the variance in the *Level of International Conflict*.

When aggregated to form the scale measuring the *Decision-Processing* faults, the combination of these variables has a major effect on the *Level of International Conflict*. The scale is highly significant ($p < .001$) and explains nearly 40 percent of the variance in the dependent variable. This means that the more problems there are during the actual decision making of the case, the more likely it is that the decision will result in higher levels of international conflict.

For some, this set of results may be a bit surprising. In the area of *National Interests*, it makes normative sense that better decision processing is likely to lead to a better course of action, as decision makers carefully weigh out information and options, essentially figuring out the best route on the map to a good outcome. But in terms of the *Level of International Conflict*, why should good decision processing result in lower levels? Rarely do decision makers define conflict avoidance as the number-one objective in a situation. In other words, it seems likely that good decision makers will always try to better national interests, but sometimes, perhaps frequently, one can imagine that to do so will require conflict escalation. Why then does better-quality decision making result in lower levels of conflict? Not only is this clearly the case in this set of decision episodes, but it turns out that high-quality decision processing actually has a greater explanatory effect on the level of international conflict than it does on national interests.

Unpacking the set of variables may prove instructive in this regard. When several of the variables in the category of decision processing are problematic, it would seem to open the door to more conflict-oriented choices. For instance, when one stereotypes the out-group, it results in such things as categorizing them in pejorative terms, dehumanizing them, and thinking of them as inherently hostile and aggressive. Ronald Reagan referred to the Soviet Union as the "evil empire"; George H. W. Bush compared Saddam Hussein to Adolf Hitler; George W. Bush called three disparate countries "the axis of evil." All three are examples of stereotyping the out-group, which essentially created space to more easily move in the direction of conflict. Similar processes can be seen in some of the other variables in this category, such as *Biased Information Processing* and *Stereotyping the Situation*. On the other hand, when decision makers do not make such reductionist assessments, they are more likely to see nuance in others, thus attributing them with a number of possible motives and reducing the likelihood of knee-jerk movement toward conflict. Recall that in the Ogaden case presented in chapter 5, Brzezinski was the member of the administration who most clearly stereotyped the situation as a cold-war case; he was also the one who most strongly advocated military escalation. It may also be the case that better analysis of information, objectives, and alternatives will lead decision makers to finding a wider range of alternatives, whereas short-circuiting these processes may lead to a more circumscribed set of options, one of which often seems to be conflict. Regardless, the data is abundantly clear here: better processes during a decision-making case are highly correlated with lower levels of conflict. If in general one prefers there to be less war and conflict in international politics, this finding is quite positive: if the quality of decision making is improved, less conflict is likely to be the result.

Multivariate Models

All of the analyses we have presented so far have been bivariate models, meaning we look at the effect of one independent variable at a time on the dependent variable. These models are helpful for looking at individual variables and for carrying out simple tests of our hypotheses. However, these simple models also lead to additional questions about such things as the relative effects of different variables and how different independent variables might work in combination to explain variance in the dependent variable. To answer these kinds of questions we turn to multivariate analysis.

Put simply, multivariate models incorporate more than one independent variable into the model at a time. Think about it this way: while any one variable by itself may highly correlate with the dependent variable, it is virtually never the case that it is the only variable that has a causal effect. Although our *Decision-Processing* scale predicts a large amount of variance in the *Level of International Conflict*, it seems likely that variables from our other two broad categories may also influence that level. It may also be the case that a bivariate model masks a spurious relationship between the independent and dependent variables. This would mean that, while we get significance in the bivariate model, the true explanatory variable is a different one altogether and, once we control for that variable, as multivariate models allow us to do, the original relationship may disappear. Finally, sometimes exactly the opposite may happen: an independent variable in a bivariate model is not significant, but when other variables are incorporated into the model, its significance emerges. All of these possibilities require the more sophisticated analysis associated with multivariate models.

There are thirty individual variables across our three categories, in addition to the three aggregated scales. Statistically speaking, we cannot include all of these variables in a single multivariate model.[7] This means that we must run models that include various combinations of the different variables. The number of possible combinations is exceedingly high, and it would be unworkable to discuss or present even a high percentage of these possible models. Instead, what we present in the rest of this chapter are models that are best representations of patterns we found in the data.

There are two broad criteria we considered in selecting the models to present here. First, we include models that are representative of consistent patterns we saw among the independent variables. For instance, if when looking at the results from several different models we saw that variable X nearly always correlated positively with the dependent variable while variable Y generally was negative, then we would include a model with both of these variables in it, each with their respective signs on the coefficient. In some cases, a variable in these presented models may not reach normal levels of statistical significance, but it will represent consistent directional patterns we saw across many tested models. Second, we present models that provide the most explanatory power for the dependent variable under consideration. This is primarily indicated by the adjusted R^2 value.[8] As we tested different models, some were more effective in accounting for variance in the dependent variable, and since one objective of statistical work in the social sciences is to account for as much causal explanation of the dependent variable as possible, this is an important criterion in our analysis. Of course, these two criteria are not mutually exclusive. Generally speaking, the models with the highest explanatory power are also those models that include variables with consistent relationships with the dependent variable.

The *Situation* variables are an excellent place to begin our multivariate investigation. Recall that Janis (1982), in his seminal work on groupthink, expected that adverse situational factors would hinder the quality of decision making and therefore have an adverse effect on the quality of outcomes. However, the bivariate results presented earlier did not provide much support for Janis's argument regarding these variables. Looking at multivariate models that include various combinations of these variables has the potential to uncover patterns that were not apparent in the simple bivariate models and thus may provide additional insight into this puzzle. And, indeed, we did find some interesting patterns.

It appears that two broad subsets of *Situation* variables emerge within which there are similar effects on the dependent variables. The first subset consists of those variables that indicate some kind of anxiety in the situation; these include *Stress*, *Crisis*, and *Short Time Constraint*. The second subset includes those variables that consider other international actors: *Views of International Organizations* and *Views of Allies*. The multivariate models we ran to explain outcomes in terms of *National Interests* demonstrated two patterns with these subsets. First, the most important *Situation* variable explaining *National Interests* is the *Views of International Organizations*, even when controlling for a variety of combinations of other *Situation* variables in the models. In this study, when the decision makers' views line up with those of key *International Organizations*, the outcome is more likely to be favorable for *National Interests* than when those views diverge. Second, all of the anxiety indicators in the multivariate models generally pointed in the same direction, though generally only approaching significance. The pattern of the three anxiety variables, however, was consistently in the direction opposite the one anticipated by Janis. It may be that heightened anxiety leads decision makers to become more vigilant, thus leading to better-quality decision making. In virtually none of the models did these variables correlate with more problematic outcomes. Among the three different anxiety indicators, *Stress* was generally the best predictor of *National Interests*. The best multivariate model demonstrating these effects can be seen in table 6.9. When the *Views of International Organizations* are favorable to those of the administration, and when the *Stress* level is high, the outcome tends to be more favorable for *National Interests*. Both variables are significant, and the adjusted R^2 is quite high at .378.

In terms of the *Level of International Conflict*, there were virtually no patterns or combinations of *Situation* variables that led to significant results among our multivariate tests. Try as we might to tease something out of the

TABLE 6.9   Multivariate model: Situation variables explaining national-interest outcomes

Situation variables	b (SE)	Beta	p
International organizations' views	.540 (.197)	.368	.019
Stress	.595 (.286)	.309	.045

Note: Adjusted R^2 = .378. n = 39. All p values are two-tailed significance tests.

data, it is simply not the case in this study that the situational factors we have coded correlate in any meaningful way with the level of conflict that comes about as a result of decision making. Certainly individual cases may be exceptions, but on average, there are simply no patterns among these variables.

There are, however, some patterns among the *Situation* variables that explain the quality of *Decision Processing* by the group during the case. Once again, we found generally a pattern that the anxiety indicators correlated with better-quality decision processing. Sometimes these variables were significant and sometimes only approached significance, but in all cases they showed the same directional pattern: more anxiety led to better decision processing. These variables tended toward increasing significance when one additional variable was entered in the model: *Views of Allies*. In the multivariate models, this variable had a surprising effect on the dependent variable in terms of the direction of the relationship: when the *Views of Allies* coincided with the views of decision makers, the quality of decision processing went down. Perhaps decision makers use allies' views as a kind of heuristic or shortcut rule in decision making; if allies have taken a clear position on the matter, perhaps decision makers perceive that less attention is required, and the result is poorer decision processes. Another possibility is that there are political costs associated with going against the in-group of allies; it may be easier to go along than to conduct thorough and independent decision making that perhaps leads to a dissenting position.[9] The multivariate model in table 6.10 demonstrates the patterns noted here. The coefficient for *Views of Allies* is positive, indicating that when allies' views were favorable for the administration, there are more decision-processing errors, whereas when there is limited time for decision making, there are fewer decision-processing errors.

Though we found some interesting patterns among these *Situation* variables, the overall pattern is that as a set they are not strong predictors of our dependent variables. Much more often than not, the *Situation* variables sim-

Table 6.10   Multivariate model: Situation variables explaining decision-processing faults

Situation variables	b (SE)	Beta	p
Allies' views	.904 (.443)	.326	.049
Short time constraint	−1.896 (.737)	−.411	.014

Note: Adjusted R^2 = .185. n = 39. All p values are two-tailed significance tests.

ply showed no relationship with outcomes or with the quality of information processing. From a prescriptive perspective, this broad pattern is good news for decision makers. *Situation* variables are those factors that are essentially givens in any decision episode. Decision makers do not choose them, nor do they have any significant control over them, generally speaking. One can imagine, as Janis did many years ago, that these contextual features, over which decision makers have little control, could be quite problematic. That is generally not the case. Indeed, while subtle, the pattern for the anxiety variables actually tends to work in the other direction. Such matters as a *Short Time Constraint* and high *Stress* levels coincided with better decision making, not the other way around. The significant exception here is that it appears to be problematic when decision makers' views differ from the *Views of International Organizations*. When the government moves against the prevailing opinion in those organizations, it is likely to have a detrimental effect on national interests.

The patterns in the models just discussed are ones that include only variables within the *Situation* category. We ran these models specifically to try to better investigate Janis's hypothesis about a provocative situational context. When we expand the multivariate models to include variables from the other two categories, we have the possibility of uncovering additional patterns and increasing the explanatory power of the models. Here our organizational focus moves away from the independent variables and toward the dependent variables as we look for best models, using variables from all three sets, to explain each dependent variable. Since a key focus of these models is explanatory power, we included in these models the aggregated scales in each category that we discussed earlier.

Two broad patterns continuously emerged in these models using variables across the three sets of independent variables. First, the aggregated *Adverse-Situation* scale is never statistically significant in the models when at least one of the other aggregated scales (*Group-Structural Faults* and *Decision-Processing Faults*) is in the model. Recall that this scale was also not significant in the bivariate models. It does not appear to be the case that an adverse situational context, as an aggregate of our *Situation* variables, has a negative effect on decision making.

The second pattern among these models is that when both the *Group-Structure Faults* and *Decision-Processing Faults* scales are entered into the same model as independent variables, only one remains significant. Statistically speaking, this is not a surprise, because the two are highly correlated; this means that when both are in one model, one accounts for a large amount of the variance in the dependent variable, leaving little left for the other, and thus it is not significant. What is interesting, however, is that the two variables have different effects across the two different outcome variables. When the dependent variable is *National Interests*, the *Group-Structures* scale is highly significant while the *Decision-Processing* scale is not. When the dependent variable is *Level of International Conflict*, just the opposite happens: the *Decision-Processing* scale is highly significant while the *Group-Structures* scale is not.

This means that, of the different aggregated variables in this study, the most important one affecting *National Interests* is the *Group-Structures* scale, even when controlling for the other two scales. Assuming states want to maximize national interests, the best way to do so is to create sound structures in their decision-making apparatus. In terms of *Level of Conflict*, the strongest predictor variable is the quality of *Decision Processing*: as there are more decision-processing faults in a case, the level of conflict is likely to increase, even controlling for the quality of group structures and for contextual variables. This suggests that taking shortcuts in decision processing, including such things as poor information search, biased information processing, and stereotyping the out-group and the situation, seems to make it easier to escalate conflict levels against opponents.

While these two patterns were consistent across our multivariate models, there were some individual variables within the other categories that were frequently significant. There are four models we will present that represent the general patterns we found in the multivariate models. The first two, tables 6.11 and 6.12, are models with *National Interests* as the dependent variable. As noted in the previous paragraph, the primary explanatory variable in these two models is the *Structural-Faults* scale, which is significant in each model and shows that more structural faults lead to worse outcomes in terms of national interests. In table 6.11, three other variables contribute to the model. The first two come from the *Situation* category: *National Interests* are generally enhanced when the *Views of International Organizations* coincide with the decision makers' views and when *Stress* is high in the decision-making episode. While we saw these two patterns in the earlier multivariate models within the *Situation* category, their significance is perhaps more notable here now that we have controlled for other variables, including the *Structural-Faults* scale that accounts for most of the variance in *National Interests*. One other variable comes from our category

Table 6.11   Multivariate model explaining national-interest outcomes

Independent variables	b (SE)	Beta	p
Structural-faults scale	−.140 (.044)	−.436	.003
International organizations' views	.455 (.171)	.310	.012
Stress	.131 (.084)	.200	.127
Stereotype of situation	−1.896 (.737)	−.155	.204

Note: Adjusted R^2 = .523. n = 39. All p values are two-tailed significance tests.

on *Decision Processing*: *Stereotyping the Situation* tends to be harmful to *National Interests*. Note that neither *Stress* nor *Stereotyping the Situation* reach our threshold of statistical significance, but both have the directional relationship with the dependent variable we saw in many models we tested, and both enhance the model overall and thus are appropriate to include in the model. The model is highly significant and the adjusted R^2 is quite high at .523.

We included the model seen in table 6.12 particularly to look at patterns involving the *Military-Differential* variable. The operational definition for this variable includes three possible values: the power differential could be *favorable* or *unfavorable* for the state we are analyzing, or the two states in the case could have *similar* levels of power. However, two problems emerged regarding this variable as we coded the cases. First, in none of the cases in this study was our subject state facing an unfavorable power differential. Second, in several of our cases this variable was simply irrelevant to decision makers as they worked through the particular case (for example, normalizing relations with China), and so for such cases we could not code any of the three possible values in the operational definition. This limited the extent to which we could include this variable in models noted earlier in this chapter. Yet, clearly, it is a variable that may affect both the quality of decision processing and the outcomes of a case. Here we have recoded the variable to allow us to conduct some analyses across all thirty-nine cases. Specifically, we recoded the variable into a dichotomous one, with the value 1 indicating that the state had a *Favorable Power* position in the case and the value 0 indicating all other cases. We recognize that this masks important differences in the concept underlying the variable and thus is limited in its meaning, but the patterns that show up using this dichotomous variable are interesting nonetheless.

Table 6.12   Multivariate model (with *Favorable-Power* variable) explaining national-interest outcomes

Independent variables	*b* (SE)	Beta	*p*
Decision processing–faults scale	−.153 (.051)	−.387	.005
International organizations' views	.585 (.190)	.399	.004
Favorable power	.464 (.245)	.245	.067

Note: Adjusted R^2 = . 379. *n* = 39. All *p* values are two-tailed significance tests.

The model presented in table 6.12 includes two variables in addition to the *Favorable-Power* variable: more *Decision-Processing Faults* produce poorer outcomes in terms of *National Interests*, while favorable *Views of International Organizations* results in better *National Interests*. The coefficient for the *Favorable-Power* variable is also positive, indicating that when the state is in the stronger position, the outcome is likely to be favorable in terms of *National Interests*. While this result may seem intuitive (that is, the strong will prevail), remember that this result happens when controlling for two other important variables. In other words, accounting for the quality of decision processing in the case and the position of international organizations in the case, if a state is strong it can essentially force a good outcome, a finding that some might find troubling.

Our next two tables shift the dependent variable to the *Level of Conflict*, with the independent variables coming from across our three categories. As noted earlier, the key explanatory variable for conflict level is the number of *Decision-Processing* faults in a case, and this pattern holds up even while controlling for variables from the *Situation* and from *Group Structures*. As seen in table 6.13, as the number of *Decision-Processing* faults increases, the outcome is likely to have a higher *Level of International Conflict*. This model also includes two variables from the set of situation factors. When the decision makers' views in a case coincide with the *Views of Allies*, there

Table 6.13   Multivariate model explaining level of international conflict

Independent variables	*b* (SE)	Beta	*p*
Decision processing–faults scale	.145 (.044)	.501	.002
Allies's views	−.220 (.105)	−.274	.044
Threat level	.235 (.121)	.259	.061
Gatekeeper	.403 (.221)	.278	.077

Note: Adjusted R^2 = . 447. *n* = 39. All *p* values are two-tailed significance tests.

is likely to be less conflict in the outcome. And, when the *Threat Level* is higher in the case, the *Level of International Conflict* is also likely to be higher.[10] One additional variable is included, this one from our list of group structures: when there are one or more *Gatekeepers* in the administration, there is likely to be a higher *Level of International Conflict*.

To this model we then added the *Favorable-Power* variable to assess its effect. The results are seen in table 6.14. Adding the *Favorable-Power* variable affects the p values for some of the other variables, though all the coefficients keep their same signs, and it increases the value of the adjusted R^2 of the model, meaning that the model is stronger with this variable. While the *Favorable-Power* variable only approaches significance, the direction of the relationship is telling: controlling for the other variables in the model, if a state is stronger than its opponent, it is more likely to make a decision that escalates international conflict.

We finish our presentation of the multivariate results by looking at the quality of *Decision Processing* as our dependent variable. The most powerful variable explaining the number of decision-processing faults is the *Structural-Faults* scale, and this pattern held up continuously throughout our multivariate analyses even while controlling for many different combinations of *Situation* variables. However, some very interesting patterns among the *Situation* variables emerged in these models. For example, when controlling for the level of *Group-Structural* faults, the anxiety indicators we discussed earlier (*Stress, Crisis,* and *Short Time Constraint*) sometimes became significant or approached significance, though this time the direction of the relationship is opposite of the one we found with our earlier models. Once we account for the quality of group structures in a case, then the anxiety indicators correlate with poorer decision processing. An example of this pattern is presented in table 6.15. As there are more *Group-Structural* faults

Table 6.14   Multivariate model (with *Favorable-Power* variable) explaining level of international conflict

Independent variables	b (SE)	Beta	p
Decision processing–faults scale	.133 (.043)	.460	.004
Allies' views	−.233 (.102)	−.290	.029
Threat level	.180 (.121)	.198	.149
Gatekeeper	.572 (.233)	.395	.020
Favorable power	.350 (.193)	.251	.079

Note: Adjusted R^2 = . 482. n = 39. All p values are two-tailed significance tests.

Table 6.15   Multivariate model explaining decision-processing faults

Independent variables	b (SE)	Beta	p
Structural-faults scale	.715 (.095)	.879	.000
Stress	.412 (.195)	.248	.041

Note: Adjusted R^2 = . 601. n = 39. All p values are two-tailed significance tests.

in the administration, the number of *Decision-Processing* faults is very likely to increase. In addition, controlling for *Group-Structural* faults, when there is high *Stress* in a case, the number of *Decision-Processing* faults goes up. In other words, as is the general pattern for the other two anxiety indicators, *Stress* can be problematic for the quality of decision making in a case, but only once we have controlled for the quality of *Group Structures*. It may be that Janis was partially correct in anticipating that some factors contributing to a "provocative situational context" (Janis 1982, 244) can adversely affect decision making. Clearly the dominant predictor variable of the quality of *Decision Processing* is the level of *Group-Structural* faults; knowing how an administration structures its decision making is the biggest single factor affecting the quality of decision processing. But, once that factor is controlled for, then the anxiety indicators tend to be harmful to decision processing.

Table 6.16 shows another interesting set of patterns affecting the quality of decision processing. As before, the most important variable in the model (as seen by the p and the Beta values) is the *Group-Structural Faults* scale. But two *Situation* variables are also significant in the model. First, when decision makers' views align with those of *Allies*, the number of *Decision-Processing* faults actually increases. Second, when the state has *Favorable Power* over its opponent, there is also likely to be an increase in the number of *Decision-Processing* faults. Both of these variables seem to provide shortcuts for the administration or result in less attention in the decision-making process. It appears that if decision makers agree with allies, then it is not

Table 6.16   Multivariate model (with *Favorable-Power* variable) explaining decision-processing faults

Independent variables	b (SE)	Beta	p
Structural-faults scale	.786 (.081)	.966	.000
Allies' views	.550 (.242)	.199	.029
Favorable power	1.818 (.486)	.379	.001

Note: Adjusted R^2 = . 718. n = 39. All p values are two-tailed significance tests.

necessary to be as thorough with their own decision-making quality. And, if the state is stronger than the opponent, likewise it seems that decision makers do not focus as much on high-quality decision making. Not only are all three variables significant in the model, but the model itself explains 72 percent of the variance in the quality of decision processing. It is clear that the quality of structures set up in advance significantly affects the quality of decision making in a case; better structures lead to better-quality decision processing. But also significant here are factors than can hamper the quality of decision making, specifically, when decision makers rely on shortcut heuristics, they fail to conduct better-quality decision making.

Conclusion

Chapters 4 and 5 provided some cases that anecdotally support the general hypothesis that decision-making structures and processes affect the quality of outcomes in foreign-policy cases. In this chapter, we have more rigorously investigated that hypothesis by looking systematically and statistically at a much larger set of cases. While no statistical model in the social sciences is definitive once and for all, and there are certainly limitations in the current dataset, something we return to below, the results seem to be quite telling: how a state structures its decision-making apparatus and how it conducts its decision processing have a high probability of affecting the quality of outcomes in a case. Good structures and processes are likely to result in better achievements in national interests and lower levels of international conflict. The data in this chapter are clear: there are better ways and worse ways to conduct decision making, and the outcomes of cases are very likely to be dependent upon these matters.

Is the quality of decision making the only thing that matters? According to our data, the answer is a qualified "no": other factors outside of the "black box" of decision making did factor into some of our models. However, these factors generally had limited effects and in some cases manifested in ways opposite the ones we might expect.

Recall that our primary research interest has been in looking inside the decision-making apparatus of the state, something that is often overlooked in other major research programs in international relations. Many of those other research programs focus primarily on state- and system-level variables to explain international politics. While it is not the case that our dataset allows us to investigate the effects of as many control variables as can be done in "large-n" quantitative datasets such as the Correlates of War, International Crisis Behavior, or Militarized Interstate Disputes, it is the case that we have included a number of state- and system-level factors in our models that might be expected to correlate with outcomes. Some of these are highly related to realist theories of international politics, such as power (*Military-Capabilities Differential, Favorable Power*) and interests (*Level of Interests*). Other variables we include deal with domestic politics (*Public Opinion, Legislative Opinion*) and the influence of other international actors (*Views of International Organizations* and *Views of Allies*). While there are major schools of thought in international relations that argue that these factors are important to understanding foreign policy and international politics, our research shows that as a set they generally pale in comparison to the effect of the decision-making variables. Indeed, of these state- and system-level factors, only two had consistent effects across our models: *National Interests* are generally enhanced when decision makers' positions align with those of key *International Organizations* and when the state has a *Favorable Power* advantage over its opponent. Even when controlling for these two system-level factors, the decision-making variables that are central to our research remain critically important and most of the time are the dominant factors affecting the outcome of a case. Based upon the data here, it is not at all hyperbole to say that in order to understand foreign policy and international relations, we must understand the quality of decision making that happens within states.

This is not to say that these state- and system-level variables are unimportant. Of course they are important. Of course it matters how powerful a country is, what its stakes are in a case, how power is aligned with the state or against it, and so on. Recall, however, that every assessment of such things as power, interests, and alliances that might matter in a case is made by people within the decision-making process. This is why the quality of the process matters. There will always be structural constraints in a case regarding such things as power differential and the role of international organizations. High-quality decision making is more likely to produce better assessments of those factors and thus lead to better policy choices and better outcomes.

What is "high-quality decision making?" The results presented in this chapter reveal certain patterns and demonstrate the variables in our model that seem to matter the most. Our model breaks "decision making" into two broad components: *Group-Structural* factors that are primarily in place before the onset of any particular decision episode and *Decision-Processing* factors that focus on mechanisms and procedures during a particular episode. Both of these broad components significantly affected outcomes in the data analyzed here. It matters significantly how an administration sets up its decision-making apparatus, which includes qualitative factors pertaining to the personnel in the administration, the traditions and norms of the decision-making group, and the precedents and expectations established by the leader. It also matters significantly how the group conducts decision processing during a case, which includes quality of information processing, specifying objectives and alternatives, and pressuring members into uniformity.

Not all of these factors are equally important, and they have different effects on our two outcome variables. Notably, our scale of *Structural Faults* was consistently the most powerful predictor of outcomes in terms of *National Interests*: fewer *Structural Faults* in the decision-making apparatus lead to better *National Interests*. On the other hand, our scale of *Decision-Processing Faults* was the better predictor of outcomes in terms of *Level of International Conflict*: as the number of *Decision-Processing Faults* increases, so does the *Level of International Conflict*. These patterns hold up solidly in virtually all of our multivariate tests, including when controlling for the other scale, individual factors within the other scale, and many different combinations of *Situation* variables.

Within the two broad categories of decision-making variables, *Group Structures* and *Decision Processing*, nearly all of the individual variables proved to be important factors in the process. Some, however, mattered more than others and thus may be the primary ones on which to focus prescriptive efforts aimed at improving the quality of decision making. Among the *Group-Structure* variables, two variables stood out more than the others: *Methodical Procedures* and *Valuing Disagreement*. If leaders and advisors want to facilitate higher-quality decision making, they would do well to create precedents and set up structures for these two areas. Other variables among the *Group Structures* that also featured prominently in our analyses were *Biased Leader*, *Illusion of Invulnerability*, and *Gatekeeping*. All of these were problematic for decision making and should be avoided.

In terms of *Decision Processes*, while nearly all variables factored into the process at some level, four stood out the most: *Biased Information Processing*, *Stereotyping the Situation*, *Stereotyping the Out-Group*, and *Surveying Alternatives*. The first three of these deal with different kinds of information processing and whether or not the decision makers get a clear view of matters before them. Engaging in these kinds of distortions is not at all uncommon in decision making. Indeed, more than two-thirds of our cases included at least one of these problems. Yet the data are clear: the more that decision-making groups can avoid these biases and stereotypes, the greater their chances of avoiding a low-quality outcome. *Surveying Alternatives*, on the other hand, is one step in the rational decision-making model that has long been offered as a prescription for higher-quality decision making (Hartle and Halperin 1980). *Surveying Objectives* is another step advocated in that model, and while this variable was less prominent in our multivariate models than *Surveying Alternatives*, it nonetheless was frequently a factor.

As noted earlier, our category of *Situation* variables factored much less prominently into our explanatory models than did the *Group-Structure* and *Decision-Processing* variables. We have already noted two variables in this category that did matter: *Views of International Organizations* and *Favorable Power*. The patterns among a few others are also worth noting. First among these are the variables we have referred to in this chapter as the "anxiety" indicators: *Stress, Crisis,* and *Short Time Constraint.* Janis expected that these factors, when present, would contribute to a problematic decision-making environment and thus would be harmful to the quality of decision making. When factored in alone or with other variables from the *Situation* category, these variables actually tend in the opposite direction: all other factors unknown, when anxiety increases, it actually leads to better decision making. However, when we account for the most prominent factor that affects the quality of *Decision Processing*—the *Structural-Faults* scale—then these variables can indeed hinder decision making. In other words, anxiety alone apparently leads to heightened vigilance in decision making, thus resulting in better quality. But the best predictor of decision-making quality is the *Structural-Faults* scale; it accounts for the lion's share of the variance in number of *Decision-Processing Faults.* Once that variable is controlled for, then anxiety indicators do indeed seem to have an adverse effect on the quality of decision making.

There are some notable limitations to our data, and it is important to keep these in mind when evaluating these results. First, the dataset, while substantially larger than any qualitative research projects in the past (Janis 1982; 't Hart 1990; Moorhead, Ference, and Neck 1991; Smith 1984; 't Hart 1994) and some of the earlier quantitative projects (Haney 1994; Herek, Janis, and Huth 1987; Schafer and Crichlow 1996, 2002; Tetlock 1979;

Tetlock et al. 1982), is still hardly a large one. The nature of collecting this kind of case-based, qualitative data will always be highly time consuming and will thus always result in smaller datasets than some of the "large-n" conflict datasets noted earlier. The consequences of having a smaller dataset are lower statistical power, perhaps higher levels of sampling error, and limited generalizability. In addition, the cases in our dataset come from only three countries, the United States, the United Kingdom, and Israel, with a large majority of the cases coming from the United States. This also places some limits on the generalizability of the project. Finally, some may wonder about subjective coding, researcher biases, and other possible factors that could affect patterns in the data. We do not doubt that such subjectivity is a possibility in coding these variables, as certainly it is in any coding endeavor, although we did take as many steps as feasible to minimize these kinds of biases. Unlike Janis's earlier work, we completely separated the coding of the explanatory variables from the outcome variables, with the former conducted by the principal investigators in the project using extensive case-study procedures and the latter coming from expert coders who were kept blind to the research hypotheses. In addition, all of the explanatory variables coded here were done based upon prespecified operational definitions, meaning that we looked for exactly the same kind of evidence and indicators for each of these variables across every case.

These limitations notwithstanding, the data presented here provide the most rigorous assessment to date of the relationship between the quality of decision making and the quality of outcomes. While Janis provided the seminal research in this area by investigating a handful of typifying cases, the evidence we have presented in this chapter goes much further. Not only is the pattern clear and significant—quality of decision making does matter—but that pattern holds even when accounting for several important state- and system-level variables. Indeed, in most of the analyses here, the decision-making variables are the most important predictors of outcome. This research has taken us systematically inside the "black box" of decision making. The evidence indicates that the quality of what happens there matters very much.

Seven

INDIVIDUAL-LEVEL FACTORS
AFFECTING THE QUALITY OF
DECISION MAKING

Overview and Methodological Issues

The case studies and data presented in the last three chapters demonstrate that group structures and decision processes have important effects on foreign-policy making: the quality of decision making has a direct, probabilistic, and measurable effect on the quality of the outcome. In this chapter, we look further back in the causal chain and investigate the following question: do psychological characteristics of the leader have an effect on the quality of decision making in his or her administration?

As we argued in chapters 2 and 3, it makes intuitive sense that who sits at the pinnacle of the government will affect not only what gets done in terms of policy but also how things get done in terms of process. It is easy to imagine different effects on policy and process under states headed by such leaders as Hitler, Clinton, or Gandhi. In this chapter, we present data that systematically assess that intuitive proposition.

This is not an easy proposition to test, and there are important limits in our data that will confine our assessments. Perhaps the most important of these limits is the number of leaders involved in our cases. While our dataset represents thirty-nine total cases, there are only nine individual leaders among those cases (Ford, Carter, Reagan, G. H. W. Bush, Clinton, G. W. Bush, Rabin, Begin, and Thatcher). This places some statistical constraints on the analysis. In addition, while those nine leaders were clearly important in their respective administrations, there were also other personalities involved in each episode. Our analysis in this chapter includes only psychological traits of the leaders themselves; each is, presumably, the central personality in their respective administrations. In addition, looking at other personalities would open a Pandora's box of methodological and statistical issues that could quickly make such a project unmanageable or even impossible given constraints on time and resources. But it is easy to see that omitting other decision makers results necessarily in underspecified models.

Given these limitations, is it worthwhile even to walk down this path, looking at the role of personalities in decision making? We believe it is, and, in the end, we let the data speak for themselves. But before we get to that point, let us make a couple of additional observations about the data and cases included in our analysis. Though having only nine leaders in the study is clearly a limitation, it is still more than has been included in any earlier study. Some scholars (Janis 1972, 1982; Preston 1997) conducted case studies pertaining to these questions and looked at only one or a few leaders. One earlier quantitative project investigating a similar question (Schafer 1999) included only five leaders in the analysis.

One thing that facilitates statistical analysis in the current dataset is that the unit of analysis remains the case, not the leader. Each occasion for decision in our data is a unique event, and as our cases and data analyses have shown, there is significant variance in processes and outcomes across the set of cases. This is true even within administrations, as seen in the Reagan cases discussed in chapters 4 and 5.

It is also possible that a leader's psychological traits may change over time. This may happen due to such psychological phenomena as learning, stimulus-response, maturation, regression, or structural adaptation, among others. Some conceive of personality traits as being relatively fixed, while others conceive of them as malleable or situation dependent (regarding this "trait-state" debate, see Mischel 1968, 1977; Bem and Allen 1974). It may also happen that one individual's traits will change notably, while another individual's will remain relatively consistent over time. While we do not purport to resolve these issues with our data, our research design allows for the possibility that traits may change or become more salient in one or another time period. Specifically, using the "at-a-distance" psychological-assessment techniques discussed in chapter 2, we measure each leader's traits for each individual case of decision in our dataset. This gives us variance on the psychological variables and on the process and outcome variables for each case and allows for statistical analysis across all thirty-nine cases.

As discussed in chapter 2, at-a-distance methods use a subject's verbal material as the basis for assessing psychological characteristics. The general idea is that what a person says and how he or she says it will give some indication of that person's underlying psychological characteristics. As the old expression suggests, we surmise that someone is an optimist when they refer to the glass as half full. In this study we are employing the traits in Margaret Hermann's (1999) Leadership-Trait Analysis (LTA) construct. The specific traits included are: *Belief in Ability to Control Events, Need for Power, Self-Confidence, In-Group Bias, Task Focus, Conceptual Complexity*, and *Distrust*. Each of these was discussed in chapter 3.

We used verbal material from press conferences and interviews as the source for the trait scores. This material is more spontaneous and directly attributable to the leader than material found in prepared speeches and thus should better reflect the leader's underlying psychological characteristics. We collected every press conference and interview available in the three months immediately preceding the onset of each case in our dataset. This provided unique, time-specific measurements for each leader for each individual case. Using material before the onset of the actual case avoids the endogeneity problem where causal direction cannot be determined. If we used material during the actual episode, then the case itself might be having a causal effect on the leader's traits instead of vice versa.

Preliminary Analysis: Leader-Based Data

Before moving onto the data using the case as the unit of analysis, we present some descriptive data that is organized by each leader. These are mean scores that average the data across all the cases in our dataset for each leader. Keep in mind while considering these data that each leader varies across the individual indicators.[1] For example, a leader whose average outcome score is poor will not necessarily have produced only poor outcomes.

Table 7.1 presents data on each leader regarding four variables: *Group-Structural Faults, Decision-Processing Faults, National-Interest Outcomes*, and *Level-of-Conflict Outcomes*. Among our nine leaders, Rabin and Thatcher had the fewest *Group-Structural Faults*, each scoring just one fault. Others scoring well on this variable include: Clinton (1.8), Carter (2.0), and G. H. W. Bush (2.75). On the other end, the most problematic group structures were found in the Reagan administration (5.83) and the G. W. Bush administration (5.8). Reagan also scored poorly in the average

Table 7.1   Decision-making variables and outcome variables per leader

Leader	Group-structural faults	Decision-processing faults	National interest	Level of international conflict
Ford	3.50	3.50	2.49	3.77
Carter	2.00	1.33	3.04	2.88
Reagan	5.83	3.58	2.83	3.53
G. H. W. Bush	2.75	3.25	3.60	3.45
Clinton	1.80	1.20	3.64	2.99
G. W. Bush	5.80	4.80	2.37	3.96
Rabin	1.00	0.00	4.45	3.30
Begin	3.50	5.00	3.45	4.28
Thatcher	1.00	2.50	3.79	4.14

number of *Decision-Processing Faults* (3.58), though by far the worst average scores on this variable belong to Begin (5) and G. W. Bush (4.8). Those with the fewest *Decision-Processing Faults* were Rabin, whose administration had none in the Entebbe case; Clinton, who averaged only 1.2 per case; and Carter, at 1.33.

We turn now to the *Outcome* variables. The Entebbe case resulted in a score of 4.45 for the Rabin administration, the highest score on this variable for any of the presidents and prime ministers in the sample. Several others clustered close together in the next tier, though well below Rabin's score: Thatcher (3.79), Clinton (3.64), G. H. W. Bush (3.60), and Begin (3.45). G. W. Bush has the distinction of earning the lowest average outcome score in terms of *National Interests* (2.37), though not far behind are Ford (2.49) and Reagan (2.83). In terms of *Level of International Conflict*, the highest scores (that is, the most conflict) belong to Begin (4.28) and Thatcher (4.14), not surprisingly, since all four of the cases for these two leaders resulted in significant military escalations. Four U.S. presidents cluster together in the next tier: G. W. Bush (3.96), Ford (3.77), Reagan (3.53), and G. H. W. Bush (3.45). The lowest conflict scores belong to Carter (2.88) and Clinton (2.99).

We can see some of the patterns we identified in chapter 6 made manifest in the average leader data here. For instance, those leaders who averaged the most *Group-Structural Faults* (Reagan and G. W. Bush) were also among those averaging the poorest outcomes in terms of *National Interests*. The two U.S. administrations that averaged the lowest number of *Decision-*

Table 7.2   Psychological-trait scores per leader

Leader	Control	Power	Self-confidence	In-group bias	Task	Complexity	Distrust
Ford	.280	.240	.560	.200	.800	.730	.00070
Carter	.318	.237	.537	.198	.793	.693	.00068
Reagan	.358	.208	.505	.155	.778	.664	.00107
G. H. W. Bush	.348	.245	.513	.193	.785	.660	.00085
Clinton	.364	.276	.498	.174	.794	.686	.00060
G. W. Bush	.364	.272	.372	.220	.760	.720	.00194
Rabin	.310	.230	.690	.230	.650	.650	.00180
Begin	.440	.270	.350	.195	.570	.665	.00190
Thatcher	.325	.265	.490	.190	.755	.625	.00070

Processing Faults (Clinton and Carter) also averaged the lowest scores on the conflict scale.

Now let us turn to our trait scores by looking at the averages by each leader across all seven of our psychological traits. These data are presented in table 7.2. The first trait is *Belief in Ability to Control Events*. This is the extent to which the leader sees himself or herself in control of situations. We anticipate that high scores on this trait will correlate with poorer decision-making processes, because these leaders "will want to maintain control over decision making," and "are less likely to delegate" to others (Hermann 1999, 14). Among our nine leaders, the highest score belongs to Menachem Begin at .44. The next three highest scores are close together and belong to U.S. presidents: Clinton (.364), Reagan (.358), and G. H. W. Bush (.348). Gerald Ford has the lowest control orientation (.280), followed by Rabin (.310) and Carter (.318).

Need for Power is about having an impact on others and enhancing one's power and influence. High scores on this trait indicate individuals who will challenge conventional constraints (Hermann 1999, 10) and "are good at sizing up situations and sensing what tactics will work to achieve goals" (Hermann 1999, 16). Such leaders may get the most out of subordinates, push them to perform at high levels, and make the most of situations, things that seem likely to improve the quality of decision making. Four of the leaders in our sample cluster near the top: Clinton (.276), G. W. Bush (.272), Begin (.270), and Thatcher (.265). The lowest score on this trait by far is Reagan, at .208.

Self-Confidence is "an individual's image of his or her ability to cope adequately with objects and persons in the environment" (Hermann 1999, 20). Conceptually speaking, this variable may affect decision making in different directions, thus resulting in rival hypotheses. High self-confidence, perhaps manifested as self-righteousness or overconfidence, may make one "immune to incoming information from the environment" (Hermann 1999, 21), which would lead to poorer-quality decision making. However, high self-confidence may manifest as healthy self-esteem, "which is involved in regulating the extent to which the self system is maintained under conditions of strain" (Ziller et al. 1977, 177). An individual who reacts well to pressure because of self-confidence may maintain a better decision-making apparatus and elicit more efficient processes from advisors. Supporting the directionality of this latter hypothesis, Hermann (1999, 22) discusses how those who score low in self-confidence may "compensate for feelings of inadequacy . . . (and) become the agents" of others who "can help to enhance their self-confidence." Such a situation may open the leader to manipulation by others. A cursory glance at the data here provides initial support for the latter hypothesis. G. W. Bush's score is among the lowest on *Self-Confidence*, coinciding with his poor scores on *Group Structures* and *Decision Processes*, while Rabin and Carter, whose structures and processes were very good, are near the top on *Self-Confidence*. Of course, in order to assess this pattern more systematically, we will need to consider the statistical models in the following section.

In-Group Bias is another trait that gives us rival hypotheses regarding its effect on the quality of decision making. Scoring high on this trait is "a view of the world in which one's own group (social, political, ethnic, etc.) holds center stage. There are strong emotional attachments to this in-group" (Hermann 1999, 29). Hermann expects that *In-Group Bias* will result in biased information processing, particularly toward external actors. This would correlate with lower-quality decision making. However, Hermann's conception of the variable also suggests that higher in-group bias may result in positive in-group maintenance. Higher involvement with and reliance upon the advisory in-group may work to enhance teamwork and empower dissenters, which would correlate with higher-quality decision making. Preliminary analysis based upon the leader data in table 7.2 does not help much in sorting out these rival hypotheses. Low scorers on *In-Group Bias* include one leader who averaged poorly and one who averaged much better on decision-making quality (Clinton). Similarly, among the high scorers on *In-Group Bias* are Rabin (high-quality decision making) and G. W. Bush (low-quality decision making).

Recall that our next trait, *Task Focus*, is a continuum having two poles: a leader scoring on one end is task-oriented, while someone scoring on the other end is focused on relationship building. High scores on this trait indicate leaders who are "always pushing a group to work on solving the particular problem of the moment . . . constantly asking for movement on a project . . . [and] for options to deal with a problem" (Hermann 1999, 26). These characteristics—problem solving, focusing on the task, and pushing for options—would seem to result in higher-quality decision making. On the other hand, low scores on this trait indicate leaders who focus on the "morale and spirit" of the group and "foster a sense of collegiality" (Hermann 1999, 26–27), things that may contribute to groupthink, according to Janis (1972, 1982). The three lowest scores (not task oriented) on this trait belong to our three non-U.S. leaders: Begin (.570), Rabin (.650), and Thatcher (.755). Among the U.S. presidents, G. W. Bush scores the lowest (.760), while Ford (.800), Clinton (.794), and Carter (.793) are the most task oriented.

Conceptual Complexity is the propensity "to differentiate things and people in one's environment" (Hermann 1999, 10). People higher in complexity are thought of as information seekers and open to alternative explanations and possibilities. Because of this, we might expect that higher-complexity individuals would have higher-quality decision-making structures and processes. However, the descriptive data on our nine leaders gives us a few surprises. G. W. Bush, who has a poor average on decision-making quality, scored near the top on *Conceptual Complexity*, while Rabin, who had very high quality decision making, scored near the bottom on this trait.

Our final trait is *Distrust*. As defined by Hermann (1999, 31), this "involves a general feeling of doubt, uneasiness, misgiving and wariness about others—an inclination to suspect the motives and actions of others." As we discussed in chapter 3, we expect that those scoring high in *Distrust* are likely to have poorer-quality decision making than those scoring lower. This is the case for at least two reasons. First, individuals who are distrusting may not adequately rely on others, delegate tasks, or trust the information provided by others within the advisory system. Second, a distrusting individual may be reticent to seek or believe information coming in from outside sources. G. W. Bush scores highest on *Distrust* (.00194), followed closely by Begin (.00190), both of whom generally had poor decision-making quality in their cases. Clinton (.00060) and Carter (.00068) score lowest on *Distrust,* which coincides with their generally high-quality decision making.

The data on the leaders' traits allow us to make some other assessments of the leaders based upon the distribution of their scores. As we discussed above, it is possible that there will be variation in the stability of traits across the different leaders. This is fairly easily assessed by looking at the standard deviations for each leader within each trait category. For instance, within the trait *Belief in Ability to Control Events,* G. H. W. Bush had the lowest standard deviation, meaning that his scores on this trait were the most stable across the leaders. On the other hand, Reagan's standard deviation on this trait was the highest, meaning that his scores across his cases varied more than any of the others.

It would consume too much time and space to go through each trait and discuss each leader's standard deviations on all of them. However, it is possible to aggregate this data in a way that may be helpful and provide some insights. We rank-ordered the standard deviations from most stable (1) to least stable (8) for the eight leaders on all seven traits.[2] We then simply computed a mean ranking score for each leader, which gives us an indication of each leader's average ranking on trait stability compared to the other leaders. This simple data is presented in table 7.3, with the leaders ranked in order of their average trait stability. Ford, Carter, Begin, and Clinton top the table, indicating that their traits were on average more stable across the dataset than the others. Reagan has the lowest average trait stability, followed by Thatcher and G. W. Bush.

These data indicate at least two things pertaining to our analysis. First, they demonstrate that there is indeed variance in trait stability across the

Table 7.3   Leaders ranked by trait stability

Leader	Average ranking on trait stability
Ford	2.43
Begin	3.57
Carter	3.57
Clinton	4.14
G. H. W. Bush	4.71
G. W. Bush	5.43
Thatcher	5.71
Reagan	6.43

Note: Lower scores indicate higher average trait stability.

different leaders. While all eight leaders had scores that varied across their cases, some varied more than others. This provides some support for our decision to use case-specific trait data for each leader. Second, the data here may have some substantive implications regarding our assessment of factors affecting the quality of decision making. Note a subtle pattern in this trait stability data: Reagan and G. W. Bush both tended to have less stable traits than most of the others, and both scored poorly on average regarding the quality of decision making in their administrations. On the other hand, Carter and Clinton are among the more stable leaders in terms of their traits, and they both tended to have higher-quality decision making. This pattern certainly is not perfect. For instance, Begin, who had problematic decision-making quality, has fairly stable traits. In addition, this pattern was discerned inductively rather than deductively (we simply found it in the data; it is not something for which we he had an a priori hypothesis). None-theless, the pattern among the leaders regarding trait stability and quality decision making is at least somewhat suggestive. Perhaps less stability in a leader's traits results in mixed messages to advisors or inconsistent signaling regarding components of the decision-making process. Though derived in-ductively, this pattern may be a fruitful area for future research.

It is also possible to conduct a type of outlier analysis with this data. This assesses which of our nine leaders on average are "most typical" and which are "most different" from the others. To conduct this analysis, we calculated the mean score in the dataset for each individual trait and then used that score to compute z-scores for each leader on each trait.[3] After that we simply averaged the absolute value of each z-score for each leader across all seven

Table 7.4   Leaders' average trait deviation

Leader	Average absolute value Z-scores
Begin	1.339227
Rabin	1.234866
G. W. Bush	0.908596
Ford	0.746471
Thatcher	0.498387
Carter	0.444731
Clinton	0.433806
Reagan	0.397083
G. H. W. Bush	0.256089

Note: Higher scores indicate higher average trait deviations from the sample mean scores.

traits. The result for each leader is a score that indicates on average how much that leader deviated from the sample's average on each of the seven traits. These results can be seen in table 7.4.

Outlier analysis can be helpful in looking for unusual patterns in the data. For instance, note that the two leaders with the highest average deviation on the trait scores are Begin and Rabin, the two Israeli leaders in the dataset. The only other non-U.S. leader, Margaret Thatcher, in the dataset, however, is not much of an outlier, ranking fifth—or right in the middle— of our nine leaders. It is not much of a surprise that the two Israeli leaders deviate on average more than the Anglo-American leaders. It seems likely that different cultural patterns, linguistic patterns, and political patterns could manifest themselves in the psychology of the leaders there. Knowing that these two leaders are outliers leads us to test our psychological models in the following section both with and without the Israeli cases, to look for spurious effects. However, while both score high on our outlier analysis, note that this does not appear to correlate with quality of decision making: Rabin scored high on decision-making quality, while Begin did not.

The most perplexing leader in this outlier analysis is G. W. Bush, who has the highest pattern of deviation among the non-Israeli leaders, averaging nearly a standard deviation away from the mean across the seven traits ($m = .91$). Bush is significantly different from average (more than one standard deviation) on four of the seven traits. He is significantly below average on *Self-Confidence* and significantly above average on *In-Group Bias*, *Conceptual Complexity*, and *Distrust*. We are not certain what to make of this, though we note that except for his level of *Conceptual Complexity*, his outlying traits are generally not ones that we expect to correlate with high-quality decision making. Combining his pattern as an outlier with his pattern of low trait stability may make G. W. Bush an interesting subject for future research as well.

Overall, this leader-aggregated data has demonstrated at least two things. First, there is broad variation, perhaps in patterned ways, across these leaders on psychological traits, decision-making procedures, and outcomes. Second, these results also reveal additional questions and uncertainties and demonstrate some limitations of using leader-aggregated data. When we average the data to the level of the leader, we see some variables that do not work in the expected direction, such as *Conceptual Complexity*; some that do not seem to show any apparent patterns, such as *In-Group Bias*; and some that seem to have clear patterns yet include obvious outliers, such as *Belief in Ability to Control Events*, which had two low scorers with high-quality decision making (Rabin and Carter), as expected, but one high scorer (Clinton) who also had high-quality decision making. In addition, several leaders had combinations of traits that seem to be at odds in terms of affecting the quality of decision making, such as Rabin, a low *Control* and high *Task-Oriented* leader, which correctly predict his administration's high-quality decision making, but who is also high on *Distrust*, which predicts the opposite. While for analytical purposes it might be nice if all leaders fell into one of four or five personality types, in reality there are numerous possible combinations of traits for any single individual. It is further complicated by the fact that leaders' traits change over time, with some changing more than others. It is appropriate, then, to move onto our case-specific data for more rigorous and systematic analysis, with particular attention paid to multivariate analysis.

Psychological Traits and Quality Decision Making

In this section, we change the analytical focus from the individual leader to the individual case. As discussed above, we use case-specific trait data for each case, which incorporates into the analysis any trait changes by leaders over time. The analytical frame then becomes the effect of a leader's psychological traits (at one particular time) upon the decision-making quality (in one particular case), thus making the case the unit of analysis. We begin with some simple bivariate analyses that correlate each of the seven traits with our two variables marking the quality of decision making: *Group-*

Table 7.5   Bivariate correlations: Traits by decision-making faults

Traits	Group-structural faults	Decision-processing faults
Belief in ability to control events	.074 (.65)	−.031 (.85)
Need for power	−.267 (.10)	−.075 (.65)
Self-confidence	−.188 (.25)	−.190 (.24)
In-group bias	−.233 (.15)	−.166 (.31)
Task orientation	−.074 (.66)	−.188 (.25)
Complexity	.100 (.55)	.230 (.16)
Distrust	.350 (.03)	.408 (.01)

Note: Cell values are Pearson's correlations with p values in parentheses; p values are two-tailed significance tests.

Structural Faults and *Decision-Processing Faults*. These results can be seen in table 7.5.

Only *Distrust* is significantly correlated with both decision-making scales: higher levels of *Distrust* correlate with more *Group-Structural Faults* ($p = .03$) and with more *Decision-Processing Faults* ($p = .01$). *Need for Power* has the same sign (direction) for each decision-making variable—higher *Need for Power* may result in fewer decision-making faults—but the correlation only approaches significance with *Group Structures* ($p = .10$). Three of the other traits (*Self-Confidence*, *In-Group Bias*, and *Task Focus*) are directionally consistent with theoretical expectations but are not significant.

The results among these correlations are not strong, and several questions remain. Two of the seven variables are particularly puzzling: *Belief in Ability to Control Events*, which does not show any patterned relationship with quality decision making, and *Conceptual Complexity*, which is opposite the direction expected (though the p values are not significant). Hermann's (1999) theoretical work on these traits provides some additional insight. While she frequently discusses how these traits work individually as explanatory variables, she also points out that sometimes they work in specific combinations. One combination she identifies involves *Belief in Ability to Control Events* and a separate one involves *Conceptual Complexity*.

Hermann argues that *Belief in Ability to Control Events* often works in combination with *Need for Power* in explaining whether a leader is likely to challenge or respect constraints in the political arena (Hermann 1999). One combination of these two traits—when the leader is high in *Control* but low in *Power*—may facilitate groupthink and problematic decision-making processes. Leaders with this combination are likely to take charge and dominate the process (high *Control*) without having the political acumen to facilitate good outcomes and get the most out of advisors and subordinates (low *Power*). Hermann suggests that these leaders "will be too direct and open . . . signaling others on how to react without really meaning to" (1999, 12). This paints a picture of a leader who dominates, signals his or her biases to subordinates, and fails to make efficient use of the advisory system, all of which are clearly problematic for decision making.

The other combination of traits that Hermann specifies is *Conceptual Complexity* and *Self-Confidence*. These two traits may work together regarding the leader's openness to contextual information (Hermann 1999, 17). The specific combination of interest here is when a leader's *Self-Confidence*

Table 7.6   Bivariate correlations: Combination variables by decision-making faults

Variable	Group-structural faults	Decision-processing faults
High control and low power	.459 (.00)	.208 (.20)
Self-confidence > complexity	−.082 (.62)	−.302 (.06)

Note: Cell values are Pearson's correlations with p values in parentheses; p values are two-tailed significance tests.

score is greater than his or her score on *Conceptual Complexity*. A leader who sees the world as a complex place may either be indicating that he or she is open to such complexities or that she or he is overwhelmed and perhaps even confused by them. *Self-Confidence* may play a critical mediating role in determining the directional effect of *Conceptual Complexity*. Leaders who are higher in *Self-Confidence* are likely to possess the self-assurance that they can manage the complexities of the world while pursuing their policy objectives. On the other hand, high *Complexity* but low *Self-Confidence* may create a condition where a leader feels overwhelmed and inadequate, leading to poorer individual functioning and increased likelihood of being manipulated by others.

We present the results of correlations using these two combination variables (*High Control and Low Power* and *Self-Confidence > Conceptual Complexity*) in table 7.6.[4] When leaders score high on *Control* but low on *Power*, they are likely to have more *Group-Structural Faults*. This correlation is highly significant ($p < .01$). The direction of the correlation is the same for *Decision-Processing Faults*, though this relationship is not significant ($p = .20$). It appears that leaders having a high *Control* orientation are unlikely to have effective decision-making processes without the mediating effect of high *Need for Power*.

Leaders who have higher *Self-Confidence* than *Conceptual Complexity* end up with fewer *Decision-Processing Faults* in their cases. It appears from this finding that high *Self-Confidence* may indeed play a mediating effect on *Conceptual Complexity*. The correlation has the same sign for *Group-Structural Faults*, but it is not significant ($p = .62$). These two combination variables give us additional information and help solve some of the puzzles in the data thus far, yet questions remain. It is now appropriate to turn to multivariate regression analysis.

Table 7.7   Multivariate models explaining group-structural faults

Psychological characteristics	"Full model"*			"Best model"**		
	b (SE)	Beta	p	b (SE)	Beta	p
Distrust	1428.63 (920.73)	.28	.07	1480.22 (716.97)	.29	.02
In-group bias	−15.11 (17.18)	−.16	.19	−	−	−
Task focus	.37 (6.99)	.01	.48	−	−	−
Self-confidence > complexity	−.98 (.95)	−.17	.15	−	−	−
High control and low power	2.80 (1.33)	.38	.02	3.08 (1.04)	.42	.00

* Adj. R^2 = .222
** Adj. R^2 = .255
Note: As all variables at this stage of the analysis have directional hypotheses, we now report one-tailed tests of significance.

We begin by looking at the effect of our psychological variables on the level of *Group-Structural Faults*. Table 7.7 presents two multivariate OLS models explaining *Group-Structural Faults* in decision making. The first model ("Full Model") includes all seven traits (the two combination variables each incorporate two of the individual traits). The second ("Best Model") is the most efficient model of those tested.

In the "Full Model," four of the five independent variables have the anticipated sign (*Task Focus* does not). Two of the variables seem to matter most. Leaders scoring high on *Distrust* are likely to have more *Group-Structural Faults* in decision making. In addition, those leaders with *High Control and Low Power* are likely to have more *Group-Structural Faults*. The "Full Model" has an adjusted R^2 of .222. The "Best" model includes just two variables (*Distrust* and *High Control and Low Power*), both of which are highly significant, and the model is more efficient, as seen by the higher adjusted R^2 (.255).[5]

Table 7.8 presents the results of two multivariate analyses explaining *Decision-Processing Faults*. In the "Full" model, all five variables have the expected sign and three of them are significant. Higher levels of *Distrust* predict higher levels of *Decision-Processing Faults*. Two other variables predict lower levels of *Decision-Processing Faults*: higher scores on *In-Group Bias* and when *Self-Confidence* is greater than *Conceptual Complexity*. The model has an adjusted R^2 of .233. The "Best Model" increases the efficiency of the model (adjusted R^2 = .271) by including just three variables: *Distrust, In-Group Bias,* and *Self-Confidence > Conceptual Complexity*. All three variables are highly significant in the expected direction.

Table 7.8   Multivariate models explaining decision-processing faults

Psychological characteristics	"Full model"*			"Best model"**		
	b (SE)	Beta	p	b (SE)	Beta	p
Distrust	1353.60 (744.20)	.33	.04	1564.46 (603.52)	.38	.01
In-group bias	−27.73 (13.89)	−.37	.03	−30.06 (11.64)	−.40	.01
Task focus	−2.05 (5.65)	−.06	.36	—	—	—
Self-confidence > complexity	−1.72 (.77)	−.37	.02	−1.66 (.74)	−.36	.02
High control and low power	.47 (1.08)	.08	.33	—	—	—

* Adj. R^2 = .233
** Adj. R^2 = .271
Note: For both models, n = 39 and p values are one-tailed significance tests.

We began this chapter by asking if psychological characteristics of the leader have an effect on the quality of decision making in his or her administration. The data in our study demonstrate that the answer to that question is "yes." Six of the seven traits included in the analyses factored into the multivariate models explaining one or both of the quality-of-decision-making variables. The psychological variables that significantly affect levels of *Group-Structural Faults* are higher levels of Distrust and when the leader has a high level of *Control* but a low *Need for Power*. The variables that significantly affect the level of *Decision-Processing Faults* are higher scores on *Distrust*, lower scores on *In-Group Bias*, and when *Self-Confidence* is greater than *Conceptual Complexity*. Put somewhat differently, what these data have shown is that specific, discernible personality characteristics of those who sit at the pinnacle of government do matter. Leaders' underlying psychological propensities are likely to have an effect on the organization and operation of the government's decision-making process.

Although this has been our primary question in this chapter, readers may recall from chapter 3 that it is also possible that leader psychology will have an effect on outcomes in addition to processes. For instance, a distrusting leader may be more likely to escalate a conflict than a leader who is more trusting, or a power-oriented leader may be more successful at getting things done than a non-power-oriented leader. Our data allow for this to be investigated, and we now turn to such analyses.

Psychological Traits and Decision Outcomes

Do the psychological traits of leaders affect the outcomes of decisions made by their administrations in terms of *National Interests* or *Level of International Conflict?* While we earlier expressed some reservations about discerning effects of psychological characteristics on decision-making processes, here the reservations are even greater. The outcome of any decision is not only influenced by the leader but is also at least in part dependent upon those who must implement the decision and upon the actions of others in the international arena. The leader of a state has much less control and influence over those factors than she or he does over internal decision-making processes. Yet a leader's psychological dispositions would not seem to be irrelevant in affecting decision outcomes. For instance, one leader's psychological characteristics might influence a decision by his or her state to quickly escalate a conflict, while another leader's characteristics might lead to a more patient, searching strategy. While it is the case that decision outcomes are influenced by a greater number of uncontrolled factors, it is still worthwhile to look in our data for patterns of outcomes associated with the traits we have investigated.

Recall that our two outcome variables, *National Interest* and *Level of International Conflict*, were coded for each case in our dataset by outside foreign-policy experts. The experts judged some cases as having advanced the national interest while others were seen as hindering national interests,

Table 7.9   Bivariate correlations: Psychological variables by outcomes

Psychological characteristic	National interests	Conflict level
Belief in ability to control events	−.075 (.65)	.030 (.86)
Need for power	.103 (.53)	.080 (.63)
Self-confidence	.215 (.19)	−.203 (.22)
In-group bias	−.102 (.54)	.136 (.41)
Task orientation	.027 (.87)	−.183 (.26)
Complexity	−.241 (.14)	.184 (.26)
Distrust	−.176 (.28)	.372 (.02)
Self-confidence > complexity	.225 (.17)	−.277 (.09)
High control and low power	−.150 (.36)	.042 (.80)

Note: Cell values are Pearson's correlations with p values in parentheses; p values are two-tailed significance tests.

Table 7.10   Multivariate models explaining national interests

Psychological characteristics	"Full model"*			"Best model"**		
	b (SE)	Beta	p	b (SE)	Beta	p
Distrust	−97.22 (338.02)	−.06	.39	—	—	—
In-group bias	−4.43 (6.31)	−.15	.24	—	—	—
Task focus	−.64 (2.57)	−.05	.40	—	—	—
Self-confidence > complexity	.42 (.35)	.23	.12	.53 (.30)	.29	.04
High control and low power	−.65 (.49)	−.28	.09	−.54 (.39)	−.23	.09

* Adj. R^2 = −.017
** Adj. R^2 = .049
Note: For both models, n = 39 and p values are one-tailed significance tests.

and they judged some decisions as having resulted in higher levels of international conflict while others resulted in lower levels. Their ratings are the dependent variables in the analyses in this section. We begin as we did in the previous section, with simple bivariate correlations between the psychological variables and the two outcome variables. The results are presented in table 7.9.

The direction of most of the correlations between the psychological variables and *National Interest* are in the expected direction, but none are significant. Regarding the *Level of International Conflict*, while again most of the correlations have signs we expect, only one is significant, while another approaches significance. Higher scores on *Distrust* correlate with a higher *Level of International Conflict* (p = .02), while lower levels of conflict may come about when the leader's *Self-Confidence* is greater than her or his *Conceptual Complexity* (p = .09).

Turning now to OLS multivariate analysis, we see the results of two models explaining the *National-Interest* outcome in table 7.10. In the "Full Model," only one variable approaches significance (*High Control and Low Power*, p = .09), and the model is highly inefficient, even generating a negative adjusted R^2 (−.017). The "Best Model" improves upon the full version in that one variable is significant (*Self Confidence > Complexity*, p = .04), the other approaches significance (*High Control and Low Power*, p = .09), and the adjusted R^2 is positive, though the model is not a strong one (adjusted R^2 = .049). While there are some patterns among the psychological variables that explain *National-Interest* outcomes, these variables do not take us very far in explaining variance in the dependent variable.

Table 7.11 Multivariate models explaining level of international conflict

Psychological characteristics	"Full model"* b (SE)	Beta	p	"Best model"** b (SE)	Beta	p
Distrust	352.80 (240.84)	.29	.08	378.74 (191.45)	.32	.03
In-group bias	.60 (4.49)	.03	.45	—	—	—
Task focus	−.05 (1.83)	−.01	.49	—	—	—
Self-confidence > complexity	−.26 (.25)	−.19	.15	−.24 (.22)	−.18	.14
High control and low power	.12 (.35)	.07	.37	—	—	—

* Adj. R^2 = −.044
** Adj. R^2 = .121
Note: For both models, n = 39 and p values are one-tailed significance tests.

The psychological variables perform slightly better in explaining the *Level of International Conflict*, as seen in table 7.11. In the "Full Model," higher scores on *Distrust* correlate positively with the *Level of International Conflict* (p = .08), meaning that leaders who are more distrusting may end up with higher conflict levels as a result of their decisions, though the relationship only approaches significance. The adjusted R^2 for the model is an unimpressive .044. The "Best Model," which includes *Self Confidence > Complexity*, improves the efficiency of the model. *Distrust* is significant in the expected direction, and the adjusted R^2 is a respectable .121.

These data demonstrate that the leader's psychological traits play a role in explaining the quality of decision outcomes, though their effect is much less than in the models explaining decision-making faults. As discussed, this is not a surprise given that leaders have more influence over the process of decision making within their administrations than in the outcomes of their decisions, which involve many other international factors. *Distrust* and the two combination variables are the psychological constructs that most affect decision outcomes. While the results here are not strong, they provide enough support for the general proposition to warrant additional investigation in future projects. Additional research might include models that add more domestic actors, such as key advisors, and perhaps external actors as well. All of the psychological data in this project have been monadic, meaning they looked only at one side of the case. Yet outcomes are also likely to be influenced by actors on the other side of the dyad, and it is possible to conceive of a research design that incorporates both sides in a better-specified model.

Conclusion

In this chapter, we tested the effects of several different psychological characteristics on decision-making processes and decision outcomes. A number of the psychological variables mattered in explaining these different dependent variables. The psychological characteristic that had the strongest effect in these data is *Distrust*. Higher levels of *Distrust* resulted in more *Group-Structural* faults, more *Decision-Processing* faults, and a higher *Level of International Conflict*. In all of these models, *Distrust* was significant even when controlling for all of the other psychological variables. A leader who has a high level of *Distrust* is not likely to have effective decision-making processes and is likely to generate more conflict in the world.

In-Group Bias, on the other hand, correlates with better decision-making processes. Those with higher scores on *In-Group Bias* had significantly fewer *Decision-Processing* faults and fewer *Group-Structural* faults, though the latter only approached significance. Recalling that we generated two rival hypotheses for this variable, the data here support the view that this variable is tapping into psychological propensities that enhance and empower the advisory in-group. There was no directional support for the hypothesis, suggesting that this variable would correlate with increased biases and poorer decision-making quality. There are some clear discordant challenges in trying to manage the decision-making process. For instance, leaders need to foster critical thinking, discourage sycophant behavior, and encourage devil's advocates while at the same time building trust, teamwork, and helpful communication patterns among advisors. These kinds of things may be discordant, but they are not antithetical. In other words, as our data in chapter 6 demonstrate, it is possible to facilitate each of these different factors and have very good decision-making quality. A propensity to have a positive focus on the advisory in-group, as the data on this trait suggest, seems to lead to better decision-making structures and procedures.

The other two psychological variables investigated in this chapter that have significant effects are the two combination variables. Ten years ago, Margaret Hermann (1999) was wise to speculate that some traits may matter most when working in combination. In her system, she only identified two specific combinations, the ones we included in our analysis here, though it is possible to imagine testing others as well. It turns out that her wisdom was well placed. When a leader's *Self-Confidence* score is greater than her or his *Conceptual Complexity* score, good things generally happen: there are fewer *Decision-Processing* faults and *National-Interest* outcomes tend to be enhanced, both of which are statistically significant. There also tend to be fewer *Group-Structural* faults and a lower *Level of International Conflict*, though those only approached significance. It appears from this that *Self-Confidence* has a mediating effect on *Conceptual Complexity*. When *Self-Confidence* is higher, it helps the leader handle the strains and complexities of the international system. When *Self-Confidence* is lower, the leader may get overwhelmed or overly anxious in dealing with the complex world. A leader with low self-confidence may also, as part of a compensatory process, be manipulated more easily by others who have ulterior motives or wish to circumvent the decision-making process, even if that leader sees the world in complex terms.

When a leader has a high *Control* orientation and low *Need for Power*, this results in more *Group-Structural* faults, more *Decision-Processing* faults, and poorer outcomes in terms of the *National Interest*. All three of these are statistically significant findings while controlling for the other psychological variables in the study. This combination variable also seems to have a compensatory component to it. A high *Control* orientation on its own was not statistically significant, but when combined with a low *Need for Power*, it is particularly problematic. As Hermann describes the *Need for Power*, it is about accomplishing things, getting the most out of people and situations, and being politically astute. These factors would seem to help compensate for a leader who is high on *Control*. If the *Control*-oriented leader's propensities to dominate and to fail to delegate are not checked by the positive, facilitating characteristics associated with a high *Need for Power*, the decision-making process ends up with more faults.

Three important criteria that are necessary for assessing causation in a hypothesis test are (1) Temporal ordering: does the independent variable temporally precede the dependent variable? (2) Association: are the independent and dependent variables correlated in some way? and (3) Plausibility: is the relationship between the independent and dependent variables theoretically grounded? The data presented in this chapter meet these three criteria as discussed in earlier sections and support the general proposition that the psychological characteristics of the leader have an effect on the decision-making process and, to a lesser extent, the outcome ratings of a decision. Our conclusions regarding these data are somewhat reserved. While meeting appropriate levels of significance, our results in this chapter are not as robust as those reported in our analyses of group structures and decision processes in chapter 6. In addition, the data are limited because there are only nine subjects in the dataset.

These kinds of reservations and hesitations are an appropriate part of social-science inquiry, but they do not negate the findings reported here. Indeed, the patterns presented in this chapter are real and represent true relationships between psychological characteristics and our dependent variables in this dataset. In addition, the results are positive enough and provocative enough to warrant additional research in this area. Among these cases, psychological characteristics affected the decision-making process and the outcomes of cases in theoretically driven, statistically significant, patterned ways. Certainly much research remains to be done. We expect to continue investigating these areas, and we encourage other scholars to take up these questions as well; it is a fruitful research area. Based upon these data, other schools of thought in the field of international relations that ignore the effect of individuals do so at the risk of positing underspecified models, while those who look only at individuals clearly run the same risk. It appears here that individuals matter in discernible ways, yet, particularly in terms of explaining outcomes, individuals alone do not tell us the whole story.

PART IV

Conclusions

Eight

THE 2003 WAR IN IRAQ

How Flawed Decision Making
Led to Critical Failures

In the preceding chapters, we saw statistically significant relationships that clearly show that the success or failure of policy decisions turns, at least in part, on the quality of the decision making that goes into them. These relationships were found to exist in a large dataset that included cases from nine administrations, three countries, and multiple policy domains over almost thirty years. The more flaws that existed in decision-making structures, the poorer the national-policy outcome turned out to be in terms of national interests. The more flaws that existed in decision-making processes, the more likely it was that a decision would result in an increase in international conflict. In addition, the particular personality characteristics of political leaders pushed them toward specific policy paths. These are general findings existing across many cases of decision making. In this chapter, we return to a specific real-world event to illustrate how these factors came to shape decision making in the most prominent foreign-policy decision in recent memory.

The decision by the Bush administration to go to war in Iraq is arguably the most important foreign-policy decision the world has witnessed since the start of the new millennium — perhaps the most important since the end of the cold war. The stakes involved have been enormous. Current projections are that the war could eventually cost the United States more than three trillion dollars (Stiglitz and Bilmes 2008). While the death toll is a matter of considerable controversy, it appears that hundreds of thousands of Iraqis have died during the war and its aftermath. Millions of Iraqis are refugees, suffering in a host of ways, while putting a destabilizing strain on the countries that host them. Thousands of Americans have been slain, and tens of thousands of Americans have been injured. And positive perceptions of the United States have collapsed. As the summary of the Pew Global Attitudes Project's "Views of a Changing World 2003" stated: "The war has widened the rift between Americans and Western Europeans, further inflamed the Muslim world, softened support for the war on terrorism, and significantly weakened global public support for the pillars of the post–World War II era—the U.N. and the North Atlantic alliance."

Relatedly, in the 2006 National Intelligence Estimate, "Trends in Global Terrorism: Implications for the United States," U.S. intelligence agencies reported that the war was a boon for terrorist recruiters. Through the actions taken in conjunction with the war, and those that may well have been taken or avoided had the war not been started, it seems safe to say that the decision to go to war in Iraq has fundamentally altered the course of several countries and that its effects will resonate in those states for many years to come.

Given the war's momentous effects, understanding why and how the U.S. government chose to prosecute it is extremely important. Great powers do not launch major wars every day. Understanding the circumstances that led to this decision will help us understand what leads a government to embark on a path toward major revisionist policies and why a government would directly challenge the status quo in a way that could lead to great costs, changes in the global power balance, and the creation of new governments.

In considering why the Bush administration elected to invade Iraq and move to war with such haste that a number of potential allies became leery of the endeavor and ultimately chose not to join the United States, we will see that the individuals involved in making the decision, the nature of the situation at hand, the group structures through which the decision was weighed, and the process by which the decision making was carried out all had an effect on the government's choice to go to war. But first it will be helpful to consider the history of the U.S. involvement in Iraq and how the decision-making team that would be responsible for taking the United States to war was formed.

In a sense, the path to war in 2003 can be traced back to decisions made in a different U.S. war with Iraq, which was prosecuted by a different President Bush, twelve years earlier. Many aspects of that war have received much praise. The building of a broad international coalition opposed to the regime of Saddam Hussein and the implementation of major military operations in that conflict were both widely lauded. Furthermore, many agreed with George H. W. Bush and Brent Scowcroft's arguments (laid out in their 1998 book *A World Transformed*) for not proceeding directly to Baghdad to depose Saddam Hussein. However, there has been criticism of the manner in which the war ended. Some say that a few more days of fighting by the coalition could have mortally weakened the forces that Saddam Hussein relied on to rule. Alternatively, greater support for the Iraqi uprisings that President Bush had encouraged in February 1991 might have produced another indirect way of removing Saddam Hussein from power.

Of course, President Bush insisted that removing Saddam Hussein from power was not a goal of the international coalition or of the United States during the 1991 war, so from the standpoint of his administration, perhaps these were not missed opportunities, presuming the administration adopted a "scorekeeping" method of evaluating victory, in which success is determined by a listing of "material gains and losses" (Johnson and Johnson 2006). In fact, it is worth noting that according to Colin Powell the administration wanted "to leave Baghdad with enough power" to contain the threat of a hostile Iran (Mann 2004). But be that as it may, in the spring of 1991, President George H. W. Bush authorized the CIA to spend over $100 million to help remove Saddam Hussein from power (Mayer 2004).

The CIA's actions aimed against Saddam Hussein continued into the mid-1990s and the Clinton administration. Famously, the United States supplied the Iraqi exile Ahmad Chalabi and his Iraqi National Congress with tens of millions of dollars to help undermine Hussein; eventually, the CIA came to decide that Chalabi was a "con man" and a "clever used-car salesman" (Isikoff and Corn 2006, 49–50) and cut off his funding in 1996.

U.S. government action against Saddam Hussein ramped up again after the Republican-controlled Congress passed and President Clinton signed the Iraqi Liberation Act in 1998. This formally committed the United States to regime change, though it did not call for this goal to be achieved through any specific means. Beyond stating a general principle the government hoped would be achieved, its great impact was that it began another round of significant funding of Iraqi opposition groups, with tens of millions of dollars going to various organizations. Chalabi's INC was one of the groups that received substantial additional funding. The INC received over $30 million in the period preceding the G. W. Bush administration's invasion of Iraq.

Of course, many other political actors supported the goal of removing Saddam Hussein from power, and over time many of these people achieved positions of great influence. By the mid-1990s, a band of prominent supporters of this cause had essentially formed a "policy community," a group of people in both the public and private sector who worked to bring this concept to fruition (Mazarr 2007). They assiduously built a network of like-minded individuals in the media, think tanks, and government. They used their influence to keep this issue in the public eye. And they were involved in a number of endeavors that kept the cause a prominent core concern for members of a number of overlapping foreign-policy and political groups.

Aside from Chalabi, who obviously had a great deal to gain personally from any movement to oust Hussein, perhaps the person most persistently arguing for regime change in Iraq was the former Harvard professor Laurie Mylroie. Mylroie went from being a go-between between the Iraqi and Israeli governments—and a supporter of Hussein's rule when the Reagan administration was backing his government in order to balance Iran—to being Hussein's most tenacious critic. She influenced several leading neocons (a collection of politicians and intellectuals who favored a vigorous and often militaristic approach to remaking parts of the world in support of certain political ideas) as well as her former co-author, the *New York Times*'s Judith Miller, with her arguments that Saddam Hussein was behind the 1993 World Trade Center bombing, the Oklahoma City bombing, the 1998 attacks on U.S. embassies in Africa, and the bombing of the *USS Cole*. Of course, U.S. intelligence agencies did not see an Iraqi hand behind all these actions, but Mylroie had become what her former co-author Daniel Pipes terms "monomaniacal" on the subject (Isikoff and Corn 2006, 74), and she had a powerful effect on certain key decision makers and opinion makers. While the FBI and CIA debunked her research in the 1990s, future Deputy Secretary of Defense Paul Wolfowitz, who wrote a blurb on the back cover of her book *Study of Revenge: Saddam Hussein's Unfinished War Against America* and who had carefully studied her work (Keller 2002), took up her cause and even pushed the CIA to reevaluate their position on Mylroie's work once he took up office in the Pentagon (Isikoff and Corn 2006). At the same time, Wolfowitz was annoyed by the White House counterterrorism chief's focus on Osama Bin Laden (Clarke 2004). Mylroie's fervor and the breadth of her connections with future administration officials and the media is a good example of the prioritization that some put on removing Hussein from power in the years before 2003.

The cause of regime change in Iraq was also being taken up by prominent political figures. Some began to write a number of papers and articles making the case for strong action to push Hussein from power. For example, in 1996 Richard Perle (the future chairman of the Bush administration's Defense Policy Board) and Douglas Feith (the future undersecretary of defense for policy) were part of a group that published the paper "A Clean Break: A New Strategy for Securing the Realm," which argued that removing Saddam Hussein from power was important for Israel's security. And on December 1, 1997, *The Weekly Standard*, one of the most influential publications among Republican leaders, published an issue with the cover headline "Saddam Must Go." The accompanying article by Wolfowitz and Zalmay Khalilzad (the future ambassador to Afghanistan, Iraq, and the United Nations) argued that the United States would have to mount a large military operation to accomplish that task.

Less than two months later, on January 26, 1998, eighteen members of an organization that became perhaps the best-known part of this policy community, the Project for the New American Century, sent President Clinton their famous letter, which stated that "removing Saddam Hussein and his regime from power" needed to be American foreign policy. These eighteen included prominent figures in the media (Bill Kristol) and the academy (Francis Fukuyama) as well as a host of prominent individuals who would hold high-ranking posts in the future Bush administration, including Elliot Abrams (who would become deputy national security advisor), Richard Armitage (future deputy secretary of state), John Bolton (future undersecretary of state for arms control and international security and future ambassador to the United Nations), Paula Dobriansky (future undersecretary of state for democracy and global affairs), Khalilzad, Perle, Donald Rumsfeld (future secretary of defense), Wolfowitz, and Robert Zoellick (future U.S. trade representative, deputy secretary of state, and president of the International Bank for Reconstruction and Development). Having long advocated for this cause, it is not surprising that many of these people placed removing Saddam Hussein from power among the goals they hoped George W. Bush's administration would achieve once it took power.

Receiving a top appointment in the Bush administration does not appear to have depended on being motivated primarily by a prioritization of the need to remove Saddam Hussein from power. In fact, if a few top appointments had gone slightly differently, the course of the Bush administration, U.S. foreign policy, and Middle East politics might have been quite different. Consider, for example, the vice presidency. In the summer of 2000, news outlets reported that Governor Bush's final decision came down to a choice between two people—former Senator John Danforth and former Defense Secretary Dick Cheney, the man Bush had tasked to run his search for a vice president (Randall 2000). Danforth was widely respected and from the electorally important "swing state" of Missouri, but Bush chose Cheney because he wanted someone he was certain would be completely loyal (Carney and Dickinson 2000; Kornacki 2007). Cheney was willing to keep Bush's secrets, including, for example, the fact that Bush had decided to pick Cheney before Danforth's name was leaked to the press (Gellman 2008).

But consider how differently things might have gone if Danforth had actually been Bush's pick. If one subscribes to the view that who leads matters, think of how differently things might have gone with a Vice President Danforth. Cheney had long prioritized removing Saddam Hussein from power. Danforth did not similarly prioritize the issue. Cheney suggested Donald Rumsfeld, another person who for years had been involved in the anti-Hussein policy community and someone Cheney had worked with for three decades, for secretary of defense. Without Cheney, that job might have gone to someone who, like Danforth, was not closely associated with the anti-Hussein activists, for example Pennsylvania's governor Tom Ridge, Colin Powell's favorite for the job (Burke 2004). With Danforth as vice president, it might have proven impolitic to name another former "Show Me"-state senator to one of the top administration positions, so someone other than John Ashcroft might have been named attorney general. In short, if even just one appointment had gone differently, the whole look of the Bush administration, and its top priorities, might have been strikingly different, particularly given that Cheney ended up wielding unprecedented power for a vice president and placed his political allies in high positions throughout the various foreign policy–making bureaucracies (Kornacki 2007; Gellman 2008).

But of course Bush did pick Cheney, and even before the U.S. Supreme Court resolved the controversial election, plans for the staffing of the administration proceeded apace, and a host of top foreign-policy jobs were filled by people who had been arguing for years that the United States needed to take strong action that would change the government of Iraq.

Bush picking Cheney because of his unquestionable loyalty fit with the president's high level of *Distrust*, noted in chapter 7. With loyalty being prized above all (Berke 2001), the Bush White House rarely listened to the opinions of outsiders. In fact, the president himself said "I have no outside advice" (Lemann 2004). He was also, in Condoleezza Rice's words, "not a big reader" (Rothkopf 2005, 404). In this situation, the preexisting priorities of those named to high office became all the more important in shaping what path the country would take. As Christopher DeMuth, the president of the American Enterprise Institute put it (Suskind 2004): "The circle around Bush is the tightest around any president in the modern era, and it's both exclusive and exclusionary. It's a too tightly managed decision-making process. When they make decisions, a very small number of people are in the room, and it has a certain effect on constricting the range of alternatives being offered."

There are reports that the possibility of removing Saddam Hussein from power began to be formally discussed at the highest levels of the Bush administration even before the new team was sworn into office. Vice President-Elect Cheney wanted Clinton's defense secretary, William Cohen, to brief the incoming president, and "Topic A should be Iraq" (Woodward 2004, 9). It was also a prominent topic in the first meeting of Bush's National Security Council (Danner 2006). In former Treasury Secretary Paul O'Neill's description of that January 21 meeting, the destabilizing influence of Iraq was a primary topic. CIA Director Tenet even presented a set of grainy surveillance pictures of what he said might be WMD-producing factories. O'Neill's reading of the scene was that from the very first meeting of its top decision-making team, the Bush administration was washing its hands of such longstanding international concerns as peace in Israel and was focusing its energies on Iraq (Suskind 2004). Others have disputed O'Neill's description of events insofar as they imply that the administration was contemplating near-term action against Iraq. But the Deputies Committee of the National Security Council met several times in the spring and summer of 2001 to contemplate ways in which Saddam Hussein's government could be pushed out of power (Woodward 2004). This was, of course, at the same time that the Bush White House's counterterrorism chief was seeing himself demoted, the size of his office cut, and finding it exceedingly difficult to get the principals of the National Security Council to hold a meeting on the threat posed by terrorism and al Qaeda—a meeting he never did get prior to September 11, 2001 (Clarke 2004).

But, of course, that was not the only division in the administration over where the government should be heading on the foreign-policy issues of the day. From January 2001 forward, the foreign-policy team was divided between "an ideologically conservative Pentagon and a more moderate State Department" (Perlez 2001a). Secretary Powell and the State Department made arguments going against the dominant views of others in the administration on issues ranging from North Korea, to peacekeeping in the Balkans, to the Kyoto Protocol. Given the White House's prioritization of loyalty and consensus, even in private, this led to seemingly more loyal aides like John Bolton being "foisted" upon Powell and a public humiliation of Powell by the White House that became "part of Washington lore" (McGeary 2001). This split extended to the Iraq issue, where Powell sought to focus on economic sanctions, while the men at the top of the White House and Pentagon favored a more "muscular" solution to the problem of Saddam Hussein (Sipress and Mufson 2001).

But if the White House had little respect for views that did not match those of the president and the vice president, if it enforced its will to crush dissent within the administration, and if it was holding preliminary meetings on Iraq prior to 9/11, why did it not move more quickly to act militarily against Saddam Hussein? One possibility is that while it was a matter the president appeared somewhat supportive of, he was not elected to be a foreign-policy president in the style of his father. He had famously called for the United States to have a humble foreign policy during the campaign, and the book that espoused the plans of his campaign, A Charge to Keep (1999), only had one reference to Iraq and none whatsoever to Saddam Hussein, terrorists, or terrorism (Woodward 2006). In its early months, much of the White House's action was being directed toward tax cuts, education reform, and matters such as the president's faith-based initiative.

Another possibility is that Powell's wariness over a rush to war, which fit with his longstanding doubts about war as a policy tool (Kaplan 2001), was sufficient to impede other actors who were pushing for it, given the Rice-led National Security Council's inability to manage disputes between the foreign-policy bureaucracies. Whether out of her own inaction or out of lacking sufficient authority from the president, Rice failed again and again to direct the administration onto a settled path on a host of issues where Secretary Powell disagreed with Vice President Cheney and Secretary Rumsfeld. Rice was more loyal to President Bush than to either faction. In addition to being a top aide, she was also a friend who watched movies with the Bush family (Perlez 2001b). She was "like a daughter" to the president (McGeary 2001). But while she had the president's respect and affection, she initially had few resources to enforce the White House's will on feuding decision makers (at the outset of her appointment she chose to cut her staff by one-third, though by the time she left office she would have a staff 50 percent larger than the one she inherited). And she received little help from the president in managing these disputes, no matter how grave the problem was. In one instance during the run-up to the war, when Secretary Rumsfeld was refusing to take her phone calls, the President "teased" Rumsfeld about his unwillingness to talk to his own national security advisor (Woodward 2006, 110). It is little wonder that the 9/11 Commission concluded that Condoleezza Rice's National Security Council was dysfunctional.

But while the president may not have had Iraq at the top of his agenda in the spring and summer of 2001, and while divisions within the administration may have been enough to slow any movement against Saddam Hussein, the 9/11 attacks created a policy window (Kingdon 1984) that those who had long sought to remove Saddam Hussein from power used to pursue their aim (Haney 2005; Mazarr 2007). The 9/11 attacks called for a quick, decisive response. There is evidence that they changed how President Bush looked at the world and how he believed the United States should act in international affairs (Robison 2006). In Secretary Powell's words, it "hit the reset button" on the administration's approach. Deputy Secretary Wolfowitz said the United States had "entered a new era" (Mann 2004, 300). President Bush let it be known that "after September the 11th, the doctrine of containment just doesn't hold any water as far as I'm concerned" (Purdum 2003). The president decided that the unilateralist approach to foreign affairs that he had pursued since his first days in office (Daalder and Lindsay 2003) needed to be wedded to more aggressive and interventionist tactics against those he believed threatened the United States. This presented those who sought regime change in Iraq with a golden opportunity. According to Richard Clarke, President Bush's chief counterterrorism advisor, the Bush administration was set on using Iraq as a test case of the "Bush Doctrine" of military domination and unilateral preventive war as early as September 12 (Haney 2005). An idea that had endured and spread throughout a set of individuals who now held the levers of policy now found itself in a situational environment that not only allowed it to be carried out but appeared to be both politically advantageous and appropriate for the president's newly espoused mission.

In the days following the 9/11 hijackings and murders in Manhattan, Pennsylvania, and Virginia, several policymakers spoke up for attacking Iraq, regardless of the fact that they lacked any clear evidence that Iraq had anything to do with the attacks. Inside the administration, these voices included those of Secretary of Defense Rumsfeld, Deputy Secretary of Defense Wolfowitz, and Lewis "Scooter" Libby (Tyler and Sciolino 2001; Woodward 2002). While largely not known beyond Washington, Libby was an unusually influential figure who held three top titles. He was chief of staff to the vice president, the vice president's top foreign-policy advisor, and an assistant to the president. It was a combination of posts no one person had ever held in American history, and it gave him immense influence. As Barton Gellman (2008, 44) describes Libby: "No one save Cheney and Bush themselves were his superiors. Like every assistant to the president, Libby would see and have the right to challenge any speech, legislation, or executive order before it reached the Oval Office. No reciprocal right came with Card's job, or Rove's, when documents flowed to or from the vice president."

Having such highly placed individuals in the Office of the Vice President and the Office of the Secretary of Defense advocating for a new prioritization on Iraq kept up the pressure on the president, although it appears he too was quickly moving in that direction of his own volition. Richard Clarke has stated that the normally incurious president asked him on September 12 to go over all the information that might possibly link Saddam Hussein to the attacks. Bush said, "I want to know any shred" (Clarke 2004). And on September 13, Pentagon officials were told to update war plans not only for Afghanistan but also for Iraq (Fallows 2004; Rothkopf 2005).

It is hard to know when the decision to go to war with Iraq was made, as there was no decision meeting, and, in fact, Secretary Powell, Secretary Rumsfeld, and CIA Director Tenet have all stated that the president never asked them for their advice on the basic question of whether or not to go to war (Mazarr 2007; Woodward 2006). And, of course, there are ample statements on the record from the decision makers, including President Bush, that any action against Iraq would have to be delayed while the situation in Afghanistan was dealt with. But at the same time, the speed with which attention became focused on Iraq, even though the United States was still involved in a war in Afghanistan and even though Osama bin Laden was still at large, is startling. It is clear that the president was giving serious consideration to going to war with Iraq as early as the days or weeks following the 9/11 attacks (Rothkopf 2005), and he settled his mind on war long before the U.S. invasion in March 2003. Mazarr states, "A de facto regime change decision was made in late 2001" (2007, 7).

Action focusing on Iraq proceeded quickly. By October 2001, the Department of State was engaging in in-depth planning for a transition in the aftermath of regime change in Iraq. This led to the "Future of Iraq" project. At thirteen volumes and twenty-five hundred pages, a great deal of analysis and forethought went into planning for a post-Hussein Iraq, though decision makers at the highest levels largely ignored the report. In fact, in several instances people associated with writing the report were banned from being further involved in U.S. planning or action in Iraq (Fallows 2004; Rothkopf 2005). The White House conducted a "purge" (Ricks 2006, 103). As Armitage described it, the people who ordered it (and it supposedly came from a source higher than Secretary Rumsfeld) did not want people who would let "the facts get into the equation." They wanted people who would, no matter what, hew to "the party line, that we'd be welcomed with garlands" (Ricks 2006, 104).

A certain type of planning and presentation was thus necessary. The Office of the Secretary of Defense wanted a report created on the larger societal, political, and historical forces behind the 9/11 attacks, so in November Rumsfeld's advisor Steve Herbits and Deputy Secretary of Defense Wolfowitz had Christopher DeMuth, the president of the American Enterprise Institute, form a group to strategize and create a report for the administration's foreign-policy principals. It boastfully termed itself Bletchley II, in reference to the center of British intelligence and codebreaking during World War II. This group, which included both former career civil servants and intellectuals such as Fouad Ajami, Bernard Lewis, Fareed Zakaria, and James Q. Wilson, produced "Delta of Terrorism," a report that described a two-generation conflict with "radical Islam." While it noted that other countries, such as Egypt, Saudi Arabia, and Iran, were more important in the battle against radical Islam (Egypt and Saudi Arabia were "the key"), removing Saddam Hussein from power mattered too. And since Saddam Hussein's government was weak and a confrontation with him was inevitable, opening the fight against radical Islam in Iraq would be the most effective way of starting the transformation of the region that many believed was required. And now was the time to prosecute this fight, since its goals would be easier to accomplish in the post-9/11 environment, where fears were heightened and the public's concern with threats from the Middle East had greatly increased. According to Woodward's account, this document had a "strong impact on President Bush," and Rice found it "very, very persuasive" (Woodward 2006, 85). For a president and advisory group already inclined to take action against Saddam Hussein, such rationalizations were key in bringing decision makers together on the need for action and the need to take action soon.

Quickly, the focus of the government moved from dealing with Osama bin Laden and the battles taking place in Afghanistan to prioritizing the removal of Saddam Hussein from power. Units began to be reassigned away from Afghanistan in late 2001. On November 21, 2001, in the midst of fighting in Afghanistan and before the Battle of Tora Bora, after which Osama Bin Laden is presumed to have escaped into Pakistan, President Bush told the Pentagon to revamp its war plan for Iraq (Woodward 2004). Suskind (2006) notes this is when plans for the invasion "officially" began, even though they had been moving forward for some time. Bush also quickly ordered an expansion of CIA covert operations aimed at ousting Saddam Hussein. These programs were allocated $100 to $200 million, "vastly more than the $70 million the CIA spent in Afghanistan" (Woodward 2002, 329).

January 2002 saw the President's famous "Axis of Evil" State of the Union address. In some drafts of the speech, Iraq was the only country mentioned, but it was felt that others needed to be added, as otherwise the implication was that the United States was going to take immediate action. So the "Axis" would be composed of Iraq, North Korea, and Iran. Rice and Stephen Hadley wanted Iran dropped from the grouping, but the president insisted it be included (Woodward 2004). As 2002 went forward, the CIA began a long series of war games (those continued into 2003, though without all the original players, as the Office of the Secretary of Defense banned Defense officials from taking part). There was also a great deal of planning relating to postwar Iraq being conducted at the Army War College. And the military continued to fine tune its plans, a months-long process that drove a deeper and deeper wedge between much of the senior officer corps and the civilians at the Office of the Secretary of Defense.

Bob Woodward's *State of Denial* is filled with stories of the antipathy and downright hostility between the two sets of national-security professionals. The most famous outcome of the split was Rumsfeld announcing the successor to Army Chief of Staff Eric Shinseki fourteen months before the general's term of office ended, essentially making him a lame duck for most of his tenure. But this hostility extended much further and deeper than a

fight between Rumsfeld and Shinseki. Rumsfeld repeatedly made personnel appointments in ways that would undermine the ability of military leaders to give independent advice, whether it was naming people to posts when
they had yet to achieve the flag rank necessary to do their job effectively or
naming deferential types to the most influential advisory posts. He worked
hard to cut the size of the joint staff and wanted its chairman to pass along
his advice to the president through him, in order to further cement his own
personal control over military affairs. And he micromanaged matters to a
degree that was comical, troubling, or depressing, depending on one's point
of view (Woodward 2006). His famous "snowflake" memos (Shanker 2006)
kept aides busy with requests or orders on a host of matters both vast and
miniscule. He sent twenty to sixty out every day (Wright 2007), and military
aides, who of course had other responsibilities as well, found it extremely
difficult to keep up with them.

These were only the most obvious example of a governing style in which
no matter was too small for his own personal direction. One of the more
extreme examples of this style was that he went so far as to rearrange the
seating on the flight to the funeral of the late congressman Floyd Spence
(R-SC), once the chairman of the House Armed Services Committee, apparently to put certain people literally in their place (like House Armed Service Committee Chairman Duncan Hunter—whose place was apparently
at the back of the aircraft). While he expected lengthy, detailed reports on a
host of subjects, the secretary only listened to his own advice and frequently
took punitive action against any who raised a dissenting word (Fallows 2004;
Woodward 2006). As Mark Danner (2006) wrote, it was striking

> the way that the most momentous of decisions were taken in the
> most shockingly haphazard ways, with the power in the hands of
> a few Pentagon civilians who knew little of Iraq or the region, the
> expertise of the rest of the government almost wholly excluded, and
> the President and his highest officials looking on . . . the systemic
> failures in Iraq resulted in large part from an almost willful determi-
> nation to cut off those in the government who knew anything from
> those who made the decisions.

Senior officials in the Pentagon were uninterested in their own study of
what might go wrong in Iraq. They sought to focus on "what would go right"
(Hersh 2004, 168–169). The Office of Special Plans was created in order to

stovepipe such information, along with information that might undermine Saddam Hussein. Oddly, given the negative associations with the seventeenth-century original, they termed themselves "the cabal" (Hersh 2004, 207). Rumsfeld believed he could win a major war with a remarkably small force and planned to leave the area as soon as possible afterward. Wolfowitz and Douglas Feith thought the war would lead to change across the region. OSP believed information that in some cases they more or less created. As Fallows (2004) put it, "they were brilliant, and they were fools." "Strong forceful military advice was bleached out of the system" (Woodward 2006, 74), and in its place were plans set by civilians that Fred Kaplan (2008) has termed "fantasists," people who had vastly different goals and who naturally had trouble coming up with coherent tactics and plans.

From the summer of 2002 forward, most of the activity involved planning the war, settling on tactics, and selling the war. The "Downing Street Memo" of July 23, 2002, included the analysis that "military action was now inevitable," and a National Security Presidential Directive signed in August 2002, "Iraq: Goals, Objectives and Strategy," formalized U.S. plans and goals relating to the removal of Saddam Hussein from power. There was even confirmation in the mainstream press months before the U.S. attack that, while the United Nations and Saddam Hussein might seemingly still have time to take action that could avert U.S. action, the president had made his decision, and he was going to take the country to war (Kessler 2003). In January, he told Colin Powell and British Prime Minister Tony Blair that he had made up his mind, and according to the British the president talked of several ways to provoke a confrontation with the Iraqis in order to further justify the war, including painting a U.S. surveillance plane in United Nations colors "in hopes of drawing fire" (Van Natta 2006).

Experts' Ratings

The decision to launch a war in Iraq has come in for immense criticism in the years since. Even some who spoke out in favor of the war have noted that it was executed in an unnecessarily costly way. The decision greatly weakened the political position of the United States with many of the world's governments, even straining relationships with longtime allies. Given these political costs, the costs that it unleashed in blood and treasure, and the demand it created to spend the bulk of the Bush presidency focused on an increasingly unpopular endeavor, it is not surprising that the expert rating of this case on the *National Interest* measure was unusually low, 1.86. And, given the scale of the military operation that was initiated, it is not surprising that this case is at the top of our *Level of International Conflict* rankings. On the five-point scale, the experts placed its effect on international conflict at 4.71.

Situation

Let us now consider in turn the independent variables, starting with the *Situational* context that the decision makers faced when choosing to go to war. There can be no doubt that decision makers involved in setting the country on a path toward war saw Iraq as a threat. They believed that Saddam Hussein had weapons of mass destruction and told the country again and again that the Iraqi dictator was a tyrant who might use them against the United States and its allies or who might give them to terrorists ("on any given day" as Bush said in his speech in Cincinnati on October 7, 2002) so that such an attack could be carried out surreptitiously, without any obvious Iraqi fingerprints (though that did beg the question of why Hussein had not done so already, if that was his intent). The president had been told that Pakistani nuclear information had been sold, and from then on the fear of a dirty bomb or even a nuclear weapon hitting the United States was a fear that "never went away" (Woodward 2004, 47). But at the same time, Hussein appears to have been considered a weak leader who could easily be defeated. In fact, the grand plans some had for the postwar period and the vice president's comments in his last *Meet the Press* interview before the fighting began, that we would be greeted as "liberators," imply a belief that this war would be short and successful. Apart from matters related to the nature of the threat and the expected outcome of the fighting, the give and take in Washington also affected how the decision makers felt about proceeding with an invasion. There was some internal disagreement, of course. But the inner circle was stable by the time the orders were given. None of the key decision makers seemed to be suffering under any particular personal crisis at the time the decision was finalized. Given the preceding remarks about the stakes, the threat, and the decision makers' personal condition and intra-administration dynamics, the *Stress* level is rated as 3 (midrange).

The situation was not a *Crisis*. It was not unexpected. After all, Iraq had let the weapons inspectors back into the country, and the United States initiated the fighting. And while there were tactical concerns about the weather, there was not a clear *Short Time Constraint* on action. There was talk of initiating a crisis (having a "United Nations" plane shot down), but that did not occur either.[1]

The United States was also not reacting in the wake of a *Recent Failure*. In fact, one could argue that the U.S. path of action was considerably more strongly shaped by what was widely seen as a recent success in Afghanistan. Secretary Rumsfeld's desire for a military force vastly smaller than the one desired by many senior officers probably became easier to achieve after the Taliban was defeated by small numbers of Americans. In fact, as early as December 2001 Rumsfeld was using the Afghanistan example to make his case for a leaner fighting force: "I'm not sure that much force is needed given what we've learned coming out of Afghanistan" (Woodward 2004, 41).

The *Level of Interests* at stake was strategic, given how this fit into larger plans for the region politically, economically, and in terms of national defense. The *Views of Allies* on the war were largely negative, though the president won and kept the support of Prime Minister Blair and a number of other states that became known as the "Coalition of the Willing." The *Views of International Organizations* were also largely negative. The most famous example of this is, of course, the Bush administration's failure to win the support of the United Nations Security Council for a resolution to back the invasion in early 2003. But it is highly debatable whether the United States really cared about these groups. Many of its senior figures had displayed a longstanding contempt for international groups. The president told Blair he was going to war no matter what the United Nations did (Van Natta 2006), and the administration planned on coordinating humanitarian issues after the war through the Pentagon, hardly an organization many international-aid groups wanted to work under.

American *Public Opinion* was with the president, however. A Gallup poll seven months before 9/11 showed a majority of Americans would have supported an invasion of Iraq even then. A majority of Americans also backed the war in the months preceding the invasion, and following it as well (that number would have been even higher if the president had won UN approval for his action). Probably relatedly, polling showed that at this time most Americans believed Iraq was responsible for the 9/11 attacks. *Legislative Opinion* was also favorable. The U.S. Congress passed a measure backing the president in the autumn of 2002, and it passed with considerable bipartisan support. Not only were almost all Republicans in favor of it, but so were many Democrats, including the Democratic leaders of the Senate and the House (Tom Daschle and Dick Gephardt) and Senator Clinton of New York.

And the *Military-Capabilities Differential* was also favorable. The "Delta of Terrorism" report notes that Iraq was an appealing target because it was weaker than many other potential threats. As far as the rest of the Axis of Evil, U.S. intelligence (hidden from Congress until after the vote on the Iraq war was held) showed North Korea was much closer to being a nuclear threat, and of course Iran was much larger and much more closely tied to terrorist networks that could harm the United States and its allies abroad. As a general rule, the top administration people felt U.S. "military power was so awesome that it no longer needed to make compromises or accommodations" (Mann 2004). Thus, given their low regard for Iraq's capabilities and its leader, it became a natural target.

In sum then, the *Situational* environment was not one where we would expect to see particularly poor decision making. We would only score this case a 2 on the scale of *Situational* impediments to high-quality decision making. Allies and international organizations were acting against the government, but otherwise the leaders of the Bush administration were not in a provocative *Situational* environment.

Group Structures

Moving on to the *Structural* variables, what stands out most was the lack of a decision-making structure. As Deputy Secretary Armitage told Ron Suskind (Suskind 2006, 225): "'There was never any policy process to break, by Condi or anyone else. There was never one from the start. Bush didn't want one, for whatever reason.' Bush believed in his own certainty and he didn't want any bureaucracy to get in the way. He wanted centralized, loyal, secretive power with clear lines of authority so his orders could be followed immediately." But are not governments supposed to engage in sober due diligence, particularly when the issue at stake is whether or not take the country to war? That "is precisely what the president didn't want, particularly after September 11; deeply distrustful of the bureaucracy, desirous of quick decisive action, impatient with bureaucrats and policy intellectuals, the President wanted to act" (Danner 2006).

The group was *Insulated*. The president said, "I have no outside advice. Anybody who says they're an outside adviser of this administration on this particular matter is not telling the truth" (Lemann 2004). And his circle became only smaller over time. Leaders as high ranking as Secretary Powell and Treasury Secretary Paul O'Neill often did not know what the president was thinking or what he wanted. This was an administration in which often the *Leader Was Biased*. President Bush almost never sought advice (Mazarr 2007), and relying on his instincts "was almost his second religion" (Woodward 2006, 11). He was remarkably incurious (Fallows 2004; Suskind 2004), and since he tended to make decisions based on instinct and that he believed were supported by his faith (Suskind 2006), being resolute in support of those positions is what mattered most to him, so hearing advice from others was less important. And the books he did read he often chose because they supported his worldview, such as Sharansky's *The Case for Democracy* (2004), and how he believed he should govern, such as Edmund Morris's *Theodore Rex* (2002).

The lack of *Methodical Procedures* at the highest levels was extreme. The fact that he never held a meeting to decide whether or not to go to war with Iraq—or even asked several of the foreign-policy principals whether they thought it was a good idea—is merely the tip of the iceberg. Those who sought a more traditional and transparent policy process were considered disloyal. "Old-style deliberations based on cause and effect or on agreed-upon precedents didn't much matter; nor did those with knowledge of prevailing policy studies, of agreements between nations, or of long-standing arrangements defining the global landscape" (Suskind 2006, 227). What the president was exposed to and what he heard was never supposed to be discussed, in order to give him the maximum freedom to construct narratives that would allow him to govern free of constraints. This hostility to set, acknowledged procedures would eventually have embarrassing and highly problematic consequences when, for example, it became obvious that neither the president nor Rice were aware of the fact that two competing chains of command had been set up for occupation-era Iraq (one reporting to Lt. General [retired] Jay Garner, the head of the Coalition Provisional Authority of Iraq, and one reporting to General Tommy Franks, the commander-in-chief of Central Command), or when Rice did not realize she had been cut out of Iraq planning by Secretary Rumsfeld (Woodward 2006). Secretary Powell complained that "huge matters" were never brought to his or the president's attention (Woodward 2008, 50). And even when matters were brought up, disputes among the decision-making principals were allowed "to fester for months and years" (Gellman 2008, 50). What little structure there was to decision making was isolated, limited, and ineffective. It was certainly not methodical.

The group in charge of the decision to invade Iraq was not *Homogenous*. Secretary Powell lacked influence within the administration even before the 9/11 attacks (Sipress and Mufson 2001). To put it bluntly and in jarring language, his tendency toward diplomacy "made Powell chum in the water for the sharks in Dubya's sea" (McGeary 2001), and he was more often than not "in the icebox" (Woodward 2002). But the presence of Powell and Armitage in decision-making circles illustrates that dissenting voices were not excluded entirely. And while the circle that the administration comprised was small and got smaller over time, it did feature members from a variety of demographic backgrounds. There were many ties among members of the administration. For example, the administration was filled with friends or former co-workers or aides to Cheney, including Rumsfeld, Wolfowitz, O'Neill, Federal Reserve Chairman Greenspan, and Deputy National Security Advisor Stephen Hadley (Lemann 2001). But the group did not entirely think alike or look alike. Given how Powell and Armitage were pushed to the side, it might be appropriate to label specific periods of the George W. Bush administration as a homogeneous group, but that would be a more of a case-specific coding, and we operationalize this variable as a structural characteristic that exists over time.

Was there an *Illusion of Invulnerability*? Yes. President Bush and Prime Minister Blair were "supremely confident" (Van Natta 2006), and, as seen in David Manning's memo to Blair, both leaders thought intra-Iraqi fighting between rival ethnic and religious groups was unlikely. Vice President Cheney said Americans were sure to be greeted as liberators. Secretary Rumsfeld was confident the job could be achieved with a fraction of the force that the Army said was necessary. Those who raised voices of caution were pushed aside. But perhaps the most important evidence of the presence of such a belief holding sway in the administration are the many writings that discuss President Bush's unusual level of certainty in the success of actions he advocates. Considering decision making in the Bush administration, Suskind has written that "a writ of infallibility . . . has guided the inner life of the White House" (Suskind 2004). In interviews and books on the administration, it becomes clear that the president's belief in his self and in both the rightness and eventual success of his agenda knew no bounds. As David Satterfield, a senior advisor to Condoleezza Rice, put it: "If Bush believed something was right, he believed it would succeed. Its very rightness ensured ultimate success" (Woodward 2008, 407). With that mindset, it is perhaps not surprising that the president would become impatient or annoyed with those who espoused doubts or were trying to brief him on competing policy options. And it would likely lead the president toward a very specific set of policies, regardless of issue briefings, policy debates, or the advice of allies. If rightness is what matters, the president would naturally be drawn to policies and arguments that "urge him to show strength and resolve" (Woodward 2008, 259). And it is striking that when asked if he had consulted his father before making the decision to go to war, Bush responded: "He is the wrong father to appeal to in terms of strength. There is a higher Father" (Woodward 2008, 432). For Bush, rightness, strength, and righteousness often folded into one.

Within the administration, there were a number of *Gatekeepers*, and it certainly could not be said that this decision-making *Group Valued Disagreement*. This was an insular, loyal group, and "dissent would not be tolerated" (Haney 2005, 296). And those who dared dissent were either fired, such as Larry Lindsey (after he stated that the war might cost up to $100 or $200 billion), or sidelined, such as General Shinseki (after he said that the troop levels needed were greater than those being proposed by Rumsfeld and Wolfowitz). This was an administration where loyalty got you hired, and it was enforced (Berke 2001; McGeary 2001; Prados 2004).

Was the *Leader Interested in Foreign Policy*? In his first months in office, George Bush did not prioritize foreign policy. It was not a major part of his campaign, he had rarely been abroad, and he appeared to have little interest in personally directing U.S. policy on most foreign-policy issues. However, after 9/11 that changed. Famously, he labeled himself a "war president" and came to see his government's actions in foreign affairs as central to his legacy. So it can definitely be said that the president was interested in foreign policy by this time. However, whether or not this mattered is debatable. The president was oddly absent from intra-administration debates over the war. Typically, the foreign-policy principals would meet to hash out plans and only take matters to the president once there was already agreement on them (Woodward 2002; Suskind 2004). This is discussed below, under *Unusual Structural Factors*.

The president did have a *Knowledgeable and Experienced* team. The Bush administration was filled with people with decades of experience in foreign policy who had served in central positions in several Republican administrations. As James Mann put it, "the Vulcans had prided themselves on their experience" (Mann 2004, 293). Staffed with men like Cheney, Powell, Rumsfeld, Armitage, and Wolfowitz, the administration entered office with old hands in most top jobs. While the president may have had little foreign-policy experience, his advisors had a great deal.

For an administration that was so tightly knit, so designed around protecting the president and his views, there was strikingly little *Teamwork*. There was close to all-out warfare between the White House, the Office of the Vice President, and the Department of Defense on one side and many of the professionals at the Central Intelligence Agency on the other. Vice President Cheney considered the CIA's work "crap," Secretary Rumsfeld stated that "Every CIA success is a DoD failure" (Suskind 2006, 77), and the Office of Special Plans was created precisely because the CIA was not providing the information the proponents of the war wanted to see. The Cheney/Rumsfeld faction was similarly aligned against much of the Department of State, and they blocked professional employees of State from holding a number of posts and dropped their own allies into State to try to control it further. Rumsfeld also regularly clashed with the National Security Council. He treated even honored staff members like "third-class citizens of dubious loyalty" (Woodward 2006, 109) and engaged in petty power plays by not returning Rice's phone calls or bringing few copies of plans to meetings, a situation that required Rice to look over material with the person next to her. And there were incessant clashes between Rumsfeld and the senior officer corps. But these fights extended beyond Secretary Rumsfeld, who had turned "breaking china to almost an art form" (Nelson 2002) as far back as his service in the U.S. House of Representatives in the 1960s. The entire administration often seemed to be seething with discord, even though the numbers of true policymakers were few and their connections tight.

Finally, there were two *Unusual Structural Factors* that impaired the quality of decision making. The first was the nearly continuous twisting of the intelligence process. Again and again the White House, the Office of the Vice President, and the Office of the Secretary of Defense clashed with much of the rest of the intelligence community. The former continually pressed forward with "evidence" of wrongdoing by Iraq that the rest of the intelligence community considered weak at best. And when support for the importance of such evidence collapsed, for example the White House's claims about Abu Zubaydah, often the White House wanted political cover more than judgments about the veracity of their claims. In some cases, for example the White House's claims about yellowcake from Niger, they were more interested in whether they could be proven wrong than in whether or not they were right (Suskind 2006, 177). This extended beyond mere problems associated with a specific case; it was a trend that existed throughout the Bush administration's first term and led to a host of exaggerated claims. Some of these ultimately resulted in the conviction of Lewis "Scooter" Libby on four counts, including perjury and obstruction of justice. Libby gave several interviews to the media that blamed administration failures on the Central Intelligence Agency, and he besmirched the reputation of Ambassador Joe Wilson, a critic of White House claims about intelligence. His statements about these interviews, and the subsequent grand-jury investigation, led to the charges that Libby lied under oath and made false claims to federal investigators.

The second *Unusual Structural Factor* was the lack of direct involvement by the president in the policy debates and planning that occurred in the run-up to the war. The president made the decision to take the country to war. But he is remarkably absent from the histories of how that decision was made and how it would be carried out. James Fallows (2004) conducted interviews for months with many of the top decision makers, in the context of his reporting on the run-up to the war for *The Atlantic Monthly*:

> In several months of interviews I never once heard someone say "We took this step because the President indicated . . ." or "The president really wanted. . . ." Instead I heard "Rumsfeld wanted," "Powell thought," "The Vice President pushed," "Bremer asked," and so on. One need only compare this with any discussion of foreign policy in Reagan's or Clinton's Administration—or Nixon's, or Kennedy's, or Johnson's, or most others—to sense how unusual is the absence of the President as prime mover. The other conspicuously absent figure was Condoleezza Rice, even after she was supposedly put in charge of coordinating Administration policy on Iraq.

Altogether, there were a staggering eight structural flaws in this decision-making group. The group was unsystematic, warring, biased, and cloistered away. This created an unstable, opaque echo chamber in which diligently carrying out carefully considered planning was next to impossible. The system was not designed to foster deliberation. Nor was it designed to be responsive to analysis and ideas that varied from a very narrow set of concerns prioritized by the handful of people at the pinnacle of power (Prados 2004).

In this environment, it is not surprising that low-quality decision making would emerge.

Decision Processing

Moving to the *Decision-Processing* variables, it is clear that the government as a whole conducted a *Good Information Search*. The professionals in the foreign-policy bureaucracies did an enormous amount of work investigating the issues at hand and creating analysis papers. But at the top level, such a careful examination did not happen. Reports went unread, and voices were blocked. This was definitely a case of *Biased Information Processing*. The diplomats, the generals, and the career intelligence professionals were, for the most part, blocked from having a voice in the process. A great deal of expertise was collected but then ignored. The consideration of their reports was often cursory at best. Mazarr wrote that "several interviewees told me that the president's entire formal briefing time on postwar Iraq amounted to a single, one-hour presentation" (2007, 18).

Given these processes, it is not surprising that there was neither a thorough *Survey of Objectives* nor a thorough *Survey of Alternatives*. The process was specifically designed to obscure such a careful consideration of goals and alternatives. As to how to overthrow Saddam Hussein, three options were considered (Mann 2004), but two, providing support for an opposition enclave within Iraq and staging a coup d'état, were quickly discarded. An American military invasion quickly emerged as the only option given serious consideration. And it was decided without much consideration for other options that the form of that invasion would fit closely with that which was advocated by Secretary Rumsfeld. Similarly, planning for the postwar era at the highest level was minimal, with only a tiny number of proposals presented to the president. Cheney and Rice were not getting them to him. And Cheney did all he could to keep things that way (Fallows 2004). After the Pentagon learned that the president would not let them install Chalabi as the new head of Iraq, the Pentagon leadership, who were ostensibly in charge of the operation, presented "virtually nothing. After Chalabi, there was no Plan B" (Risen 2006). Of course, this also meant that there was no transparency with the American people or the Congress either, and many matters tied to the invasion were not evaluated at all, lest the outcome of such an evaluation might imperil the mission. The administration "refused to hazard even the vaguest approximation of what financial costs" (Fallows

2004, 66) the war might entail until months after the shooting started. When they did hazard guesses about costs related to the war, they were ridiculous and obviously not tied to any remotely serious investigation of likelihoods associated with the conflict. For example, Andrew Natsios of USAID said the U.S. contribution to rebuilding Iraq would be no more than $1.7 billion. And Deputy Secretary Wolfowitz said U.S. taxpayers would not have to pay for the war at all.

It is clear that the decision-making group both *Stereotyped the Situation* and *Stereotyped the Out-Group*. As to the situation, the chorus about what the nature of the threat was and how an invasion would succeed was constant. For months on end, all of those closest to the president, and the president himself, talked of a supporter of terrorism, the threat of weapons of mass destruction, and a war that would be little more than a cakewalk. As to stereotyping the out-group, the president compared Hussein to Hitler and Stalin. He saw a vicious, corrupt killer devoid of empathy. But he also regularly saw a weak leader, one whose people would turn against him. The president and many of those around him saw an enemy that neatly fit the description of a "degenerate," according to Herrmann and Fischerkeller's (1995) description of the types of dominant images leaders rely on when classifying the world around them. And the administration never wavered from the script of Hussein being a corrupt but fundamentally weak monster.

The *Pressures for Uniformity* were strong. Few questioned the president (Suskind 2004), and those who went off message were swiftly punished. As mentioned earlier, Larry Lindsey said the war would cost $100 to 200 billion and was promptly fired; General Shinseki was made a lame duck and isolated for most of his tenure as Army chief of staff. Deputy Secretary Wolfowitz's rebuke of Shinseki's comments regarding the number of troops needed for war in Iraq was "as direct a rebuke of a military leader by his civilian superior as the United States had seen in fifty years" (Fallows 2004, 73). Army Secretary Thomas White's refusal to rebuke Shinseki's statement led Rumsfeld to dismiss him as well.

The total number of problems with the decision processing in this case therefore stands at 6. That is out of a total of seven, and the one thing the government did well in this area, the scope of the information search, is arguably the least important, as those at the top of the decision making process chose to ignore a great deal of that information and twist other information into facts that were badly skewed.

Conclusion

Things did not go as the Bush administration planned in Iraq. The much-discussed stockpiles of weapons of mass destruction did not exist. The American forces were greeted with things much harsher than smiles, thanks, and bouquets of flowers. Thousands of Americans have been killed, and tens of thousands of Americans have been wounded. Iraq plunged into a civil war that left hundreds of thousands of Iraqis dead and far more than that displaced. The stream of Iraqi refugees threatens the stability of surrounding countries. And if Iraq was meant to be a victory in the Global War on Terror, it is hard to see the war as anything but a failure, given that "the administration's own 2006 National Intelligence Estimate explains, 'The Iraq War has become the cause célèbre for jihadists . . . and is shaping a new generation of terrorist leaders and operations'" (Bergen 2007).

Given the results, it is not surprising that the war is rated negatively by the foreign-policy experts. And its failures surely result, at least in part, from the decision-making factors we have considered in this study. The situational environment was not especially problematic. The administration had much on its side when planning the invasion. But both the structure of the decision-making group and the processes carried out as the principals worked toward war evinced a host of negative attributes. The structure was seemingly designed to prevent careful analysis by people with relevant expertise. For example, like Fallows (2004, 74), one can ask: "How could the administration have thought that it was safe to proceed in blithe indifference to the warnings of nearly everyone with operational experience in modern military occupations?" But that was clearly by design. The system was created so that only a tiny handful of individuals would direct policy or even know what decisions had been made and why. Predictably, this left the bureaucracy struggling, working in circles, and lacking any position by which it could have helped guide decision makers who knew relatively little about key aspects of many issues before them. And the decision processes and norms within that structure (or lack of structure) worked to reinforce existing biases and stereotypes more than to raise questions about how workable the strategies and tactics stemming from those stereotypes really were.

Many of the mistakes associated with the war and its aftermath can be laid at the feet of "an inexperienced and rigidly self-assured president who managed to fashion, with the help of a powerful vice president, a strikingly disfigured process of governing" (Danner 2006). A less opaque, insular, and isolated decision-making group would likely have performed much better, as in retrospect it is clear that experts from the Department of State, the Department of Defense, and the Central Intelligence Agency had a much better handle on what was going on in Iraq and the likely consequences of an invasion than the president and his closest advisors did. But those bureaucrats, specialists, and analysts were creating reports and plans that the policymaking principals either put aside or never read. And while they worked, "there was a momentum toward war and a lack of caution that the president embraced. His convictions were driving the march to war like a locomotive gaining steam" (Woodward 2008, 432), even though he was disconnected from most of the policy debates and planning that were proceeding apace.

This case shows the importance of looking inside the "black box." The choices the United States made in this matter were clearly tied to the preferences of a handful of people in Washington, D.C., more than they were the rational outputs of the U.S. government efficiently and systematically acting as whole. There simply was no decision-making structure in place to carefully evaluate policy alternatives or gauge the effects of possible outcomes. And while the United States would surely have faced many difficulties from any invasion of Iraq, the nature of the weaknesses in the decision-making structure and process would seem to imply that surely some of the problems the United States encountered were avoidable. Again, this is not to say that a more competently and efficiently managed war would have been a smashing success. There are several reasons to think that any war would have been an uphill battle in the longer term. But the low quality of the decision making appears to have definitely hurt the U.S. cause and led to a lower-quality outcome than would have been the case with a more careful decision-making structure that better integrated the views of the relevant parts of the bureaucracy. The administration's mismanagement of its own affairs hurt its cause, and the United States suffered as a result.

Nine

GROUPTHINK VERSUS HIGH-QUALITY DECISION MAKING

Lessons and Prescriptions

In the preceding chapters, we have seen that the quality of foreign-policy decisions, group structures and processes, and the personality traits of decision makers all vary, and they vary in predictable ways. Group structures and processes significantly affect the quality of foreign-policy decision making, whether that quality is rated according to the decision's impact on the national interest or effect on international conflict. The direct effect of leader personality on the quality of decision outcomes is weaker than the structural and process effects related to the decision group, but it does exist. These results reaffirm the basic literature associated with political psychology and the field of foreign-policy analysis. But, more importantly, they clarify this literature by pointing to specific structures, processes, and personality traits that significantly move governments toward a greater or lesser chance of success and to more or less conflict in the international system.

Seeing which specific variables or combinations of variables have significant effects across dozens of cases helps us build better specified models. It also helps us evaluate debates in the current literature about what precisely is going on in these relationships. In general, our findings are supportive of Janis's general proposition that the quality of group decision making matters. Yet there are some patterns in our results that refute some of Janis's contentions, and there are some that make significant qualifications to his earlier work. Janis's seminal work was critical in attracting attention to group decision making. Now we have a more refined view of the elements that affect the quality of the process.

These findings have valuable prescriptive benefits. The results herein show that the chances of policy making leading to better or worse results is greatly affected by matters that occur long before that policy is set. We see that how decision-making groups are structured and perform have a powerful effect on the policies that come out of them. Leaders can affect their administrations and move them toward either greater successes or greater losses, depending upon how they form their government and upon what processes that government uses as it takes in information, evaluates options, and comes to a decision. While leaders may exist in a turbulent world and face many foreign and domestic obstacles, the results of our analyses show that they have a strong hand in determining the outcomes of their initiatives. Their opportunities for success are greater than some observers of the international scene would imagine. So is their responsibility for their failures.

We have seen a great deal of variance in the leaders we have examined and in their administrations. This is true across the decision-making variables, the outcome variables, and the personality attributes of the leaders in our study. As to this last factor, we found that more distrustful leaders oversee governments that have more poorly structured decision-making groups. Their governments also feature a more flawed process of decision making when they are in the midst of settling on an answer to a specific policy problem. In addition, more distrustful leaders make decisions that increase the level of conflict in the international system. While a number of other personality traits, either individually or in combination, were found to have effects on political behavior, the *Distrust* variable has the broadest impact. These effects have an intuitive appeal. One could easily expect distrustful individuals to only take in information from a limited number of voices, to process that information in ways that privilege parts of that already-constricted information flow, to stereotype their surroundings, and to see limited opportunities for cooperation. We see that such relationships are indeed significant and hold up across dozens of foreign-policy cases.

The effects of *Distrust* can be seen in our case study on Iraq in chapter 8. Among our sample of leaders, President G. W. Bush had the highest average level of *Distrust*. In the Iraq war case study, the administration had a high number of structural faults, several of which seem to have conceptual ties to a distrusting leader, such as *Gatekeeping* and failing to *Value Dis-*

agreement. A similar pattern can be seen in the *Decision Processing* in the case; several of them related to the concept of *Distrust*, such as *Stereotyping the Out-Group* and *Pressures for Uniformity*. This was an insular administration where contrarian information and voices were systematically silenced, a select few advisors had disproportionate sway, and the system was set up so as to reinforce and protect the biased views at the top.

While *Distrust* has the broadest effect among our psychological variables, we see other connections between the personality of the leader and the workings of their government. Presidents and prime ministers who have a considerable *In-Group Bias* are likely to oversee decision-making processes that feature fewer faults. This might seem surprising if one were to match our findings with some of Janis's assumptions. After all, he believed that cohesive groups were a danger to high-quality decision making. But as we noted when reviewing Paul 't Hart's (1998) critique of this literature, groups serve multiple functions. Groups exist in part to solve problems. But their ability to do that is related to how well they perform *other* functions, such as coordinating multiple organizations, sharing ideas, and overseeing the implementation of policy by a large and complex bureaucracy. For groups to perform these roles effectively, they must have a healthy belief in their abilities and efficacy. It appears that leaders who support and believe in their group at higher levels tend to oversee groups that carry out decision making in superior ways. This an important finding, given the division in the literature between those who see a strong belief in group cohesion as necessary for groups to work efficiently and those who see it as a problem that leads to lazy, poorly considered decisions by groups who overestimate their talents and power. On *In-Group Bias*, Yitzhak Rabin scored highest in the sample. Despite the enormous strains associated with the Entebbe case, his advisory group performed incredibly well as a team, and we found only one *Decision-Processing* fault in the case and no *Structural* faults.

Another Hermann (1999) trait variable nears significance. It appears leaders who have a high *Need for Power* may put in place better group structures, structures that we show are more likely to advance the national interest. This fits with Hermann's understanding of the variable, which describes high-*Power* leaders as those who are especially skilled at both increasing their own influence and at organizing their subordinates in particularly effective ways. It also fits with Peterson et al.'s (1998) critique of the groupthink literature that we discussed in chapter 2. Peterson and his colleagues argue that the appropriate response to groupthink and similar group dynamics is not the creation of a slower, more unbiased system advocated by Janis's "vigilant decision making." Instead, what is needed for better-functioning groups is a strong, activist leader, one who will question easy answers and entrenched interests. Leadership matters.

As noted above, in our statistical analyses the *Power* variable only nears significance. However, another statistical analysis leads us to be more confident that the variable does indeed matter. We also found that leaders who have *Higher Control* and *Lower Power* oversee significantly worse group structures than those for whom that is not true. Believing oneself to be able to control events but lacking the political acumen to do so is very problematic. It is not surprising that such a leader would lack the ability to organize his or her aides and would reign over a seriously flawed group structure that would have difficulty fulfilling important objectives. Much as Machiavelli (2008, 82) noted that it is the "prudence of the prince" that matters in the end, it appears that Hermann (1999) and Peterson and his colleagues (1998) were correct: the power and political acumen of a leader may have an important effect on guiding groups past the shoals of dangerous and destructive group structures and in successfully collecting and managing advice. The leader who most exemplifies the problematic side of this pattern in our dataset is Ronald Reagan, whose *Control* score is above average but who has the lowest *Power* score in our sample. His administration averaged the highest number of *Group-Structural* faults and was second in the sample in number of *Decision-Processing* faults.

The final personality variable we find to have an impact on decision making is one of the combination variables. Leaders whose *Self-Confidence* is greater than their *Conceptual Complexity* run administrations that commit fewer decision-processing faults when they are setting policy. This is an interesting finding. There are intuitive reasons to think that both *Self-Confident* leaders and *Complex* leaders would be able to avoid decision-processing faults. For example, someone who is *Self-Confident* may feel secure enough to work outside the boundaries of stereotypes. Likewise, we could expect *Complex* leaders, who see many shades of grey in the world, to be willing to do the same thing and to demand a thorough information search before making a decision. But it appears from our results that high *Complexity* without high *Self-Confidence* may be of little use. And that, in fact, high *Self-Confidence* can mitigate some of the negative effects of low *Complexity*. These leaders who are willing to take the initiative, challenge complacency, and are comfortable in difficult situations may also be the sort Peterson et al. (1998) suggested would be especially effective at avoiding groupthink. Leaders with high *Self-Confidence*, as discussed in chapter 7, may also be more likely to avoid overcompensating behavior and be willing to be assertive with poorly performing subordinates. This relationship is significant across our sample, and by way of illustration it is worth mentioning that President G. W. Bush was both the least *Self-Confident* president in our sample and the president whose administration committed on average the most decision-processing faults.

Together, these results show that even though there are limitations on the impact that the personality traits of a president or prime minister can have on decision making and the outcomes of state policy, there is nonetheless evidence that a number of these psychological characteristics have meaningful effects. That said, the results of chapter 6 show that there are even more powerful predictors of the nature and quality of a state's choices. How the decision group is structured prior to decision making during specific events and the processes a group employs during discrete decision-making events both significantly affect the quality of decision outcomes. We repeatedly saw these relationships in the cases in chapter 4. For example, in late 1978 and early 1979 we saw in the Carter administration the presence of gatekeepers, acrimonious decision makers, disconnected decision processes, and a biased president. These factors greatly limited the government's ability to reliably collect and process information, objectively weigh alternatives, and carefully plot the path the United States should take regarding Iran. Similarly, in the SDI case we saw major foreign-policy principals cut out of decision making entirely, a biased leader, and an insulated group suppressing dissent that was not in a position to effectively coordinate policy making. With decision making impaired in these ways (and, of course, other harmful decision-making variables were also present in these cases), given our significant findings, it is not surprising that these decision processes resulted in policy outcomes that score very low in terms of their effect on the national interest.

Across the full set of cases, our data clearly show that the structure of decision-making groups has a powerful effect on the quality of decision results. We found seven of the *Group-Structure* variables to have significant independent effects on the quality of decision outcomes when measured in terms of the national interest. More *Insulated* groups produced more negative results. Groups that lacked *Methodical Procedures* produced poorer results, as did groups that acted under an *Illusion of Invulnerability*. The presence of *Gatekeepers* was significantly associated with more negative results. Groups that *Valued Disagreement* produced higher-rated decisions, as did groups that operated with a notable level of *Teamwork*. Finally, groups that had higher levels of *Knowledge and Experience* also produced higher-rated decisions. When all the *Group-Structure* variables we tested were collapsed into a scale, we found that it explained 44 percent of the variance in the *National Interest* dependent variable. These findings are some of the most dramatic in our set of analyses. How a government is structured at the highest level has a powerful effect on the quality of that government's decisions. This means that governments can secure better outcomes in foreign policy simply by adopting structures that will be more likely to produce positive results. Such structures are in place across time, and before any particular decision is made—hence their broad, general effects.

Regardless of outside events, governments have the ability to improve their chances of success by altering their own form. On the whole, our findings in this regard fit with some of Janis's basic ideas and expectations. Setting clear lines of authority and communication, keeping groups open to new and different ideas, keeping them connected to a variety of other political actors and sources of information, fostering teamwork, keeping a healthy eye on potential problems and vulnerabilities, and filling top jobs with experienced and knowledgeable individuals all fit with Janis's preferred solution to negative group dynamics: "vigilant decision making."

There were also five *Group-Structure* variables that had significant effects on the *Level of International Conflict*. A *Biased Leader*, an *Illusion of Invulnerability*, and *Gatekeepers* are all likely to increase the level of conflict in the international system. If a group has *Methodical Procedures* in place and *Values Disagreement*, it is likely to produce lower levels of international conflict. But group structure has its strongest effect on the processes of making a decision during a case. The *Group-Structure* variables explain 60 percent of the variance in decision processes, with eight of the variables having a significant effect when tested independently: *Insulation, Biased Leader, Methodical Procedures, Illusion of Invulnerability, Gatekeepers, Values Disagreement, Teamwork,* and *Knowledgeable and Experienced Team*. In total, group structure affects how decisions are processed in specific instances, the degree to which national interests are achieved, and the level of conflict introduced into the international system.

But this last outcome variable, *Level of International Conflict*, is more strongly affected by the decision processes carried out in a specific case of decision making. Six decision-processing variables are significantly related to variation in international-conflict outcomes: *Biased Information Processing, Surveying Alternatives, Surveying Objectives, Stereotyping the Situation, Stereotyping the Out-Group,* and *Uniformity Pressures.* When the process variables are combined into a scale, they explain 38 percent of the variance in the *Level of International Conflict* outcome variable. These variables are not as strong as the *Group-Structure* variables in predicting national interests, but four of them have significant independent effects on national interests: *Biased Information Processing, Surveying Alternatives, Surveying Objectives,* and *Stereotyping the Situation.* When the decision-process variables are combined into a scale, they predict 18 percent of the variation in the *National Interest* outcome variable. These findings provide empirical support for notions that have been discussed in this literature for decades and illuminate key details. That *structure* more strongly affects the national interest while *process* more strongly affects the level of international conflict is an important finding.

While the pattern of structures and processes affecting outcomes is solid throughout our data, it is interesting to note that some administrations went through significant adjustments during their tenure. For example, though the Reagan administration had many cases in our sample that were problematic, by 1986 the structures and decision processes had notably improved, as seen in the case study on easing Ferdinand Marcos of the Philippines out of power. Reagan was *Biased* in this case—he wanted to help an old cold-war ally—and he generally was not *Interested in Foreign Policy* nor an expert in it. But in spite of these drawbacks, the administration as a whole had come to be well structured by 1986, including much better *Teamwork* than in the early Reagan years, more *Methodical Procedures,* and *Less Insulation;* the administration also *Valued Disagreement* and had no *Illusion of Invulnerability,* both of which had been problems for some of the earlier Reagan cases. These better structures contributed to much better *Decision Processing,* and we found only one fault in this case: the administration continued to *Stereotype the Situation,* as they had so many others, as being part and parcel of the cold war. Just as Janis observed the Kennedy administration dramatically improve its decision making between the Bay of Pigs episode and the Cuban Missile Crisis, the Reagan administration showed similar improvements by the time the Marcos case occurred, though it took a long time for the administration to learn those lessons.

Finally, we tested the effect of several situation variables in our model.

Many foreign-policy debates discuss decisions in terms of the level interests at stake, stress, the views of allies, and the like. We found little evidence that such variables have a powerful effect, though a few have an effect on *Outcomes* measured in terms of *National Interest*. Some of these findings were potentially counterintuitive. For example, we found that decision making that occurs in high-anxiety situations, where high *Stress* levels and a *Short Time Constraint* are present, produces better results. Other findings were expected. When an administration's chosen policy converges with the views of allies and international organizations, the chances for a positive result increase.

We also found some evidence in the statistical results that suggests that more powerful states may be able to force a success regardless of the quality of the decision making that occurred during the decision event. In addition, stronger states are more likely than others to increase military conflict in the world. The pattern seems to be that the strong are in a better position to endure policy choices that may be inefficient and costly, and thus their decision-making procedures are sometimes less effective. Of course, that is not to say that powerful countries should not take steps to lessen those inefficiencies or avoid them completely through high-quality decision making. It simply notes that they are usually in a stronger position to survive a poor, inefficient, or haphazard decision. And, of course, being strong enough to survive a case that has such poor decision making may mask some of the real consequences associated with that decision making. For example, the U.S. wartime commitment to Iraq may be winding down, which may lead some from the Bush administration to claim that it was successful after all, essentially glossing over the significant consequences paid by the United States, Iraq, and many others in the international system. The more accurate description is that the administration had very poor decision-making procedures that lead to very poor consequences, yet the United States was militarily and economically strong enough to survive and move on from those consequences.

But while we see a few individual relationships like these, overall, the *Situation* variables are poor predictors in our model. This further heightens the prescriptive implications of our findings. Many *Situation* variables are matters over which decision makers have limited control, and they are noticeably less influential on the quality of decision outcomes than the *Group-Structure* and *Decision-Processing* variables, over which decision makers have much greater influence. Decision makers may sometimes feel like they are victims of circumstances, but these data imply something quite different: effective leaders will construct good decision-making procedures that will function efficiently and soundly despite difficult circumstances.

Our study on South Asia is an excellent case in point. The Clinton administration was surprised in the case and found itself dealing with a *Crisis* involving high *Stress, Short Time Constraints,* potentially huge consequences, and perhaps as many *Situational* distractions as any other case in our dataset. And yet the group functioned at a very high level. The decision-making apparatus was set up very effectively, and we found only one *Group-Structural* fault in the case. This had a positive effect on the actual decision making in the case, where we noted only one *Decision-Processing* shortcoming. The Kargil conflict ended fairly quickly—with the fewest number of fatalities of any of the four wars between the two combatants—in no small part because of the actions of the U.S. government.

We do not wish to leave readers with sense that all cases fit nicely into the pattern seen in our data: that high-quality decision making correlates with high-quality outcomes. Clearly this is what the data show, but, as with so much of social science, while the pattern is statistically and substantively significant and accounts for a large percentage of variance in the cases, high-quality decision making is not determinative. In the making of foreign policy, even the best procedures cannot account for other factors that might affect outcomes; many things are simply beyond the control of decision makers. A good case in point is the Carter administration's decision to try to rescue U.S. hostages held in Iran in 1980. Though our experts coded this case as one that negatively affected U.S. *National Interests,* our coding of the case-study materials showed that the administration featured good *Group Structures* and *Decision Processes.*

The administration was not perfect—no case in our sample met that criteria. We found a notable problematic *Group-Structural* fault in the case: when the final decision was made to attempt the rescue, Secretary of State Cyrus Vance—the most significant voice opposed to the plan—was out of town and therefore not at the key meeting of the decision group. His absence is a central reason behind Steve Smith's (1985) labeling of this case as an example of groupthink. But the negative impact of Vance's absence was mitigated by the fact that Vance had already clearly articulated his views regarding the rescue plan. They were very well known by others in the administration, including President Carter, and after Vance returned to Washington, Carter granted him a special meeting in which he was allowed once again to voice his concerns. Even though by this point in the administration Vance had come to feel like a minority voice on several major foreign-policy issues, accommodations were made to keep his perspectives included and heard. And this was not a decision where there was an unconsidered rush to action, even though the stakes were great and many Americans were in peril. The planning was carefully drawn up over months. While Smith has argued that decision makers "did not critically evaluate the probability of success" or examine the weak points of the plan "in any detail" (Smith 1985, 182), in the same paragraph he notes that the mission was planned "in considerable detail" and judged to be workable. His criticisms are difficult to deal with in that he does not give us specific operationalized measures that would allow us to independently judge what qualifies as a critical evaluation or not. Further, he lumps in other criticisms of the process, such as the fact that a possible rehearsal of the mission did not occur due to operational security concerns, which is of limited relevance to measuring the norms of the decision-making group. Of course, we agree that this decision did not turn out well. But the decision making that led to the rescue mission was not marked by a high number of *Group-Structural* or *Decision-Processing* faults. Based upon our systematic comparative methods, it was a good decision-making process.

Yet the case turned out terribly. How can these two facts—good process, bad outcome—be reconciled? First, just because an administration conducts a good decision-making process does not mean the leader will make the "right" decision. A good process includes careful consideration of options and alternatives, checking biased processing, searching for the best and latest information, and listening to disparate opinions. Our data show that, on average, when an administration does these things, the better choice is more likely to emerge. But it is entirely possible that the group will get to that final point and it will not be clear which is the "better choice," yet the leader must choose. Remember that decision making always takes place under the condition of imperfect information. It is true that effective decision making should result in the best information possible, but it will never be perfect and complete. In addition, even if the "better choice" is made, there are still factors well outside of the control of the administration that will affect the outcome. In the hostage-rescue case, the operation was disrupted by a significant and unexpected sandstorm that caused major damage to helicopters, and the operation had to be aborted.

Did Carter come to the fork in the road and make the wrong choice? We cannot answer that question, because the kind of counterfactual analysis involved is beyond the scope of this book—and even if it could be done, it would result in nothing much more than speculation. We know this much: the decision-making process did not have the level of faults we saw in many other cases—it was a good process. And we also know that the case turned out poorly. Process does not always determine outcome. Yet, it would be dead wrong to draw from this case the conclusion that process does not matter. It does matter; it is not, however, determinative. What our data show is that high-quality decision making significantly increases the *probability* of having higher-quality outcomes. If we were giving advice to a leader who is setting up her or his decision-making apparatus, we would suggest setting up high-quality structures and procedures along the lines of those we have discussed thus far. Then, cases are much more likely to turn out well. Yet we would acknowledge that such structures cannot be a panacea. On the other hand, failing to set up effective structures is very likely to lead to poor outcomes. In Texas hold 'em poker, while being dealt two aces at the start of a hand is the best one can possibly do, that particular hand will also lose some of the time. But we would much rather bet on a good outcome with that starting hand than when holding a 7-2 off suit!

When looking over the results of all these analyses, what can we say we know? This study is premised on the notion that there may indeed be better and worse forms of group-based decision making. Does this study find that to be true? After all, works like Kowert's (2002) study of Eisenhower and Reagan have made the entirely reasonable point that appropriate decision-making structures will depend upon the experience, personality, and needs of those occupying the top offices of state, a contention that is individual based rather than group based. If that is true, can we still say there are "good" and "bad" forms of group decision making? Yes we can. There is considerable variation across the thirty-nine cases in both the decision-making variables and the outcome variables. And we find significant effects that show there are better structures and processes that in turn produce better outcomes. This is not to say that there is a one-size-fits-all structure or process that every president or prime minister should use regardless of what they bring to their office. But on the whole there are many factors that have broadly positive effects, regardless of the individual leader's personal characteristics. And, likewise, there are many factors that have broadly negative effects.

Can we affirm that Janis's findings in his classic works were correct? Across our much larger sample of cases, in many respects, Janis's classic "symptoms of groupthink" have the negative effects he anticipated. However, we find that some of his assertions are contingent, a few are not significant in our sample, and we find that low-quality decision making can stem from a variety of circumstances not discussed in *Victims of Groupthink*.

If Janis's work appears to have new holes in its details and reasoning, does that mean that we have support for the leading critiques of his classic work? Perhaps, in some qualified ways. Consider Kramer's (1998) contention that what was driving Janis's findings in some of his classic studies was not a negative group effect but simply the triumph of convenient politics. Our case studies show some support for Kramer's view. Clearly, some of the decisions that were rated poorly in our sample were made for political reasons. For example, as we discussed in chapter 4, the Reagan administration's policy to support the Contras was driven by their political agenda. But while political priorities may drive certain choices, a better decision-making process might have eliminated certain costs and hazards or resulted in policy adaptations that lessened the negative effects of that policy.

What of Whyte's (1998) contention that groupthink stems not from the stresses placed on a decision-making group but on a group suffering under excessive efficacy? Our results tend to support Whyte. Some of our significant findings involving situation variables suggest that stressful situations may lead to decision making that produces better outcomes, not worse ones. And we see significant relationships involving a number of variables, perhaps most obviously *Illusion of Invulnerability*, that suggest that excessive efficacy can be a serious problem.

While it is notable that many of our findings fit with Janis's proposed cure for harmful group dynamics, vigilant decision making, let us be explicit about where our conclusions diverge from and move significantly beyond Janis's original conception. Janis argued that poor-quality decision making, made manifest as groupthink, stems from two primary factors: an adverse situational context marked by high pressure and anxiety and an overly cohesive in-group that produces premature consensus. As discussed earlier, our results refute his argument that situational pressures are significantly detrimental. Across our larger and more diverse set of cases, the statistics are clear: an adverse situational context does not systematically co-vary with poor-quality decision making.

Regarding Janis's argument about a cohesive group, our data provides some support. Several things related to this are clearly problematic in decision making, such as group insulation, failing to value disagreement, suppressing dissent, and gatekeeping. When the group focuses inordinately on maintaining group cohesion and preventing contrarianism, the quality of its decision making is greatly compromised.

Yet our results find that Janis is short-sighted in implying that reducing group cohesion is the key to improving the quality of decision making. Our data show that advisory systems must be able to work together and communicate across diverse and dispersed elements of the bureaucracy and the decision-making apparatus. Some level of teamwork and group cohesion is essential. Note that in several of our problematic cases the heart of the problem seemed to reside in a contentious and damaging rivalry between key foreign-policy advisors. Others featured weak leadership by the president, the national security advisor, or both, which allowed drift, inaction, or unresolved disputes to continue unabated. While too much in-group cohesion can be problematic, as Janis anticipated, too little cohesion may be just as bad or worse.

What then might tilt the balance on this divide? It appears from this research that leadership may be key. A leader with sharp political skills and acumen, including self-confidence and a high need for power, is more likely to achieve positive outcomes. As Peterson et al. (1998) note, an activist leader who is willing to take risks may be an important part of the dynamic needed to secure the highest group functioning. A leader must know how to develop his in-group positively, sending signals that contrarian viewpoints are more than welcome but that teamwork and communication are also essential. It takes a strong leader to invite competing voices to be heard and at the same time manage them and get them to work efficaciously as a team.

Finally, given the prescriptive focus of this literature dating back to Janis, it merits mentioning once more that these findings have positive implications for real-world decision making. The negative decision-making dynamics we study are mostly the product of group structures and processes, not the combination of stress and group cohesion noted by Janis and others. Decision makers have the ability to control how their own groups are structured and which processes they will implement. This gives them a considerable tool through which they can alter the likelihood of their policies succeeding. From a prescriptive standpoint, holding them responsible for how they choose to wield this tool would seem to encourage the growth of more efficient and effective foreign policies. At the very least, it would seem to encourage moves that could lead a government in that direction and pull leaders and groups away from dynamics that are associated with sub-par outcomes. Our research has undertaken the task of increasing our knowledge of the linkages between individual-level psychology, group structure and process, and the quality of decision outcomes. It is up to policymakers to build better structures and implement better procedures.

Appendix A

Cases Included in the Analysis

Case 1: MAYAGUEZ. Decision by the Ford administration on May 14, 1975, to land marines in Cambodia to search for the *Mayaguez* hostages, to board and seize the *Mayaguez*, and to conduct air strikes targeting the Cambodian mainland.

Case 2: U.S. INVOLVEMENT IN ANGOLA. Decision by the Ford administration in the summer of 1975 to increase covert aid to Zaire. This aid was to be funneled to the FNLA and UNITA, organizations combating the Marxist-oriented MPLA for control of Angola.

Case 3: ENTEBBE. Decision by the Rabin government on July 3, 1976, to launch Operation Thunderbolt, a military engagement aimed at rescuing the hostages held at the Entebbe airport.

Case 4: "DEEP CUTS"/SALT II. Decision by the Carter administration on March 19, 1977, to propose a substantial increase in the arms reductions sought by the United States. This included reducing U.S. and Soviet nuclear launchers and a cut in Soviet heavy missiles from 300 to 150.

Case 5: OGADEN WAR. Decision by the Carter administration in February 1978 not to become involved in the Ogaden War. Proposals had been made to send a carrier task force to the region to restrain Soviet action or to grant covert aid to Somalia. The Soviets had responded to Ethiopia's requests for aid in repelling the Somali invasion.

Case 6: RELATIONS WITH CHINA. Decision by the Carter administration, finalized in December 1978, to proceed with the normalization of relations with China.

Case 7: SUPPORTING THE SHAH. Decision by the Carter administration to continue its support for the shah's rule in Iran in November and December 1978, after domestic unrest began to dramatically intensify.

Case 8: NONINTERVENTION IN NICARAGUA. Decision by the Carter administration not to intervene militarily in Nicaragua in the summer of 1979 to prevent the Sandinistas from coming to power.

Case 9: IRAN HOSTAGE RESCUE ATTEMPT. Decision by the Carter administration on April 11, 1980, to proceed with an attempt to rescue American hostages held in Iran.

Case 10: ATTACKING OSIRAQ. Decision by the Begin government in October 1980 to bomb Iraq's Osiraq nuclear reactor. The implementation of this decision was delayed until June 1981.

Case 11: FUNDING THE CONTRAS. The decision by the Reagan administration to begin supporting and organizing paramilitary groups in Nicaragua in November 1981.

Case 12: FALKLANDS I. Decision by the Thatcher government on April 2, 1982, to respond to the Argentinean invasion of the Falkland Islands by sending a naval task force to the area.

Case 13: FALKLANDS II. Decision by the Thatcher government in May 1982 to implement Operation Sutton, landing troops on the Falkland Islands.

Case 14: INVASION OF LEBANON. Decision by the Begin government on June 5, 1982, to invade Lebanon and clear out a twenty-five-mile strip north of the border in order to protect northern Israeli communities from PLO artillery raids.

Case 15: CONFRONTING THE SIEGE OF BEIRUT. Decision by the Reagan administration on August 4, 1982, not to sanction Israel but instead to publicly and privately condemn that country's violations of the Beirut ceasefire. Israeli troop movements and shelling were occurring as the PLO was presenting what was widely seen as a workable plan to implement their departure from the city.

Case 16: REJECTING THE "WALK IN THE WOODS." Decision by the Reagan administration in September 1982 to reject the "Walk in the Woods" proposal in the Intermediate-Range Nuclear Forces Talks. The "Walk in the Woods" proposal, negotiated privately between Paul Nitze and Yuli Kvitinsky, was aimed at overcoming a number of disagreements in the official talks.

Case 17: DEVELOPING SDI. The decision by the Reagan administration in February 1983 to develop the Strategic Defense Initiative.

Case 18: GRENADA. Decision by the Reagan administration on October 22, 1983, to launch a military operation aimed at securing the safety of Americans in Grenada and restoring civilian rule in that country.

Case 19: ACHILLE LAURO. Decision by the Reagan administration on October 10, 1985, to have U.S. military aircraft intercept the 737 transporting the hijackers of the Achille Lauro from Egypt to Tunisia, force it to land at a NATO base in Sicily, and bring the hijackers to the United States for trial.

Case 20: IRANIAN ARMS SALES. Decision by the Reagan administration, finalized on January 6, 1986, to authorize arms sales to Iran.

Case 21: REMOVING MARCOS. Decision by the Reagan administration on February 23, 1986, to act to ease Ferdinand Marcos out of power in the Philippines. Steps quickly taken toward this end included an offer of asylum and a threat to cut off aid if forces supporting him attacked the rebels.

Case 22: ATTACKING LIBYA. Decision by the Reagan administration in April 1986 to launch an air attack against Libya, as a reprisal for the regime's support of international terrorism.

Case 23: FUNDING UNITA. Decision by the Reagan administration on November 12, 1985, to begin providing covert aid to the UNITA rebels in Angola.

Case 24: EXCEEDING SALT II. Decision by the Reagan administration in May 1986 to deploy the 131st ALCM-armed B-52, thereby exceeding the nuclear-arsenal subceilings prescribed by the unratified SALT II agreement.

Case 25: NEGOTIATING NORIEGA'S DEPARTURE. Decision by the Reagan administration in May 1988 to try to negotiate Noriega's departure from Panama.

Case 26: ATTACKING PANAMA. Decision by the Bush administration in December 1989 to launch Operation Just Cause and remove Manuel Noriega from power by force.

Case 27: GULF WAR I/DESERT SHIELD. Decision by the Bush administration in early August 1990 to protect Saudi Arabia from a potential Iraqi attack by sending a large U.S. military force to the region.

Case 28: GULF WAR II/DESERT STORM. Decision by the Bush administration on October 30, 1990, to increase the size of the American force to the level that the military felt was necessary to enable a successful attack against Iraq.

Case 29: GULF WAR III/THE END. Decision by the Bush administration on February 26, 1991, to end the war against Iraq after one hundred hours of fighting on the ground.

Case 30: ADOPTING "LIFT AND STRIKE." Decision by the Clinton administration on May 1, 1993, to propose the "Lift and Strike" policy in the former Yugoslavia. This proposal called for lifting the arms embargo and using air strikes against the Serbians if they attempted to strengthen their position before the Bosnians were armed.

Case 31: LEAVING SOMALIA. After the failed attempt to capture Mohamed Farah Aideed, the Clinton administration's decision in early October 1993 to boost troop strength to protect the remaining U.S. forces in Somalia and to begin a disengagement process that would remove all U.S. troops from the area by March 31, 1994.

Case 32: NORTH KOREA. Negotiation between the Clinton administration and the North Korean government following the threat by North Korea on March 12, 1993, to withdraw from the Nuclear Non-Proliferation Treaty.

Case 33: PAKISTAN/INDIA NUCLEAR CRISIS. Decisions by the Clinton administration regarding South Asia from May 1998 through July 4, 1999, in relation to nuclear tests by each country and the subsequent Kargil conflict.

Case 34: KOSOVO. Decision by the Clinton administration to assist the NATO intervention in Kosovo on March 12, 1999.

Case 35: ISRAEL/PALESTINE. The decision by the Bush administration following his inauguration on January 20, 2001, to refuse to deal with Palestinian leader Yasser Arafat unless he renounced terrorism.

Case 36: REMOVING THE TALIBAN. Decision by the Bush administration to invade Afghanistan on October 7, 2001, in order to remove the ruling Taliban government and attempt to capture Osama bin Laden.

Case 37: ABM TREATY. The decision by the Bush administration on December 13, 2001, to give notice to the Russian government in order to resign from the Anti-Ballistic Missile Treaty of 1972.

Case 38: STEEL TARIFFS. Decision by the Bush administration on March 3, 2002, to place a 8 to 30 percent tariff on steel imports in an attempt to protect American steel manufacturers from bankruptcy.

Case 39: IRAQ WAR. Decision by the Bush administration on March 20, 2003, to go to war with Iraq in an attempt to remove Saddam Hussein.

Appendix B

Operational Definitions of Situational-Context Variables

1. STRESS LEVEL: The degree to which the situation being dealt with was stressful for the principals involved. This variable is coded on a 1–5 scale (Holsti 1972; Janis and Mann 1977; Schafer and Crichlow 1996).

2. CRISIS: The situation confronting decision makers is unexpected, must be dealt with in a short time period, and is perceived as threatening highly valued interests. Coded 1 if a crisis, coded 0 if not a crisis (C. Hermann 1969; Krasner 1972; Janis and Mann 1977; Wallace and Suedfeld 1988; 't Hart 1990; McCalla 1992).

3. RECENT FAILURE: A recent political or military defeat weighs on the minds of members of the decision-making group. Coded 1 if present, coded 0 otherwise (Janis 1982; Schafer and Crichlow 1996).

4. SHORT TIME CONSTRAINT: The group suffers under perceived temporal limits in the situation at hand. Coded 1 if present, coded 0 otherwise (C. Hermann 1969; Lebow 1981; Schafer and Crichlow 1996).

5. LEVEL OF INTERESTS AT STAKE: The degree to which the situation is perceived as threatening the national interest. This variable is coded on a 1–3 scale depending on the type of concerns that are endangered. 1 = peripheral interests; 2 = strategic interests; 3 = vital interests (C. Hermann 1969; Janis and Mann 1977; McCalla 1992).

6. ALLIES' VIEWS: The stance taken by most of the country's allies regarding the issue being confronted. Whether they have an opinion on the policy favored by the government, and, if they do, whether they are favorably or unfavorably disposed to the preferences of the decision makers. This variable is coded −1 if allies' opinions are negative, 0 if they are not relevant, and 1 if they are favorable (Kegley and Wittkopf 1996; Haney 1997).

7. INTERNATIONAL ORGANIZATIONS' VIEWS: The stance taken by key international organizations regarding the issue being confronted. Whether they have an opinion on the policy favored by the government, and, if they do, whether they are

favorably or unfavorably disposed to the preferences of the decision makers. This variable is coded −1 if the international organizations' views are negative, 0 if they are not relevant, and 1 if they are favorable (Karns and Mingst 1987; Kegley and Wittkopf 1996).

8. PUBLIC OPINION: The group is affected by the perception of a high level of public interest in the situation being addressed. This variable is coded −1 if public opinion hinders the adoption of a favored policy, 0 if it is not relevant, and 1 if it is beneficial to the adoption of a favored policy (Barnett 1990; James and O'Neal 1991; James and Hristoulas 1994; Russett 1990; Powlick 1995; Kegley and Wittkopf 1996).

9. LEGISLATIVE OPINION: The group is affected by the existence of a high level of interest by the national legislature in the situation being addressed. This variable is −1 if legislative opinion hinders the adoption of a favored policy, 0 if it is not relevant, and 1 if it is beneficial to the adoption of a favored policy (Hagan 1993; Kegley and Wittkopf 1996; Milner 1997).

10. MILITARY-CAPABILITY DIFFERENTIAL: This is the difference in the level of power between the parties involved. This variable is coded −1 if the difference is the favor of another actor(s), 0 if the capabilities are similar, and 1 if the difference favors the actor under examination (Morgenthau 1978; Mearsheimer 1983; Huth 1988; Rothgeb 1993; Kegley and Wittkopf 1996).

11. SITUATIONAL DISTRACTIONS: The group is dealing with the situation at hand while it is distracted by other pressing events. These may include such occurrences as the development of a separate major international situation, domestic political issue, or a decline in the leader's health. This variable is coded 1 if one or more distractions exist, 0 if not.

Appendix C

Operational Definitions of
Group-Structural Variables

1. GROUP INSULATION: Decision makers isolate themselves from others not in the immediate decision-making circle. The others here include bureaucrats, intelligence officers, diplomats, allies, area experts, and those on location at the scene of a crisis. A decision-making group is isolated if it relies almost exclusively on members of its own group for information and counsel. Coded 1 if the group isolates itself, 0 otherwise (Janis 1982; Hybel 1993; Thomson 1968; Schafer and Crichlow 1996; George 1991).
2. BIASED LEADERSHIP: The leader conducts decision-making processes in a manner that limits the consideration of a wide range of alternatives because of his or her previously stated preferences. Such a leader typically makes clear that he or she has a predisposition toward a particular course of action before consulting with advisors. Coded 1 for biased leadership, 0 for unbiased leadership (Janis 1982; Schafer and Crichlow 1996; Haney 1997; Vertzberger 1998).
3. METHODICAL PROCEDURES: The group has established a tradition of using methodical procedures in the decision-making process in terms of routine and systematic decision-making meetings and the analysis of pros and cons. Coded 1 if methodical procedures are used, 0 otherwise (Janis 1982; 't Hart 1990; Kerr 1981; Schafer and Crichlow 1996; Vertzberger 1990; Vertzberger 1998).
4. GROUP HOMOGENEITY: A lack of disparity exists in the social background and ideology of members of the decision-making group. Coded 1 if the group is homogeneous, 0 otherwise (Janis 1982; George 1980; Schafer and Crichlow 1996; Vertzberger 1998).
5. ILLUSION OF INVULNERABILITY: The group overestimates its ability to control events. This may be due to a belief that it is pursuing the "moral" position in a situation or simply a belief in an overly high level of efficacy. Coded 1 if the group has an illusion of invulnerability, 0 otherwise (Janis 1982; Schafer and Crichlow 1996; Mackie 1986; Vertzberger 1990).

6. GATEKEEPERS: The group includes one or more members who prevent information and arguments that conflict with their own position from entering into the decision-making process. Coded 1 if gatekeepers are present, 0 otherwise (Janis 1982; Burnstein and Vinokur 1977; Kerr 1981; Sanders and Baron 1977; Baron et al. 1996; Vertzberger 1990).

7. GROUP VALUES DISAGREEMENT: The leader and/or other prominent members of the group value disagreement as a way of improving the policies that come out of the decision-making process. They do not try to suppress dissenting opinions. Coded 1 if the group values disagreement, 0 otherwise (Janis 1982; George 1980; Haney 1997; Vertzberger 1990).

8. FOREIGN-POLICY INTEREST: The leader is regularly engaged in the design of foreign policy, as opposed to simply approving decisions made by others or leaving that sphere of issues unaddressed. Coded 1 if the leader shows such an interest in foreign policy, 0 otherwise (Hermann 1980; Hermann and Preston 1994).

9. KNOWLEDGE AND EXPERIENCE: The group in charge of foreign-policy making is knowledgeable about the matters that come under its domain and significantly experienced in the complexities of international politics. Coded 1 if the group is knowledgeable, 0 otherwise (Wallace and Suedfeld 1988; Thomson 1994; Haney 1997).

10. TEAMWORK: The group in charge of foreign policy works well together, communicates across bureaucratic divisions, and facilitates cooperative activities in the decision-making process. It is not frequently impaired by divisive personalities or disagreements. Coded 1 if the group is characterized by teamwork, 0 otherwise ('t Hart 1990).

11. UNUSUAL STRUCTURAL FACTORS: The group has one or more specific structural anomalies that do not fall into the categories listed above.

Appendix D

Operational Definitions of Decision-Processing Variables

1. POOR INFORMATION SEARCH: The group does a poor job of searching for information and fails to obtain available information necessary for critically evaluating the policy options considered by the decision-making group. This may include a failure to contact experts whose knowledge could be particularly useful. Coded 1 if the group performs a poor information search, 0 otherwise (George 1980; Herek et al. 1987; Janis 1989; Haney 1997; Vertzberger 1990).

2. BIASED INFORMATION PROCESSING: The group shows a definite tendency to accept new information from experts, the mass media, and outside critics only when it supports preferred alternatives. Members generally ignore, distort, or refute other information to which they are exposed. Coded 1 if information is processed in a biased manner, 0 otherwise (Jervis 1976; Herek et al. 1987; Janis 1989; 't Hart 1990; Haney 1997; Burnstein and Vinokur 1977; Sanders and Baron 1977; Baron et al. 1996).

3. SURVEY OF OBJECTIVES: The group discusses its objectives and the nature of its goals and values in a particular situation before deciding on a course of action. Coded 1 if such a survey is conducted, 0 otherwise (George 1980; Herek et al. 1987; Janis 1989; Haney 1997; Vertzberger 1990).

4. SURVEY OF ALTERNATIVES: The group thoroughly considers a variety of alternative policies, including their risks and their prospects for success, before adopting a course of action. Coded 1 if such a thorough consideration is conducted, 0 otherwise (George 1980; Herek et al. 1987; Janis 1989; Haney 1997; Burnstein and Vinokur 1977; Sanders and Baron 1977; Baron et al. 1996; Vertzberger 1990).

5. STEREOTYPE OF SITUATION: The group stereotypes the situation in which it finds itself. Coded 1 if the group, or a significant section of it, stereotypes the situation, 0 otherwise (Jervis 1976; Janis 1989; Khong 1992; Hybel 1993; Thomson 1994; Vertzberger 1990; Vertzberger 1998).

6. STEREOTYPE OF OUT-GROUP: The group stereotypes the out-group upon which its behavior is focused. Coded 1 if the group, or a significant section of it, stereotypes the out-group, 0 otherwise (Jervis 1976; Janis 1989; Khong 1992; Hybel 1993; Thomson 1994; Vertzberger 1990; Vertzberger 1998).

7. PRESSURES TOWARD UNIFORMITY: One or more of the following exist that curtail the free exchange of perspectives on the situation at hand: self-censorship, an illusion of unanimity, direct pressure on dissenters, self-appointed mind guards. Coded 1 if such pressures exist, 0 otherwise (Janis 1989; 't Hart 1990; Schafer and Crichlow 1996; Burnstein and Vinokur 1977; Sanders and Baron 1977; Baron et al. 1996; Vertzberger 1990).

8. UNUSUAL PROCESS FACTORS: The decision-making process is affected by specific, anomalous factors that do not fit into any of the other process variables.

Notes

1. Introduction

1. See chapter 3. For works that deal with a concept similar to our *Poor Information Search*, see George (1980), Haney (1997), and Herek et al. (1987).

2. The Group and the Individual in Foreign-Policy Decision Making

1. The International Crisis Behavior Project (ICB) includes a few variables that pertain to decision making, such as decision-maker stress and size of the decision-making group. Including these kind of variables in major-conflict data sets moves in the direction of more rigorous research in these areas, though perhaps due to their specific operationalizations and limited scope, the ICB variables have not been regularly incorporated into the extensive research agenda focused on process.
2. Greenstein uses this distinction is his famous work *Personality and Politics* (1969, esp. 3–6).
3. Suedfeld and Rank (1976), however, argue that complexity (at least their version of it) varied based upon situational constraints and thus acted more as a "state" variable than a nonshifting "trait."
4. For a complete discussion of all eight types and their likely leadership styles, see Hermann (1999).
5. For more information on VICS, the coding system, and its indexes, see Schafer and Walker (2006b).
6. For a discussion of this and several other at-a-distance methodological issues, see Schafer (2000).

3. The Decision-Making Model

1. Appendices B, C, and D provide the complete list of variables in each of these three categories, along with their operational definitions and possible coding values.

4. Case Studies in Low-Quality Decision Making

1. Regarding this, see Cannon (1991) and Talbott (1988). Shultz (1993, 246) says it explicitly: "He [Reagan] hoped for the day when there would be no nuclear weapons."
2. We use the term *group* as our generic reference to the set of individuals involved in the case, but here it is a very small and isolated set consisting only of Clark, MacFarlane, and Reagan, and even those three did not act as a decision-making group per se: Reagan heard what he wanted to hear from the joint chiefs, facilitated by MacFarlane, who told Clark, and then Reagan made the decision; there were no additional meetings to evaluate or assess the policy.

5. Case Studies in High-Quality Decision Making

1. This case is sometimes referred to as the "Ogaden crisis," and indeed the ICB dataset codes it as a crisis, but only for the African countries involved (Brecher and Wilkenfeld 1988). The case literature regarding the Carter administration's views is clear that they did not see it as a crisis for the United States.
2. This is often marked by the simple slogan coined by James Carville, "It's the economy, stupid," and used by the 1992 Clinton campaign.

6. The Effect of Groupthink Versus High-Quality Decision Making on Outcomes

1. Standard deviation is a measure of dispersion of the values in the variable. It may be used to indicate whether any one value of a variable is significantly different from the mean. If a value is more (or less) than one standard deviation away from the mean, we consider that to be statistically significant. For example, if our experts gave an average score of 2.05 for *National Interests* on a case, we would say that they rated the *National-Interests* outcome as significantly poorer than the average case in our dataset.
2. Recall that we discussed the general directional expectations of the independent variables in chapter 3. One example is *Group Insulation*. If the group is insulated, which is coded as a higher value than noninsulated groups, our expectation is that it will be problematic for the outcome of the case, which would show up as a lower score on the *National-Interests* dependent variable. Hence, we would expect a negative linear relationship.
3. In this figure one set of variables is left out—*Leader's Psychology*—which is covered separately in chapter 7.
4. *Military-Capability Differential* is not included in the aggregate scale. It was relevant in only twenty-nine of the cases. Had we included it, it would have meant that we would have had to eliminate those extra ten cases, resulting in much weaker statistical analyses.

5. This requires reversing the coding of several variables: *Methodical Procedures, Group Values Disagreement, Foreign-Policy Interest of the Leader, Knowledgeable/Experienced Team,* and *Teamwork.*
6. Recall that these are bivariate models, for which R^2 values are probably elevated. In multivariate models, the amount of variance accounted for by any one variable will be lower. We turn to multivariate models later in this chapter.
7. Technically speaking, there are (barely) enough degrees of freedom to allow all thirty-three variables in one model where $n = 39$, but given the restrictions on the degrees of freedom along with very high multicolinearity among the independent variables, the results would be essentially meaningless.
8. Merely adding one or more independent variables to a model has the effect of increasing the R^2 value regardless of whether the added variables actually contribute to additional explained variance. To account for this, we use the adjusted R^2 statistic, which essentially controls for the number of independent variables in the model.
9. Note that this explanation is an interesting variant on Janis's groupthink argument regarding problematic group cohesiveness.
10. Note that both of these variables are examples where the underlying patterns did not show up in the bivariate models earlier, but only when controlling for other factors.

7. Individual-Level Factors Affecting the Quality of Decision Making

1. Except for Rabin, who has only one case in the dataset, and therefore there is no variance.
2. Rabin could not be included in this analysis because there is only one case in the dataset from his administration, meaning that there is no variance in his scores and therefore no standard deviations can be calculated.
3. Z-scores are calculated by subtracting the sample mean score for the trait from the individual leader's score on that trait and then dividing by the sample standard deviation for the trait. The result is a standardized score indicating how far the leader's score is from average.
4. *High Control and Low Power* is operationalized using the mean scores of the two variables. *Self-Confidence > Conceptual Complexity* is operationalized using *z*-scores for the two variables, which standardizes their scores.
5. As noted earlier, because of the outlier analysis that showed the two Israeli leaders as averaging higher deviations from the sample mean scores for the traits than the other leaders, we tested for possible spurious effects regarding this by adding a dummy variable (coded 1 if the leader is from Israel, 0 otherwise) to all tested multivariate models in this chapter. Including the dummy variable caused some of the *p* values to change, rarely notably, and never caused the sign of the coefficient to change for any of the significant variables in the model. Because these effects were negligible and nondirectional, the models reported here do not include this dummy variable.

8. The 2003 War in Iraq

1. It is possible to conceive of the subsequent war initiated by the United States as a *Crisis*, which is how the ICB dataset codes it starting in September 2002 (http://www.cidcm.umd.edu/icb/). But that does not fit our operational definition, which requires it to be an unexpected event with a short time constraint. In addition, we focus on the decision-making process that took place before the onset of the war, and during that time the situation in Iraq was not a crisis at all. In fact, if one determines that the situation in Iraq eventually became a crisis, it was the decision making beforehand that brought that crisis about.

References

Ahlfinger, Noni R., and James K. Esser. 2001. Testing the groupthink model: Effects of promotional leadership and conformity predisposition. *Social Behavior and Personality* 29 (1): 31–41.

Allen, Mike, and Jonathan Weisman. 2003. Steel tariffs appear to have backfired on Bush. *Washington Post* (September 19).

Allison, Graham T. 1971. *Essence of decision: Explaining the Cuban missile crisis.* Boston: Little, Brown.

Anderson, Harry, Melissa Liu, Richard Vockey, Zofia Smardz, and Kim Willenson. 1985. Saving Marcos from himself. *Newsweek* (November 11).

Anderson, Harry, Melissa Liu, Richard Vokey, Zofia Smardz, Kim Willenson, John Walcott, and Morton M. Kondracke. 1985. The Philippines: Another Iran? *Newsweek* (November 4).

Anderson, Martin. 1988. *Revolution.* New York: Harcourt Brace Jovanovich.

Axelrod, Robert. 1972. Psycho-algebra: A mathematical theory of cognition and choice with an application to the British Eastern Committee in 1918. *Papers of the Peace Research Society (International)* 18: 113–131.

——. 1976. The analysis of cognitive maps. In *Structure of Decision*, ed. Robert Axelrod. Princeton, N.J.: Princeton University Press.

Barber, James D. 1968a. Adult identity and presidential style: The rhetorical emphasis. *Daedalus* 97: 33–68.

——. 1968b. Classifying and predicting presidential styles: Two weak presidents. *Journal of Social Issues* 24, no. 3: 51–80.

——. 1972. *Presidential character: Predicting performance in the White House.* Englewood Cliffs, N.Y.: Prentice-Hall.

Barnett, Michael N. 1990. High politics is low politics: The systemic and domestic sources of Israeli security policy, 1967–1977. *World Politics* 42, no. 4: 529–562.

Baron, Robert, Sieg I. Hoppe, Chuan Feng Kao, Bethany Brunsman, Barbara Lin-
neweh, and Diane Rogers. 1996. Social corroboration and opinion extremity. *Journal of Experimental Social Psychology* 32: 537–560.

Becker, Elizabeth. 2003. U.S. tariffs on steel are illegal, World Trade Organization
says. *New York Times* (November 11).

Bem, D. J., and A. Allen. 1974. On predicting some of the people some of the time:
The search for cross-situational consistencies in behavior. *Psychological Review*
81: 506–520.

Bergen, Peter. 2007. War of error: How Osama bin Laden beat George W. Bush. *New
Republic* (October 22).

Berke, Richard L. 2001. This time, dissent stops at the White House door. *New York
Times* (December 16).

Bidwai, Praful, and Achin Vanaik. 2000. *New nukes: India, Pakistan, and global nuclear disarmament*. New York: Interlink Publishing Group.

Bloom, William. 1993. *Personal identity, national identity, and international relations*.
New York: Cambridge University Press.

Bonham, G. Matthew, Daniel Heradstvei, Ove Narvesen, and Michael J. Shapiro.
1978. A cognitive model of decision making: Application to Norwegian oil policy.
Cooperation and Conflict 13: 93–108.

Bonham, G. Matthew, Victor M. Sergeev, and Pavel B. Parshin. 1997. The limited
test-ban agreement: Emergence of new knowledge structures in international negotiation. *International Studies Quarterly* 41: 215–240.

Bonham, G. Matthew, and Michael Shapiro. 1976. Explanation of the unexpected:
The Syrian intervention in Jordan in 1970. In *Structure of Decision*, ed. Robert
Axelrod. Princeton, N.J.: Princeton University Press.

Bonner, Raymond. 1987. *Waltzing with a dictator: The Marcoses and the making of
American policy*. New York: Times Books.

Boulding, Kenneth E. 1956. *The image*. Ann Arbor: University of Michigan Press.

——. 1959. National images and international systems. *Journal of Conflict Resolution*
39, no. 2: 120–131.

Brands, Henry W. 1992. *Bound to empire*. New York: Oxford University Press.

Branigin, William, and John Burgess. 1986. Marcos is named winner; Reagan disputes
outcome; Opposition quits assembly session. *Washington Post* (February 16).

Brecher, Michael. 2008. *International political earthquakes*. Ann Arbor: University of
Michigan Press.

Brecher, Michael, Blema Steinberg, and Janice Stein. 1969. A framework for research
on foreign policy behavior. *Journal of Conflict Behavior* 13, no. 1: 75–101.

Brecher, Michael, and Jonathan Wilkenfeld. 1988. *Crises in the twentieth century:
Handbook of international crises*. Oxford: Pergamon Press.

——. 1997. *A study of crisis*. Ann Arbor: University of Michigan Press, 1997.

Brzezinski, Zbigniew. 1983. *Power and principle: Memoirs of the national security advisor, 1977–1981*. New York: Farrar, Straus & Giroux.

Burke, John P. 2004. *Becoming president: The Bush transition, 2000–2003*. Boulder,
Colo.: Lynne Rienner.

Burnstein, Eugene, and Amiram Vinokur. 1977. Persuasive argumentation and social
comparison as determinants of attitude polarization. *Journal of Experimental Social Psychology* 13: 315–332.

Bush, George, and Karen Hughes. 1999. *A charge to keep*. New York: William Morrow.

Byman, Daniel, and Kenneth Pollack. 2001. Let us now praise great men: Bringing the statesman back in. *International Security* 25: 107–146.

Callaway, M. R., R. G. Marriot, and James K. Esser. 1985. Effects of dominance on group decision making: Toward a stress-reduction explanation of groupthink. *Journal of Personality and Social Psychology* 49: 949–952.

Cannon, Carl, and Alexis Simendinger. 2002. The evolution of Karl Rove. *National Journal* (April 26).

Cannon, Lou. 1991. *President Reagan: The role of a lifetime*. New York: Simon & Schuster.

Carney, James, and John F. Dickinson. 2000. How Bush decided. *Cable News Network* (July 31). Available online at http://www.cnn.com/ALLPOLITICS/time/2000/07/31/decided.html.

Carney, Jay. 2002. General Karl Rove, reporting for duty. *Time* (September 29).

Carter, Jimmy. 1982. *Keeping faith: Memoirs of a president*. Toronto: Bantam Books.

Clarke, Richard. 2004. *Against all enemies: Inside America's war on terror*. New York: Free Press.

Clinton, Bill. 2005. *My life*. New York: Vintage Books.

Cottam, Martha L. 1985. The impact of psychological images on international bargaining: The case of Mexican natural gas. *Political Psychology* 6: 413–439.

——. 1986. *Foreign policy decision making: The influence of cognition*. Boulder, Colo.: Westview.

——. 1992. The Carter administration's policy toward Nicaragua: Images, goals, and tactics. *Political Science Quarterly* 107: 123–146.

——. 1994. *Images and intervention: U.S. policies in Latin America*. Pittsburgh, Penn.: University of Pittsburgh Press.

Cottam, Richard. 1977. *Foreign policy motivation: A general theory and a case study*. Pittsburgh, Penn.: University of Pittsburgh Press.

Crichlow, Scott. 1998. Idealism or pragmatism? An operational code of analysis of Yitzhak Rabin and Shimon Peres. *Political Psychology* 19: 638–706.

——. 2002. Legislators' personality traits and congressional support for free trade. *The Journal of Conflict Resolution* 46, no. 5: 693–711.

——. 2005. Lincoln, Seward and the United Kingdom. *White House Studies* 5, no. 3: 411–422.

——. 2006. The eyes of Kesteven: How the worldviews of Margaret Thatcher and her cabinet influenced British foreign policy. In *Beliefs and leadership in world politics: Methods and applications of operational code analysis*, ed. Mark Schafer and Stephen G. Walker, 77–99. New York: Palgrave Macmillan.

Daalder, Ivo H., and James M. Lindsay. 2003. *America unbound: The Bush revolution in foreign policy*. Washington, D.C.: Brookings Institution Press.

Danner, Mark. 2006. Iraq: The war of the imagination. *New York Review of Books* 53 (December 21).

Destler, I. M., Leslie Gelb, and Anthony Lake. 1984. *Our own worst enemy: The unmaking of American foreign policy*. New York: Simon & Schuster.

Dickey, Christopher. 1985. *With the Contras: A reporter in the wilds of Nicaragua*. New York: Simon & Schuster.

Drew, Elizabeth. 1978. A reporter at large, "Brzezinski." *New Yorker* (May).

Driver, Michael J. 1977. Individual differences as determinants of aggression in the inter-nation simulation. In *A psychological examination of political leaders*, ed. Margaret G. Hermann. New York: Free Press.

Drury, A. Cooper. 2006. Economic sanctions and operational code analysis: Beliefs and the use of economic coercion. In *Beliefs and leadership in world politics*, ed. Mark Schafer and Stephen G. Walker, 187–200. New York: Palgrave Macmillan.

Dugger, Ronnie. 1983. *On Reagan: The man and his presidency.* New York: McGraw Hill.

Erikson, Erik H. 1958. *Young man Luther: A study in psychoanalysis and history.* New York: Norton.

Esser, James K. 1988. Alive and well after twenty-five years: A review of groupthink research. *Organizational Behavior and Human Processes* 73, no. 2/3: 116–141.

Etheredge, Lloyd S. 1978. *A world of men: The private sources of American foreign policy.* Cambridge, Mass: The MIT Press.

Fallows, James. 2004. Blind into Baghdad. *Atlantic* (January).

Feng, Huiyun. 2005. The operational code of Mao Zedong: Defensive or offensive realist? *Security Studies* 14: 637–662.

——. 2006. Crisis deferred: An operational code analysis of Chinese leaders across the strait. In *Beliefs and leadership in world politics: Methods and applications of operational code analysis*, ed. Mark Schafer and Stephen G. Walker, 151–170. New York: Palgrave Macmillan.

Flowers, M. L. 1977. A laboratory test of some of Janis's groupthink hypothesis. *Journal of Personality and Social Psychology* 33: 888–895.

Fuller, Sally Riggs, and Ramon J. Aldag. 1997. Challenging the mindguards: Moving small group analysis beyond groupthink. In *Beyond groupthink: Group decision making in foreign policy*, ed. Paul 't Hart, Bengt Sundelius, and Eric Stern, 55–93. Ann Arbor: University of Michigan Press.

——. 1998. Organizational Tonypandy: Lessons from a quarter century of the groupthink phenomenon. *Organizational Behavior and Human Processes* 73, no. 2/3: 163–184.

Gellman, Barton. 2008. *The Cheney vice presidency.* New York: Penguin.

George, Alexander L. 1969. The "operational code": A neglected approach to the study of political leaders and decision making. *International Studies Quarterly* 13: 190–222.

——. 1979. The causal nexus between cognitive beliefs and decision-making behavior: The "operational code" belief system. In *Psychology models in international politics*, ed. Lawrence S. Falkowski. Boulder, Colo.: Westview.

——. 1980. *Presidential decisionmaking in foreign policy: The effective use of information and advice.* Boulder, Colo.: Westview.

George, Alexander L., and Eric K. Stern. 1998. Presidential management styles and models. In *Presidential Personality and Performance*, by Alexander L. George and Juliette L. George, 199–280. Boulder, Colo.: Westview.

Glad, Betty. 1980. *Jimmy Carter: In search of the great White House.* New York: W. W. Norton.

Greenstein, Fred I. 1969. *Personality and politics: Problems of evidence, inference, and conceptualization.* Chicago: Markham.

Hagan, Joe D. 1993. *Political opposition and foreign policy in comparative perspective.* Boulder, Colo.: Lynne Rienner.

Halliday, Fred. 1997. U.S. policy in the Horn of Africa: Aboulia or proxy intervention? *Review of African Political Economy* 10: 8–32.

Halperin, Morton H. 1974. *Bureaucratic politics and foreign policy.* Washington: Brookings.

Haney, Patrick J. 1994. Decision making during international crises: A reexamination. *International Interactions* 19: 177–191.

———. 1997. *Organizing for foreign policy crises: Presidents, advisers, and the management of decision making.* Ann Arbor: University of Michigan Press.

———. 2005. Foreign-policy advising: Models and mysteries from the Bush administration. *Presidential Studies Quarterly* 35, no. 2: 289–302.

Harris, John F. 2005. *The survivor: Bill Clinton in the White House.* New York: Random House.

Hart, Jeffrey. 1976. Comparative cognition: Politics of international control of the oceans. In *Structure of Decision,* ed. Robert Axelrod. Princeton, N.J.: Princeton University Press.

't Hart, Paul. 1990. *Groupthink in government: A study of small groups and policy failure.* Amsterdam: Swets & Zeitlinger.

———. 1998. Preventing groupthink revisited: Evaluating and reforming groups in government. *Organizational Behavior and Human Processes* 73, no. 2/3: 306–326.

't Hart, Paul, and Irving L. Janis. 1991. Victims of groupthink. *Political Psychology* 12, no. 2: 247–278.

't Hart, Paul, Eric K. Stern, and Bengt Sundelius. 1997. Foreign policy making at the top: Political group dynamics. In *Beyond groupthink: Group decision making in foreign policy,* ed. Paul 't Hart, Bengt Sundelius, and Eric K. Stern, 3–34. Ann Arbor: University of Michigan Press.

Hartle, T. W., and M. J. Helperin. 1980. Rational and incremental decision making: An exposition and critique with illustrations. In *Managing public systems: Analytic techniques for public administration,* ed. M. J. White et al. North Scituate, Mass.: Duxbury Press.

Herek, Gregory M., Irving Janis, and Paul Huth. 1987. Decision making during international crisis: Is quality of process related to outcome? *Journal of Conflict Resolution* 31, no. 2: 203–226.

Hermann, Charles. 1969. International crisis as a situational variable. In *International Politics and Foreign Policy,* 409–421. New York: Free Press.

Hermann, Margaret G. 1976. Circumstances under which leader personality will affect foreign policy. In *In Search of Global Patterns,* 326–333. New York: Free Press.

———. 1980. Explaining foreign policy behavior using the personal characteristics of political leaders. *International Studies Quarterly* 24, no. 1: 7–46.

———. 1984. Personality and foreign policy decision making: A study of fifty-three heads of government. In *Foreign policy decision making: Perceptions, cognition, and artificial intelligence,* ed. Donald A. Sylvan and Steve Chan. New York: Praeger.

———. 1987. Assessing the foreign policy role orientations of sub-Saharan African leaders. In *Role theory and foreign policy analysis,* ed. Stephen G. Walker. Durham, N.C.: Duke University Press.

——. 1999. Assessing leadership style: A trait analysis. Social Sciences Automation, Inc.

——. 2001. How decision units shape foreign policy: A theoretical framework. *International Studies Review* 3, no. 2: 47–81.

Hermann, Margaret G., and Charles F. Hermann. 1989. Who makes foreign policy decisions and how: An empirical inquiry. *International Studies Quarterly* 33, no. 4: 361–387.

Hermann, Margaret G., and Thomas Preston. 1994. Presidents and their advisers: Leadership style, advisory systems, and foreign policy making. In *Domestic sources of American foreign policy*, ed. Eugene Wittkopf, 340–356. New York: St. Martin's Press.

Hermann, Margaret G., Thomas Preston, Baghat Korany, and Timothy M. Shaw. 2001. Who leads matters: The effect of powerful individuals. *International Studies Review* 3, no. 2: 83–131.

Herrmann, Richard K. 1984. Perceptions and foreign policy analysis. In *Foreign policy decision making: Perception, cognition, and artificial intelligence*, ed. Donald A. Sylvan and Steve Chan. New York: Praeger.

——. 1985. *Perceptions and behavior in Soviet foreign policy*. Pittsburgh, Penn.: Pittsburgh University Press.

——. 1986. The power of perceptions in foreign-policy decision making: Do views of the Soviet Union determine the policy choices of American leaders? *American Journal of Political Science* 30, no. 4: 841–875.

Herrmann, Richard K., and Michael P. Fischerkeller. 1995. Beyond the enemy image and spiral model: Cognitive-strategic research after the cold war. *International Organization* 49, no. 3: 415–450.

Herrmann, Richard K., James F. Voss, Tonya Y. E. Schooler, and Joseph Ciarrochi. 1997. Images in international relations: An experimental test of cognitive schemata. *International Studies Quarterly* 41: 403–433.

Hersh, Seymour M. 2004. *Chain of command: The road from 9/11 to Abu Ghraib*. New York: HarperCollins.

Holsti, Ole. 1970. The "operational code" approach to the study of political leaders: John Foster Dulles' philosophical and instrumental beliefs. *Canadian Journal of Political Science* 3: 123–157.

——. 1972. *Crisis, escalation, war*. Montreal: McGill-Queen's University Press.

——. 2004. *Public opinion and American foreign policy*. Ann Arbor: University of Michigan Press.

Hoyt, Paul D. 1997. The political manipulation of group composition: Engineering the decision context. *Political Psychology* 18, no. 4: 771–790.

Huth, Paul. 1988. Extended deterrence and the outbreak of war. *American Political Science Review* 82, no. 2: 423–443.

Hybel, Alex R. 1993. *Power over rationality: The Bush administration and the Gulf crisis*. Albany: State University of New York Press.

Hyland, William G. 1999. *Clinton's world: Remaking American foreign policy*. Westport, Conn.: Praeger.

Isikoff, Michael, and David Corn. 2006. *Hubris: The inside story of spin, scandal, and the selling of the Iraq War*. New York: Crown.

James, Patrick. 2002. *International relations and scientific progress: Structural realism reconsidered*. Columbus: Ohio State University Press.

James, Patrick, and Athanasios Hristoulas. 1994. Domestic politics and foreign policy: Evaluating a model of crisis activity for the United States. *Journal of Politics* 56: 327–348.

James, Patrick, and John R. O'Neal. 1991. The influence of domestic and international politics on the president's use of force. *Journal of Conflict Resolution* 35: 307–332.

Janis, Irving. 1972. *Victims of groupthink: A psychology study of foreign-policy decisions and fiascoes.* Boston: Houghton Mifflin.

———. 1982. *Groupthink: Psychological studies of policy decisions and fiascoes.* Boston: Houghton Mifflin.

———. 1989. *Crucial decisions: Leadership in policymaking and crisis management.* New York: Free Press.

Janis, Irving, and Leon Mann. 1977. *Decision making: A psychological analysis of conflict, choice, and commitment.* New York: Free Press.

Jervis, Robert. 1976. *Perception and misperception in international politics.* Princeton, N.J.: Princeton University Press.

———. 1985. Perceiving and coping with threat. In *Psychology and deterrence,* ed. Robert Jervis, Richard Ned Lebow, and Janice Gross Stein, 13–33. Baltimore, Md.: The Johns Hopkins University Press.

Johnson, Dominic D., and Dominic Tierney. 2006. *Failing to win: Perceptions of victory and defeat in international politics.* Cambridge, Mass.: Harvard University Press.

Johnson, Loch K. 1977. Operational codes and the prediction of leadership behavior: Senator Frank Church at midcareer. In *A psychological examination of political leaders,* ed. Margaret G. Hermann. New York: Free Press.

Kaarbo, Juliet, and Margaret G. Hermann. 1988. Leadership styles of prime ministers: How individual differences affect the foreign policy making process. *Leadership Quarterly* 21: 511–527.

Kahn, Joseph, and David E. Sanger. 2002. Bush officials meet to seek a compromise on steel tariffs. *New York Times* (March 1).

Kaplan, Fred. 2008. *Daydream believers: How a few grand ideas wrecked American power.* Hoboken, N.J.: Wiley.

Kaplan, Lawrence F. 2001. Yesterday's man: Colin Powell's out-of-date foreign policy. *New Republic* (January).

Karns, Margaret P., and Karen A. Mingst. 1987. International organizations and foreign policy: Influence and instrumentality. In *New Directions in the Study of Foreign Policy,* ed. C. Hermann. New York: Routledge.

Kegley, Charles W., and Eugene R. Wittkopf, Jr. 1996. *American Foreign Policy.* New York: St. Martin's Press.

Keller, Bill. 2002. The sunshine warrior. *New York Times* (September 22).

Kerr, Norbert L. 1981. Social transition schemes: Charting the group's road to agreement. *Journal of Personality and Social Psychology* 41: 684–702.

Kessler, Glenn. 2003. U.S. decision on Iraq has puzzling past. *Washington Post* (January 12).

Khong, Yuen F. 1992. *Analogies at war: Korea, Munich, Dien Bien Phu, and the Vietnam decision of 1965.* Princeton, N.J.: Princeton University Press.

Kingdon, John. 1984. *Agendas, alternatives, and public policies.* New York: HarperCollins.

Kornacki, Steve. 2007. The first Bush mistake: Choosing Cheney over Danforth. *New York Observer* (June 28).

Kowert, Paul A. 2002. *Groupthink or deadlock: When do leaders learn from their advisors?* Albany: State University of New York Press.

Kramer, Roderick M. 1998. Revisiting the Bay of Pigs and Vietnam decisions twenty-five years later: How well has the groupthink hypothesis stood the test of time? *Organizational Behavior and Human Processes* 73: 236–271.

Krasner, Stephen D. 1972. Are bureaucracies important? (Or Allison Wonderland). *Foreign Policy*: 159–179.

Lebow, Richard N. 1981. *Between war and peace: The nature of international crisis.* Baltimore, Md.: The John Hopkins University Press.

Leites, Nathan. 1951. *The operational code of the Politburo.* New York: McGraw-Hill.

——. 1953. *A study of Bolshevism.* New York: Free Press.

Lemann, Nicholas. 2001. The quiet man: Dick Cheney's rise to unprecedented power. *New Yorker* (May 7).

——. 2004. Remember the Alamo: How George W. Bush reinvented himself. *New Yorker* (October 18).

Levi, Ariel, and Phillip E. Tetlock. 1980. A cognitive analysis of Japan's 1941 decision for war. *Journal of Conflict Resolution* 24: 195–211.

Machiavelli, Niccolo. 2008. *The prince.* New York: Oxford University Press.

Mackie, Diane M. 1986. Social identification effects in group polarization. *Journal of Personality and Social Psychology* 50: 720–728.

Malici, Akan. 2005. Discord and collaboration between allies: Managing external threats and internal cohesion in Franco-British relations during 9/11 era. *Journal of Conflict Resolution* 49: 90–119.

——. 2006. Reagan and Gorbachev: Altercasting at the end of the cold war. In *Beliefs and leadership in world politics: Methods and applications of operational code analysis*, ed. Mark Schafer and Stephen G. Walker, 127–149. New York: Palgrave Macmillan.

Mann, James. 2004. *Rise of the Vulcans: The history of Bush's war cabinet.* New York: Penguin.

Marfleet, B. Gregory. 2000. The operational code of John F. Kennedy during the Cuban missile crisis: A comparison of public and private rhetoric. *Political Psychology* 21, no. 3: 545–558.

Marfleet, B. Gregory, and Colleen Miller. 2005. Failure after 1441: Bush and Chirac in the UN Security Council. *Foreign Policy Analysis* 1: 333–359.

Mayer, Jane. 2004. The manipulator. *New Yorker* (June 7).

——. 2006. The hidden power: The legal mind behind the White House's war on terror. *New Yorker* (July 3).

Mazarr, Michael J. 2007. The Iraq War and agenda setting. *Foreign Policy Analysis* 3: 1–23.

McCalla, Robert B. 1992. *Uncertain perceptions: U.S. cold war crisis decision making.* Ann Arbor: University of Michigan Press.

McCauley, Clark. 1989. The nature of social influence in groupthink: Compliance and internalization. *Journal of Personality and Social Psychology* 57, no. 2: 250–260.

——. 1998. Group dynamics in Janis's theory of groupthink: Backward and forward. *Organizational Behavior and Human Processes* 73, no. 2: 142–162.

McClelland, David. 1951. *Personality*. New York: Sloane.
——. 1961. *The achieving society*. Princeton, N.J.: Van Nostrand.
McDermott, Rose. 2004. *Political psychology in international relations*. Ann Arbor: University of Michigan Press.
McGeary, Johanna. 2001. Odd man out. *Time* (September).
McLellan, David. 1971. The operational code approach to the study of political leaders: Dean Acheson's philosophical and instrumental beliefs. *Canadian Journal of Political Science* 4: 52–75.
Mearsheimer, John. 1983. *Conventional deterrence*. Ithaca, N.Y.: Cornell University Press.
Milner, Helen V. 1997. *Interests, institutions, and information: Domestic politics and international relations*. Princeton, N.J.: Princeton University Press.
Mischel, Walter. 1968. *Personality and assessment*. New York: Wiley.
——. 1977. On the future of personality measurement. *American Psychologist* 32: 246–254.
Moens, Alexander. 1990. *Foreign policy under Carter: Testing multiple advocacy decision making*. Boulder, Colo.: Westview.
Moorhead, Gregory, Richard Ference, and Chris P. Neck. 1991. Group decision fiascoes continue: Space Shuttle Challenger and a revised groupthink framework. *Human Relations* 44: 539–550.
Morgenthau, Hans. 1978. *Politics among nations: The struggle for power and peace*. 5th ed. New York: Alfred A. Knopf.
Nelson, Suzanne. 2002. Stint on the Hill offered hints of Rumsfeld's style. *Roll Call* (March 11).
Oberdorfer, Don. 1983. Applying pressure in Central America. *Washington Post* (November 23).
Pastor, Robert A. 1987. *Condemned to repetition: The United States and Nicaragua*. Princeton, N.J.: Princeton University Press.
Perlez, Jane. 2001a. Bush team's counsel is divided on foreign policy. *New York Times* (March 27).
——. 2001b. Rice on the front lines as adviser to Bush. *New York Times* (August 19).
Persico, Joseph E. 1990. *Casey: From the OSS to the CIA*. New York: Penguin.
Peterson, Randall S., Pamela D. Owens, Phillip E. Tetlock, Elliot T. Fan, and Paul Martorana. 1998. Group dynamics in top management teams: Groupthink, vigilance, and alternative models of organizational failure and success. *Organizational Behavior and Human Processes* 73: 272–305.
Post, Jerrold M. 1993. The defining moment of Saddam's life: A political psychology perspective on the leadership and decision making of Saddam Hussein during the Gulf crisis. In *The political psychology of the Gulf War leaders: Leaders, publics, and the process of conflict*, ed. Stanley A. Renshon, 49–66. Pittsburgh, Penn.: University of Pittsburgh Press.
Powlick, Philip J. 1995. The sources of public opinion for American foreign policy officials. *International Studies Quarterly* 39, no. 4: 427–451.
Prados, John. 2004. The pros from Dover. *Bulletin of the Atomic Scientists* (January 1).
Preston, Thomas. 1997. Following the leader: The impact of U.S. presidential style upon advisory group dynamics, structure, and decision. In *Beyond groupthink: Group decision making in foreign policy*, ed. Paul 't Hart, B. Sundelius, and E.

Stern, 191–248. Ann Arbor: University of Michigan Press.

——. 2001. *The president and his inner circle: Leadership style and the advisory process in foreign policy making*. Ann Arbor: University of Michigan Press.

Purdum, Todd S. 2003. The brain's behind Bush's war. *New York Times* (February 1).

Randall, Gene. 2000. Cheney, Danforth emerge as Bush's top choices. *Cable News Network* (July 22). Available online at http://archives.cnn.com/2000/ALLPOLITICS/stories/07/22/bush.veepstakes.

Raven, Bertram H. 1998. Groupthink, Bay of Pigs, and Watergate reconsidered. *Organizational Behavior and Human Processes* 73: 352–361.

Renshon, Jonathan. 2008. Stability and change in belief systems: The operational code of George W. Bush from governor to second-term president. *Journal of Conflict Resolution* 52, no. 8: 820–849.

Renshon, Stanley A. 1996. *High hopers: The Clinton administration and the politics of ambition*. New York: New York University Press.

Renshon, Stanley A., and Deborah Welch Larson. 2002. *Good judgment in foreign policy: Theory and application*. New York: Rowman & Littlefield.

Ricks, Thomas E. 2006. *Fiasco: The American military adventure in Iraq*. New York: Penguin.

Risen, James. 2006. *State of war: The secret history of the CIA and the Bush administration*. New York: The Free Press.

Roberts, Fred. 1976. Strategy for the energy crisis: The case of computer transportation policy. In *Structure of Decision*, ed. Robert Axelrod. Princeton, N.J.: Princeton University Press.

Robison, Sam. 2006. George W. Bush and the Vulcans: Leader-advisor relations and America's response to the 9/11 attacks. In *Beliefs and leadership in world politics*, ed. Mark Schafer and Stephen G. Walker, 101–124. New York: Palgrave Macmillan.

Rothgeb, John M. 1993. *Defining power: Influence and force in the contemporary international system*. New York: St. Martin's Press.

Rothkopf, David J. 2005. *Running the world: The inside story of the National Security Council and the architects of American power*. New York: PublicAffairs.

Russett, Bruce. 1990. *Controlling the sword: The democratic governance of national security*. Cambridge, Mass.: Harvard University Press.

Sanders, Glenn S., and Robert S. Baron. 1977. Is social comparison irrelevant for producing choice shifts? *Journal of Experimental Social Psychology* 13: 303–314.

Schafer, Mark. 1999. Explaining groupthink: Do the psychological characteristics of the leader matter? *Political Psychology* 18: 813–829.

——. 2000. Issues in assessing psychological characteristics at a distance. *Political Psychology* 21: 511–527.

Schafer, Mark, and Scott Crichlow. 1996. Antecedents of groupthink: A quantitative study. *Journal of Conflict Resolution* 40, no. 3: 415–435.

——. 2002. The process-outcome connection in foreign policy decision making: A quantitative study building on groupthink. *International Studies Quarterly* 46, no. 1: 45–68.

Schafer, Mark, and Stephen G. Walker. 2001. Political leadership and the democratic peace: The operational code of Prime Minister Tony Blair. In *Profiling political leaders and the analysis of political leadership: The cross-national study of personal-*

ity and behavior, ed. Ofer Feldman and Linda Valenty, 21–35. Westport, Conn.: Greenwood Press.

——. 2006a. Democratic leaders and the democratic peace: The operational codes of Tony Blair and Bill Clinton. *International Studies Quarterly* 50: 3.

——. 2006b. Operational code analysis at a distance: The verbs in context system of content analysis. In *Beliefs and leadership in world politics: Methods and applications of operational code analysis*, ed. Mark Schafer and Stephen G. Walker, 25–51. New York: Palgrave.

Schafer, Mark, Sam Robinson, and Bradley Aldrich. 2006. Operational codes and the 1916 Easter rising in Ireland: A test of the frustration-aggression hypothesis. *Foreign Policy Analysis* 2: 63–82.

Scott, James M. 1996. *Deciding to intervene: The Reagan doctrine and foreign policy.* Durham, N.C.: Duke University Press.

Selassie, Bereket Habte. 1984. The American dilemma on the Horn. *The Journal of Modern African Studies* 22, no. 2: 249–272.

Shanker, Thom. 2006. Snowflakes. *New York Times* (December 24).

Shapiro, Michael J., Matthew G. Bonham, and Daniel Heradstveit. 1988. A discursive practices approach to collective decision making. *International Studies Quarterly* 17: 147–174.

Shultz, George. 1993. *Turmoil and triumph: My years as secretary of state.* New York: Macmillan.

Sipress, Alan, and Steven Mufson. 2001. Powell takes the middle ground. *Washington Post* (August 26).

Smith, M. B. 1968. A map for the analysis of personality and politics. *Journal of Social Issues* 24: 15–28.

Smith, Steve. 1984. Groupthink and the hostage rescue mission. *British Journal of Political Science* 15, no. 1: 117–123.

Snyder, Jack L. 1991. *Myths of empire: Domestic politics and international ambition.* Ithaca, N.Y.: Cornell University Press.

Snyder, Richard C., H. W. Bruck, and Burton Sapin. 1954. *Foreign policy decision making.* New York: Free Press of Glencoe.

——, eds. 1962. *Foreign policy decision making: An approach to the study of international politics.* New York: Free Press of Glencoe.

Sprout, Harold, and Margaret Sprout. 1965. *Man-milieu relationship hypotheses in the context of international politics.* Princeton, N.J.: Princeton University Press.

Stern, Eric K. 1997. Probing the plausibility of newgroup syndrome: Kennedy and the Bay of Pigs. In *Beyond groupthink: Group decision making in foreign policy*, ed. Paul 't Hart, Bengt Sundelius, and Eric Stern, 153–190. Ann Arbor: University of Michigan Press.

Stern, Eric K., and Bengt Sundelius. 1997. Understanding small group decisions in foreign policy: Process diagnosis and research procedure. In *Beyond groupthink: Group decision making in foreign policy*, ed. Paul 't Hart, Bengt Sundelius, and Eric Stern, 123–150. Ann Arbor: University of Michigan Press.

Stevenson, Matthew. 2006. Economic liberalism and the operational code beliefs of U.S. presidents: The initiation of NAFTA disputes, 1989–2002. In *Beliefs and leadership in world politics: Methods and applications of operational code analysis*, ed. Mark Schafer and Stephen G. Walker, 201–217. New York: Palgrave Macmillan.

Stiglitz, Joseph, and Linda Bilmes. 2008. *The three trillion dollar war: The true cost of the Iraq conflict*. New York: W. W. Norton.

Stuart, Douglas, and Harvey Starr. 1981. The "inherent bad faith model" reconsidered: Dulles, Kennedy, and Kissinger. *Political Psychology* 3: 1–33.

Suedfeld, Peter, and Susan Bluck. 1988. Changes in integrative complexity prior to surprise attacks. *Journal of Conflict Resolution* 32: 626–635.

Suedfeld, Peter, and Dennis Rank. 1976. Revolutionary leaders: Long-term success as a function of changes in conceptual complexity. *Journal of Personality and Social Psychology* 34: 169–178.

Suedfeld, Peter, and Phillip E. Tetlock. 1977. Integrative complexity of communications in international crisis. *Journal of Conflict Resolution* 21: 168–178.

Suedfeld, Peter, Phillip E. Tetlock, and C. Ramirez. 1977. War, peace, and integrative complexity: UN speeches on the Middle East problem. *Journal of Conflict Resolution* 21: 427–442.

Suskind, Ron. 2004. *The price of loyalty: George W. Bush, the White House, and the education of Paul O'Neill*. New York: Simon & Schuster.

——. 2006. *The one-percent doctrine: Deep inside America's pursuit of its enemies since 9/11*. New York: Simon & Schuster.

Talbott, S. 1988. *The master of the game: Paul Nitze and the nuclear peace*. New York: Vintage.

——. 2006. *Engaging India: Diplomacy, democracy, and the bomb*. Washington, D.C.: Brookings Institution Press.

Teller, Edward, and Judith Shoolery. 2001. *Memoirs: A twentieth-century journey*. New York: Basic Books.

Tetlock, Philip E. 1979. Identifying victims of groupthink from public statements of decision makers. *Journal of Personality and Social Psychology* 37: 1314–1324.

——. 1981. Personality and isolationism: Content analysis of senatorial speeches. *Journal of Personality and Social Psychology* 41: 737–743.

Tetlock, Philip E., Randall S. Peterson, Charles McGuire, Shi-jie Chang, and Peter Feld. 1992. Assessing political group dynamics: A test of the groupthink model. *Journal of Personality and Social Psychology* 63: 403–425.

Thies, Cameron G. 2006. Bankers and beliefs: The political psychology of the Asian financial crisis. In *Beliefs and leadership in world politics: Methods and applications of operational code analysis*, ed. Mark Schafer and Stephen G. Walker, 219–233. New York: Palgrave Macmillan.

Thomson, James C. 1968. How could Vietnam happen? An autopsy. *Atlantic Monthly* 221, no. 4: 47–53.

Tuckman, Bruce. 1965. Developmental sequence in small groups. *Psychological Bulletin* 63, no. 6: 384–399.

Tuckman, Bruce, and M. Jensen. 1977. Stages of group development revisited. *Group and Organizational Studies* 2, no. 4: 417–427.

Tyler, Patrick E., and Elaine Sciolino. 2001. Bush advisers split on scope of retaliation. *New York Times* (September 19).

Van Natta, Dale. 2006. Bush was set on path to war, British memo says. *New York Times* (March 27).

Vance, Cyrus. 1983. *Hard choices: Critical years in America's foreign policy*. New York: Simon & Schuster.

Vertzberger, Yaacov. 1990. *The world in their minds: Information processing, cognition, and perception in foreign policy decision making.* Palo Alto, Calif.: Stanford University Press.

——. 1997. Collective risk taking: The decision-making group. In *Beyond groupthink: Group decision making in foreign policy,* ed. Paul 't Hart, Bengt Sundelius, and Eric Stern, 275–308. Ann Arbor: University of Michigan Press.

——. 1998. *Risk taking and decision making.* Palo Alto, Calif.: Stanford University Press.

Walker, Stephen G., and Lawrence S. Falkowski. 1984. The operational codes of U.S. presidents and secretaries of state: Motivational foundations and behavioral consequences. *Political Psychology* 5: 237–266.

Walker, Stephen G., and Mark Schafer. 2000. The political universe of Lyndon B. Johnson and his advisors: Diagnostic and strategic propensities in their operational codes. *Political Psychology* 21: 529–543.

——. 2006. Belief systems as casual mechanisms: An overview of operational code analysis. In *Beliefs and leadership in world politics: Methods and applications for op code analysis,* ed. Mark Schafer and Stephen G. Walker. New York: Palgrave.

——. 2007. Theodore Roosevelt and Woodrow Wilson: Realist and idealist archetypes? *Political Psychology* 28, no. 6: 747–776.

Walker, Stephen G., Mark Schafer, and Greg Marfleet. Forthcoming. British learning patterns toward Nazi Germany: Why did Britain persist with an appeasement strategy in the face of negative feedback? In *Change in foreign policy direction,* ed. Charles Hermann. College Station: Texas A&M University Press.

Walker, Stephen G., Mark Schafer, and Michael Young. 1998. Systematic procedures for operational code analysis: Measuring and modeling Jimmy Carter's operational code. *International Studies Quarterly* 42: 175–190.

Wallace, J., and R. Kaylor. 1986. Nightmare for U.S.; Groping for a way on Philippines. *U.S. News* (February 24).

Wallace, Michael D., and Peter Suedfeld. 1988. Leadership performance in crisis: The longevity-complexity link. *International Studies Quarterly* 32: 439–451.

Weissman, Stephen R. 1995. *A culture of deference: Congress's failure of leadership in foreign policy.* New York: BasicBooks.

Winter, David G. 1980. An exploratory study of the motives of southern African political leaders measured at a distance. *Political Psychology* 2: 75–85.

——. 1987. Leader appeal, leader performance, and the motive profiles of leaders and followers: A study of American presidents and elections. *Journal of Personality and Social Psychology* 52: 196–202.

——. 1992. Personality and foreign policy: Historical overview of research. In *Political Psychology and Foreign Policy,* ed. E. Singer and V. Harper. Boulder, Colo.: Westview.

——. 1993. Power, affiliation, and war: Three tests of a motivated model. *Journal of Personality and Social Psychology* 65: 532–545.

——. 2002. Motivation and political leadership. In *Political leadership for a new Century: Personality and behavior among American leaders,* ed. L. O. Valenty and O. Feldman, 27–47. New York: Praeger.

——. 2003. Personality and political behavior. In *Oxford handbook of political psychology,* ed. David O. Sears, Leonie Huddy, and Robert Jervis, 110–134. New York: Oxford University Press.

Weissman, Stephen R. 1995. *A culture of deference: Congress's failure of leadership in foreign policy*. New York: BasicBooks.

Welch, David A. 1992. The organizational process and bureaucratic politics paradigms: Retrospect and prospect. *International Security* 17, no. 2: 112–146.

——. 2005. *Painful choices: A theory of foreign policy change*. Princeton, N.J.: Princeton University Press.

White, M. 1986. U.S. may decide to quit bases. *Guardian* (February 20).

Whyte, Glen. 1998. Recasting Janis's groupthink model: The key role of collective efficacy in decision fiascos. *Organization Behavior and Human Decision Processes* 73: 185–209.

Wittkopf, Eugene R., Christopher M. Jones, and Charles W. Kegley, Jr. 2007. *American foreign policy: Pattern and process*. Wadsworth.

Wolfowitz, Paul, and Zalmay Khalilzad. 1997. Overthrow him. *Weekly Standard* (December 1).

Woodward, Bob. 2002. *Bush at war*. New York: Simon & Schuster.

——. 2004. *Plan of attack*. New York : Simon & Schuster.

——. 2006. *State of denial*. New York: Simon & Schuster.

——. 2008. *The war within*. New York: Simon & Schuster.

Wright, Robin. 2007. From the desk of Donald Rumsfeld. *Washington Post* (November 1).

Young, Michael D. 1994. Foreign policy problem representation and President Carter. Ph.D. dissertation, Ohio State University.

Ziller, Robert C., William F. Stone, Robert M. Jackson, and Natalie J. Terbovic. 1977. Self-other orientations and political behavior. In *A psychological examination of political leaders*, ed. Margaret G. Hermann. New York: Free Press.

Index

GPSR Authorized Representative: Easy Access System Europe, Mustamäe tee 50, 10621 Tallinn, Estonia, gpsr.requests@easproject.com

www.ingramcontent.com/pod-product-compliance
Lightning Source LLC
Chambersburg PA
CBHW021852020426
42334CB00013B/298